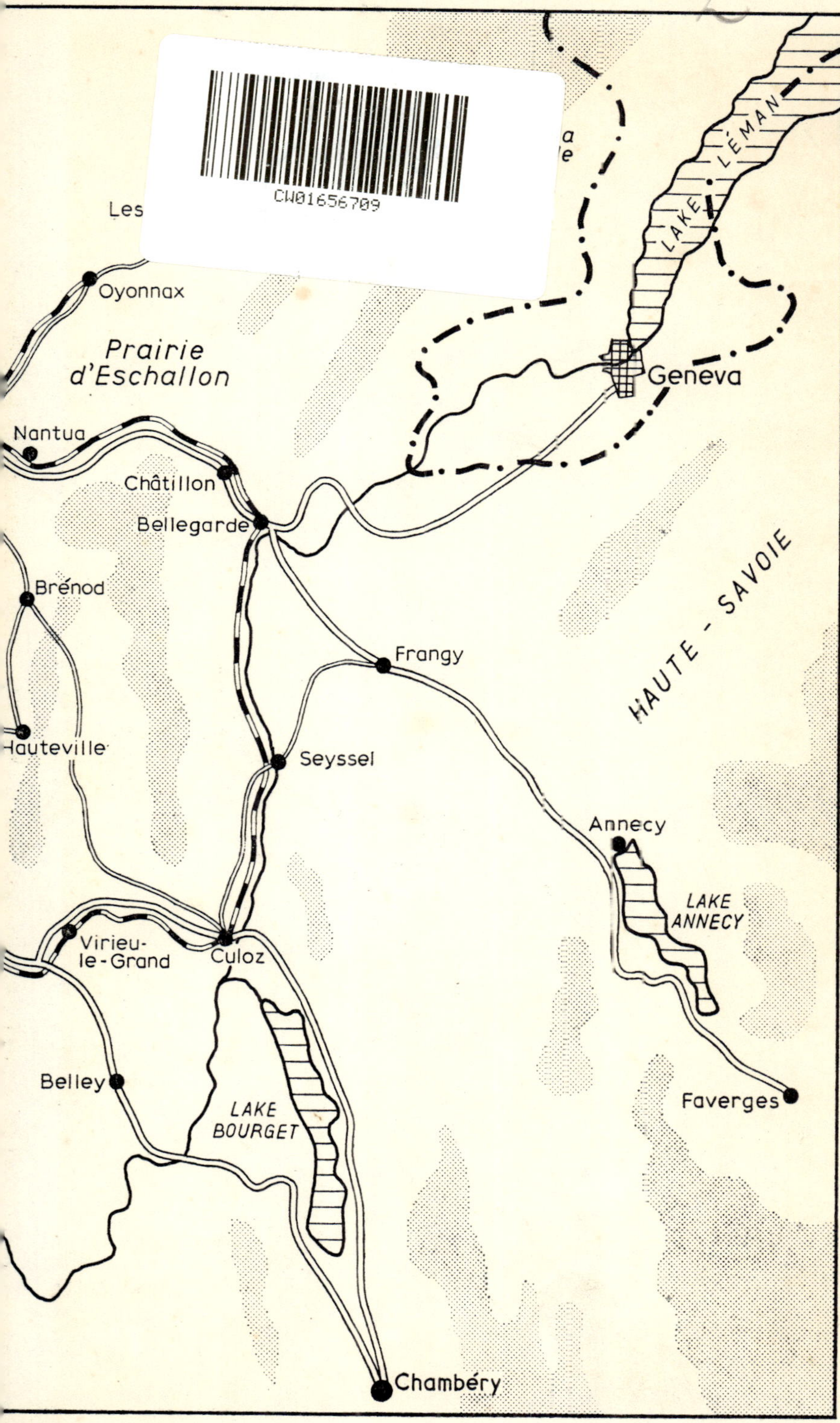
Les
Oyonnax
Prairie d'Eschallon
Nantua
Châtillon
Bellegarde
Geneva
LAKE LÉMAN
Brénod
Hauteville
Frangy
HAUTE - SAVOIE
Seyssel
Annecy
LAKE ANNECY
Virieu-le-Grand
Culoz
Belley
LAKE BOURGET
Faverges
Chambéry

XAVIER

XAVIER

The Famous British Agent's
Dramatic Account of his work
in the French Resistance

RICHARD HESLOP

*Foreword by Major-General Sir Colin McV. Gubbins,
KCMG, DSO, MC*

Rupert Hart-Davis London 1970

First published 1970 by Rupert Hart-Davis Ltd.,
3 Upper James Street, London W1

Printed in Great Britain by Cox & Wyman Ltd,
London, Fakenham and Reading

SBN 246 63989 X

I dedicate these memoirs of courage, devotion to duty
and determination, in the first place
to my brave and faithful companions
ALEX, PAUL and ROMANS.
And in the second place, to D.E.L., whose patience
and encouragement made them possible.

I feel indebted to so many people in England
and France who have helped in so many seemingly
small but often vital ways that it would need an
appendix to name and pay tribute to them all.
I must however mention in particular my friend
Bob Taylor, a journalist of repute, for his
patience and tireless assistance in the writing
of this book.

Lieutenant-Colonel Richard Heslop DSO
Herne Bay, Kent.

List of Illustrations

Foreword

by Major-General Sir Colin McV. Gubbins, KCMG, DSO, MC

It is difficult enough for those who have never suffered it to imagine life in an occupied country under a brutal and utterly ruthless despotism. How much harder to appreciate properly the daily life in such conditions of a foreigner whose declared mission is actually to build up armed resistance to the oppressor among the populace, whatever the retaliation that would inevitably fall on him. Such was the author's role, and the country—France.

In his favour was the fact that so many of the French people had refused to accept defeat and surrender and who, after the first traumatic shock, sought only the means to continue the struggle by forming clandestine groups of patriots of all classes. But among the populace as a whole there were followers of Pétain who accepted the status quo, followers of de Gaulle and of Moscow (after June 1941) who rejected it totally, and others who would have none of these things but fought for *la Patrie* alone. These acute political differences bedevilled the work of organising resistance, and made it doubly dangerous for those most active in it.

The build-up of successful resistance in all occupied countries during the war depended on two indispensable lifelines: developments in clandestine wireless telegraphy and in supply by aircraft whether of weapons or personnel. Without these material aids it would have been impossible to create and equip underground forces significant enough to affect the operations of regular forces. Given adequate aid, given the right spirit of the people, all this was rendered possible.

Colonel Heslop (Xavier) describes feelingly his sense of

frustration and impotence during his first mission in France with no direct communication with Special Operations Executive in London. On his second mission to the Maquis in south-eastern France his whole position and his local standing are completely transformed. Now he can ask directly for the arms so desperately needed. Now he can report suitable dropping zones and the dates for parachuting can be mutually agreed. Now he can report in detail at any time on the local situation, and plans can be agreed for the development of his sector for specific operations against the enemy, and other urgent matters. All his demands could not of course be met: no occupied country or any individual sector ever got its full requirements—our means were limited by higher decree. But during the war there were delivered by air to France more than 10,000 tons of weapons, ammunition and equipment. On D-day, 6th June 1944, some 150 undergronnd wireless stations were in touch with SOE from occupied France and Belgium. Xavier's sector certainly received its fair share—and made most effective use thereof. For his services in France he was awarded the Distinguished Service Order, Légion d'honneur, Croix de Guerre with three palms and the American Medal of Freedom with palm.

This is an absorbing book. Its interest lies in the author's factual narrative of what actually happened to him and of his hopes and fears through the trials and tribulations of underground and open warfare in France, where guerilla warfare was being waged long before an allied soldier set foot on Norman soil, to the final dramatic meeting on his own stamping-ground with the invading American armies from the south. It is told with a wealth of detail which is at all times relevant and enlightening. The questions that spring to mind are answered immediately, the little happenings of daily life that are so important for security are faithfully reproduced. But what stands out in high relief is the courage, the endurance and the magnificent spirit in conditions of incredible hardship of those alongside whom he fought—the men and women and even the boys and girls of France. The seas that surround our island saved us from this ultimate test.

I

The job which led to my most disturbing incident as a British agent started quite simply when I met one of the many dozens of resistance men I had worked with in the Angers area. I saw him in a bar, and as we sat over a coffee one morning in mid-1943, he told me that he could let me have all the future train movements for months to come, every ammunition train, every troop train, every food train, which had been planned with characteristic German efficiency and listed in one slim file which rested in a steel drawer inside the movement control office at Le Mans station.

I was, of course, instantly aware of the value of this information. Armed with it, I could brief the Royal Air Force to attack the trains and could let the saboteurs in the groups know when food trains were passing so that they could be derailed and the goods taken into the secret stores of the Resistance. How, I asked, were these plans to reach me?

'Monsieur, I have a contact at Le Mans who is a movements control officer. He can tell you where they are kept and you can come in and get them.'

That was all very well, I told him—but what about guards, locked doors and so on? And if he worked there, why couldn't he collect the papers?

He explained that there was only one guard on at nights, a Frenchman, and that he could be tempted away by the offer of a couple of brandies in a bar close by the offices. He would leave a shutter open in a ground-floor room and the window unlocked so I could come in that way. There would be no problem. As for locked doors, he would give me wax impressions of the only key I would need which opened the door from the room with the open shutter into the room where the file was kept, but he would even try to keep that unlocked for the night I would make my burglary.

'I cannot take the file out as I am a Frenchman. Every Frenchman is searched when they leave the offices and I could not risk smuggling the papers through myself,' he told me.

But there was another snag. If the file disappeared, the Germans would know that it had been stolen and they would change the whole of the schedule. If I took the file, I asked my contact, could he smuggle it back the following day without being discovered?

'Yes, they don't search people going in. If you photograph the documents and let me have them back in a day or so, then I can cover up for that length of time. If a German asks to see the file I can put him off by pretending that another officer is looking at it, and put it back later without anyone knowing that it has been out of the office.'

That settled all my inquiries. He told me when I could have the impression of the key and I made arrangements for this to be picked up. I also arranged that he would give the date on which the raid could be made to another contact I would send to him.

I received the impression of the key a few days later and, as I was working legitimately as a lathe operator in a factory making tungsten drills—perfect cover for me—I was able to make my own key from the wax impression. I was ready for the burglary from then on. I was told the day by a courier who reached me at Angers and I arranged to be taken by van out to Le Mans. The driver knew nothing of the job I was on, just that I wanted transport there and back. I dressed in my dark-blue overalls and my black beret, as they would help to conceal me in the dark, got into the van and was driven off. At 11 p.m., the time arranged, I was hiding in the shadows by the offices, when I saw my contact come out and chat to a guard who had been paying little interest in his job of sentry. After a few minutes the two moved off towards the café, from which I could hear, distantly, the clatter of glasses and the hum of talk.

I waited for the two to get out of my sight and then, with my heart beating heavily at the thought of my coming burglary and the chances of being captured, strolled over to the offices and to the shutters.

The shutters opened at a touch and without any noise—he must have oiled them. The window, too, was opened as he had promised and I pulled myself up into the dark, quiet room. I stood listening for steps, but all I heard were the voices from the café. I pulled my ·45 revolver out, carried it in one hand after pushing off the safety catch, and took out a pencil-slim electric torch from another pocket.

I eased myself quietly across the room to the door which led into the office where the files were kept, and leaned my shoulder against it as I turned the handle. That, too, was open and there was no need for my key. I opened this slowly—again there was no noise—entered the room and closed the door behind me. I switched my torch on, shone it on to the floor and took two paces towards the files.

Then, all at once, the lights in the room came on and a girl's voice ordered:

'Stay where you are, don't move.' I swung to my left and saw a pretty young girl of twenty-three or twenty-four standing there dressed in a white blouse and a blue skirt. In her right hand she held a pistol which was pointing straight at me, but wavering so much that the muzzle seemed to be blurred. I fired from the hip. She fired at the same time. Her shot hit the ceiling, mine hit her in the left breast, and I had the crazy thought that my pistol instructor would have been proud of me. The heavy ·45 bullet flung her across the room and she crashed on her back on the floor. She gasped and started to moan, and the blood seeped into her trim white blouse.

I should have shot her in the head, snatched the plans and run before the noise of the shots brought searchers. But I was sickened because I had shot a pretty girl, so I put my gun down, knelt on the floor beside her and cradled her head in my lap. I stayed like that for some minutes, as the girl gasped her last breaths, and then died. Shocked, I still held her for another minute or two. I laid her down gently, picked up the two guns and switched the lights off. I leaned against the wall and thought for a moment that I was going to be sick. The room reeked of gunpowder and mingled with it was a trace of the girl's perfume. I can smell it even now. I pulled myself together and then realised that the blast from my ·45 must have been heard a long way off. But I heard no shouts, no running feet. Automatically I turned to the right file, switched on my torch and brought out the plans which I tucked into one of my big, overall pockets. I stepped over the body of the girl, walked to the door, went into the next office and stood by the open window. I looked out, saw no one, and the only sounds were those from the bar. I dropped to the ground and ran into the darkness towards the van which was tucked away a few streets off.

I stopped, panting. It was only then that I realised I had committed a murder. I leaned against a wall catching my breath as the shock of this hit me for the first time. Murder was a frightening word at any time. But to have committed a murder oneself, and that of a pretty girl, was enough to turn one's senses. I wanted to run, run anywhere, but I fought the panic that rose in me and forced myself to be calm.

Then another thought came into my mind. How the hell did that girl know I was going to be there? Who had talked and who was she? Had my contact betrayed me? What had happened and how was I going to escape being caught and tried?

But reason told me that the Germans could not trace me for I had left no fingerprints and they would not be too thorough just because a slip of a girl had been killed. I would photograph the plans and have them delivered back to my man as we had planned.

And in the meantime I would try to find out the identity of the girl.

I was driven back to Angers and dropped at my house. The next day I arranged for the plans to be photographed and asked for information to be obtained for me on the previous night's events.

I heard within a few hours that the girl, who was named Marthe —I never did know more than that—was a recent recruit to the Milice, the French plainclothes equivalent of the Gestapo. Her boy friend worked at the movement control and by chance overheard my contact discussing my coming raid on their offices. The boy friend told Marthe about this as an interesting anecdote —he was a loyal Frenchman—not realising his girl was a member of the Milice.

Marthe was young and eager and, I presumed, had sought to impress her new chief by catching a thief single-handed. It was her misfortune to meet a fully armed and trained British army officer instead of a frightened, unarmed French thief. I felt a little better when I knew that the girl was an enemy of France. But I shall never forget that I was forced to kill a girl. Until now no one has known I was Marthe's killer—not even SOE. I was too ashamed.

As it was, the plans were not as vital as I had been led to believe. They were useful, but only covered a small section of the future movements of the railways through Le Mans junction. The Germans hunted the murderer, checks were made in Le Mans, but no one, outside my contact at the control office, found out the killer.

The final reaction set in a couple of days after her death. I could not stop trembling, I could not eat. I was very tensed up and preoccupied for many days. At night I lay awake, hearing again the sound of her cries as she lay dying, and smelling again the fresh, exciting perfume she had worn. I was remorseful and wondered why the hell I had wanted to become a British agent. How, I asked myself, had I managed to become an assassin? I thought back to the beginning of the war when I, and many like me, still thought that war was an awfully big adventure.

It started when a friend walked into my golf club and said: 'Here you are, Richard—just the job you were looking for,' and he handed over an advertisement asking for recruits of good education, speaking several languages, who would have a hard but interesting life in the Field Security Police.

'Well, that seems all right,' I told him. 'But I'm not all that interested in being a policeman chasing drunken soldiers who've run off with someone's wife.'

'No, no—it's not that sort of job at all. It's security, checking up on spies and seeing that the Germans don't steal our secrets. Should be just the thing.'

That sounded much more interesting, so I applied. I was called for an interview in February 1940, passed the language tests, and I was in.

I went through the normal military training of the day when I reported to Sheerness in April—square bashing, bull, and the rest of it. Then came lectures on field security, which were much more to my liking. We were taught how to follow a person without being seen, how to spot false papers, and so on. I realised as the weeks passed that I had found just the sort of work I wanted.

Dunkirk came and went. There were a few bombs in the distance, but, apart from that, the war seemed a long way off. It came fairly close, though, when there were two serious invasion threats, and in one I was sent to a defensive position with a rifle and five rounds of ammunition. Five rounds did not seem very many to hold off the German Army, and I asked the company sergeant-major what I should do when my five rounds were used.

'Run like hell,' was his succinct reply.

They made me a Lance Corporal, unpaid. I joined a group doing port control work in the north and was then ordered back to the depot of the Security force, which now had the title

'Corps' rather than Police—a word that smacked too much of the Gestapo. There I found many hush-hush preparations going on and I was ordered to brush up my French, Spanish, and Portuguese, and finally joined Section 52 of the Field Security Corps on board the Polish ship *Sobiesky* at Liverpool. We sailed for Scapa Flow on 20 August, where there were some of the Royal Marines, an independent company, and some Free French soldiers.

The ship steamed south, the weather became hotter and life aboard the Polish ship increasingly difficult because we were living in the airless stifling afterhold with the Royal Marines. The smell of dozens of sweaty soldiers became overpowering, and we looked forward to our brief hours on deck. Still the mystery of our voyage was maintained.

Finally our officer, Captain C. P. Henzell, called the section together and told us that we were part of a force going to take over Dakar and that he hoped this would be done without violence. We were to form part of the fifth wave and would use landing craft to do specific jobs.

'Sergeant Robbie, Corporal Heslop and a sergeant from the Independent company will have a difficult job,' Henzell said. 'You're to kidnap the Governor of Dakar, a chap called Boisson, and bring him back in one piece. Here are maps of the city and all the news we have been able to get on his habits. So study them and make your own plans for getting him out. We want him.'

We put into Freetown for final storing to be made by ourselves and other ships, and steamed off again towards Dakar. This was it.

'Attention all troops. General de Gaulle has sent repeated signals to the Governor of Dakar to parley but they have been ignored. He is now sending envoys ashore. That's all for now.' The loudspeakers of the *Sobiesky* clicked off. So things did not look too good. We waited, and the ship steamed around off shore.

'Attention all troops. General de Gaulle's envoys have been fired on. The situation is tensing up. Prepare for possible immediate action. That's all.' Click, and the speakers went off again.

We still steamed round waiting. Two French planes came snooping, and suddenly they swooped on the rest of the ships and dropped bombs. No damage.

Click again. 'Attention all troops. It has been decided to call off the engagement. Action stations are now cancelled. That's all. We are heading back to Freetown.'

It was an anti-climax. But Robbie and I were secretly rather glad, for everything seemed to have been such chaos that our chances of getting the Governor—just three against who knows how many guards—were slim.

When we got back to Freetown I was made a sergeant and the section was put on port control. My job was to board ships three miles offshore to vet the officers, crews, and cargoes. It was now that I first became involved with Intelligence and found the importance of the small snippets of news passed on to me by the merchant seamen I talked with. Some of the neutral ships gave me information on enemy warships they had met, and others would pass on information about morale in the neutral ports, all of which was transmitted to London.

My job was now becoming routine and rather tedious. As usual in wartime most of the time was spent waiting for something to happen. Nothing much did. We went up country to follow and check a tip-off that a member of the African Frontier Forces was preaching mutiny, but we found it was a pack of lies made up by a man whose girl friend had been taken over by the alleged *agent provocateur*.

I was relieved when we left for England at the end of January 1941. Perhaps something exciting might come my way yet. But in Britain, although promised a place in an officer training unit, I was again put on port control—this time in the Isle of Wight. The only thing I remember about that part of my war was the day the Intelligence Corps—as the Field Security Corps had now been named—tried to capture a man who loved to cut telephone wires, especially if they were new ones. We set a trap. New wire was stretched along from the HQ, and listening posts were set up at intervals, one of which was manned by myself. I waited in a hole in a thicket with a pair of earphones which would tell me the instant anything touched the sparkling new copper. I could not move, as the earphone leads were too short, and I was forced to watch in just one direction. As soon as I settled down on that warm evening a Wren and a soldier, hand in hand, strolled into a clear patch of grass not thirty feet from my observation post. I only hope that they are as happy now as they were then. Admittedly they did not teach me much, and soon dusk spared my blushes and the falling dew sent them on their way. The wire-cutter did not strike that night, but the police caught him a few days later.

Finally I was called to a selection board. They wanted to know what unit I would like to join if I became an officer, and seemed surprised when I said the Intelligence Corps, even though I had been working in it for two years. But they passed me, and sent me to Bulford Camp, and then to Dunbar in Scotland.

Half-way through this course some officers from the War Office came up to interview those cadets who had asked to join the Intelligence Corps. I was most upset when they turned me down and was thinking 'just like the bloody army, teach you to do one thing and just as you're some use, put you into something fresh.'

But as this group left, one of them took me aside and told me that he thought the War Office had something up its sleeve for me, although he could not tell me what it was.

Well this set my imagination going, and for days I was tensed up waiting for some word which, mercifully, came in a brief note telling me to report to Room 055A at the War Office.

I was shown into a room where there was a Major in uniform, a girl, and a man in civilian clothes. The Major shook me by the hand, offered me a cigarette and showed me to a seat. No army officer at an interview had ever been this friendly before. He asked me some routine questions, the answers to which he must have known, but I supposed he was weighing me up. Then came a string of other questions.

'Have you ever flown?'

'No, sir.'

'Do you think you would like jumping from an aeroplane by parachute?'

'I don't really know, sir—I don't think I'd mind.'

He paused here and lit another cigarette.

'How would you like to be dropped by parachute into France?'

I could hardly speak for sudden excitement. At last, at last. I finally managed to say that I would like it very much.

'Are you courageous?' was the next question.

'I don't know, sir. I suppose about the same as everyone else.'

'Well we think you have the sort of nervous courage needed for the work we want you to do,' and the Major grinned. It really was a friendly interview.

'I have got to say this. You realise that if you are dropped and caught, things will be most unpleasant for you—torture, prison, unpleasant death. This is a volunteer job and I know you want to do it. But go away and think about it a little more, and then let me know your decision. If you decide not to go ahead we shall understand, and that decision will not affect your army career.'

I knew that I wanted to go and that thinking about it would only whet my appetite even more, but I agreed to let him know shortly. I walked down Whitehall in a bit of a daze. As the first wave of exhilaration passed, I put myself on trial. Would I be brave enough to drop and operate in France? Could I stand torture if I was caught? But my fear of pain was linked with a much more important consideration; how long would it be before I betrayed my friends and our secrets? That was the important thing, and that was the background fear that I sensed through all the months ahead. Would I break? We were to be taught, before I went to France, that forty-eight hours was enough. Last out for forty-eight hours and this gives the other agents the opportunity of getting clear and closing down operations which one might talk about. At the end of forty-eight hours one could talk. But two days is a hell of a long time if the best brains in the Gestapo are at work on a man's body: the pulled finger-nails, electric shocks, the damaged testicles, the raw edge of nerve in a broken tooth, the kidney beatings.

I walked out of Whitehall into a telephone box, called a girl I knew and asked her to lunch. She was pretty and we were young, and the Châteauneuf-du-Pape over the meal brought just the right frame of mind.

'You are on good form today, Richard,' she said, as the brandy arrived. 'What's put you in such a good temper?'

'Well, darling . . .' and suddenly I stopped, mouth open. I had been about to tell her the job I was going to do; I was bursting to tell someone. This was my first lesson. Keep your mouth shut, Heslop, and do not drink too much wine—it makes you expansive.

For a week I curbed my impatience to write to the Major. Then I simply dropped him a note saying: 'I would like the job.'

He wrote back: 'I think you might like to know that, following our recent conversation, I am asking to have you on attachment as from 28 November 1942. You will get orders through regular channels in due course.'

A few days later I passed out from the OCTU head of the class, much to my amazement and, I think, to the amazement of many others there. For I was an old man in terms of cadets. So many of them were straight from school and in their late teens or early twenties. But I was the best there, and that gave me an added sense of confidence. The end of term seven-day leave completed my sense of well being.

When it ended I was sent to a most unmilitary sounding address—2 Orchard Court, in London, a block of modern flats with a large entrance hall, thick carpets, and uniformed porters. I took the lift, as I had been told, to the third floor and rang the bell. The door was opened by a slightly bald, middle-aged man, with a gold tooth that flashed in the artificial light. He spoke to me in English, with a foreign accent. He quickly showed me into a room with no carpets and a desk, two chairs, two full-length mirrors and the inevitable blackout boards as the only furnishings. On the desk was a blotter, a dirty inkpot, a pen, and some scraps of paper on which someone had been doodling. This was part of Special Operations Executive, hub of a spy, sabotage, and intelligence ring, which ranged from North Cape down to the Balkans, and I hoped that the bareness of the room did not mean that SOE was operating on a shoestring.

Eventually an officer in uniform came in, who told me, without preamble, that I was going on a preliminary course, and that if, at the end of it, I wanted to back out, that was all right with him. The course, he said, would also give them—the mysterious 'them' of whom I was to hear so much in the next months—a chance to size me up. But he thought I should be dropped in France after my training if I wanted to be. And, as from then, I was to be known as Raymond Hamilton and not Richard Heslop. He shook hands and left. I have often wondered what would have happened if I had decided, at the end of my preliminary training, that I did not want to go on, for by then I was in possession of all sorts of secrets that were valuable to our enemies. It was not until a couple of years ago that I learned that those men or women who decided to pull out, or who failed the preliminary course, had been sent off to the north of Scotland by SOE. There they carried out some war work, but were virtual prisoners for some months, until all the knowledge they had gained was old hat and of no future importance to anyone.

My conducting officer was André Simon, son of the gourmet of the same name. He became known to us as the Blue Draught, because, dressed in RAF uniform, he would breeze into a room, make a hurried statement, and then breeze out again. He explained that his job was to look after me and the rest of the would-be British agents on the course. He would watch everyone of us to see what sort of agents we might make, and report to SOE when the course was over.

He then took me to see my 'classmates', Vladimir, Ely, Auguste, Albert, Henri, Jean Marie, Peter, Roland, Antoine and Guy. One was to become my firm friend and was to die within too short a span of months. They were of all ages, some in uniform, some in scruffy civilian clothes, but none of them had that sinister look that spies are supposed to be born with. They were just an ordinary bunch of people you might meet any day on the seafront, or having a beer at any bar.

We were then taken by train to Guildford, bundled into a 30 cwt army truck, and driven for an hour through the night to Wanborough Manor, a medium-sized country house with wooded grounds, set in an area cleared of all civilians so the budding agents could carry on their training without risk of discovery. We were met on the doorstep by the Commandant, a very proper soldier who was a major in the Coldstream Guards, and he set out to make our motley bunch feel at home. Our dormitory beds were comfortable, and there was always hot water. Regrettably we did not heed the Government's orders to run only five inches of water into the bath to save fuel. We wallowed in a few feet of it. We also devoured mountains of food, the best I had eaten for a long time. It was luxury to me, the atmosphere was friendly and everyone leaned over backwards to be helpful and kind. However, we had to work hard for our hot water and full stomachs. There were courses in map reading and sabotage, morse sending and receiving, unarmed combat, and weapons training.

All the subjects were first explained by lecturers, and then came the practical. For instance, we were introduced to plastic explosive, and told the best way of carrying it was to put it in one's trouser pockets, as the body warmth would soften it, and make it easier to mould round the object to be destroyed. I learned it could be dropped, kicked, and heated without anything happening. That was reassuring.

We learned, too, about how to place detonators in the plastic to set off a charge. Detonators, unlike plastic, are very temperamental and have to be handled carefully. Some of them, made of fulminate of mercury, could not be carried in the hand because the heat of the body exploded them. Many hands and fingers have been blown off through incautious handling, and most agents or saboteurs kept detonators in their caps or hats, as this way they kept cool and were not likely to go off if you bumped into something in the dark. Others kept them in breast pockets, but I was always fearful that I would knock my chest against a tree or post, and that would be the end of Heslop. It was stressed that it was unwise to run when you carried them, because if you tripped and fell . . .

In the grounds of Wanborough I learned to set charges to destroy railway tracks. I was taught how to secure two pieces of plastic to a line, fix the detonator, a time-fuse for, say, ten minutes' delay, and then walk away unhurriedly. I fixed my first plastic, a two pound 'split' charge which I shaped to fit in the 'T' of a rail, smoothed it over so it could not be seen except by very close inspection, crimped the fuse, and knew that I had a couple of minutes to get clear. I was tempted to run, for two minutes does not sound long when a damn great 'bang' is due. But I remembered to walk away calmly.

'Never run away from a charge, you might trip up after a step or two and knock yourself out. Then you'll go up with the target. That is not the object of the exercise,' the explosives expert told us.

My charge went off with a very satisfactory bang, and I went back to examine the effect of plastic on railway lines. I found the steel cut through as cleanly as a blunt knife going through wartime margarine. There was a gap of several inches in the line, which was quite sufficient to derail a train or engine. There were different instructions on blowing bridges, dams, or transformers, and we went through the lot, using plastic or amatol—a powder explosive that has to be tamped down before it works properly.

I worked very hard at Wanborough and thoroughly enjoyed the course. I knew I wanted to continue and be sent to France, but I did not know until later in the war that I nearly did not pass. That was when I was at Orchard Court and was left for a few minutes alone in a room where I had been talking to one of the chiefs. He had my personal file open on his desk and when he walked into another room the opportunity was too good to miss. So I flipped through and found a chit from Wanborough which read: 'This man is disappointing, and has not borne out the high promise which one was led to expect.'

I have often wondered why this report was put in by the Commandant, and there are three possible reasons, I think. One of the skills we were taught at Wanborough was how to creep, undetected in the daytime, past guards. The Commandant and his staff would stand on a slight rise and shout at the men they spotted, who then got to their feet to be told where they went wrong. I managed, when it was my turn, to creep around the back of them, and the first the Commandant knew of me was when I threw a dummy grenade from a few feet behind him and shouted: 'You're dead.' He did not like that very much.

Then I was not a talker, and the Commandant was a very friendly man who wanted to get to know his men. After my time in the Field Security, I was acutely conscious of the seemingly innocent question of an interrogator, so I would volunteer no information to the friendly Commandant. He probably thought I was a typical, wartime-only-officer—rude and tactless.

There was also one subject at which I was completely useless—radio. I just could not get the hang of sending or receiving morse. Perhaps I felt it was too mechanical a job, even if a vital one. I became all thumbs when I had to sit down and tap out messages. The Commandant may have had that in mind when he wrote his report.

At the end of the fourteen-day course, despite the report, I was asked if I wanted to continue, and I said I did. From then on everything was geared to my future operations on enemy soil. 'Learn the lessons well,' I was told, 'for your life, and the lives of others, depend on them.' It had not really struck me that lives depended on the use of correct methods in the field. From then on I listened, and remembered. It was no longer a wartime game.

The next step was Arisaig, on the west coast of Invernesshire, in Scotland—a most beautiful stretch of country, rugged, rocky, filled with small ravines and small streams. Here SOE had set up another school. Groups of future agents were given instructions to blow up certain targets, and I was told I must take five men and blow up an old engine in daylight. I was given a map reference and told to brief my party. From the map we devised a scheme where one couple would approach the target from one direction, two more from another, and I and my companion from a third. We had to plot our course beforehand so that we could keep out of sight of the 'enemy guards', a part played by the instructors, always vigilant, and ready to advise us where we went wrong.

We split up the following morning after I had made a recce of the area—for however well one can map read, the actual terrain always looks very different. Then we set off on a seven or eight mile clamber through the Invernesshire countryside. After two or three miles I slipped, fell, cracked the tibia in my left leg, and collected a fine gash to go with it. But my companion and I on that January day in 1942 pressed on, keeping in the cover of small ravines, out of sight of obvious high points where a watcher might be. We slipped round the back of the engine, and slapped our explosives in place. There was a loud 'crump', and we were very happy. We were the first couple on the target.

My leg hurt, and later I was taken to hospital. The next day I was standing in the hospital lobby when the matron came hustling in, asked, in scandalised tone, if I was 'her tibia', and insisted on me being carried off to bed, where everyone called me 'Major' and took X-rays which did not show any great damage. I was there four weeks, and great was the surprise when I dressed to leave and they discovered I was a humble subaltern, and nothing as grand as a major.

Shortly afterwards SOE sent me down to Beaulieu, in Hampshire, for what was probably the most important part of an agent's training. For it was here that one was taught how to survive, how to communicate, and how to take on a false identity. Up to this time I had been Raymond Hamilton and apart from the change of name I had no cover story to remember. If challenged, when I was wearing uniform or civvies, all I had to do was produce my service identity card in the name of Heslop, and that was that. If anyone still doubted me, I did not have to worry, because I could quite happily describe my earlier life, my parents, my jobs and so on.

At Beaulieu I was trained to take on false identities by making up a name, and fabricating a life to cover the new name. Having manufactured a new identity, I would be interrogated by an expert to see what holes he could find in my story. And at first it was quite easy to be caught out. For instance, I might be asked the date of my birth and give a false date. Later in the conversation the question would be slipped in again, and this time, by reflex, I would give the proper date. The mistake would be pointed out, and I was told that a similar slip in France would lead to torture and death in a very short time. It was important to remember the details—survival depended on remembering, and it is surprising how many details you have to remember to stay alive.

We were sent on an exercise to Bournemouth to test out our training on passing messages, remembering code introductions, and using methods to make certain one was not being followed. It was a simple exercise really, but important. I was told that my headquarters would be a small hotel and that I would have to walk through the town to deliver a message to a man in another hotel. The first thing I said to him had to be the phrase which would identify myself correctly, and I had to memorise the actual message. He would identify himself by using another introductory phrase, and if I did not get the correct reply, then I must walk away. I saw my man and, to avoid being followed, used all the tricks that later were to become second nature to me. When

I came out of my hotel I walked a little way down the street, suddenly fumbled in my pocket as though I had forgotten something, and then turned round quickly and returned to the hotel. That enabled me to see who was on both pavements and walking towards me. The next time I came out I checked to see that none of these people was still about. It was essential to re-enter the hotel, otherwise you tipped the trained follower that you were suspicious.

Other methods we were taught were simple and effective. For instance, if you knew you were being followed, you kept your eye open for a bus and hopped on it at the last moment, which normally meant the follower would not have a chance to catch up. Just to make certain, you hopped off and caught a bus going in another direction. Or you could walk into a busy store like, say, Selfridges, take a lift up three flights, walk up two more, take a lift down four, and then walk out a back door. That got rid of most people. Another trick was to choose a gentlemen's lavatory with an exit and an entry. You would walk in in the normal way, wait a couple of minutes and then walk out the same way you went in. Simple but effective.

Back at Beaulieu we were shown how to write messages in invisible inks and how to search people properly. We were told that collaborators would leave a maquis or village to pass information to the Germans, and that some of them did not write messages on paper but on their bodies. Women have been known to write messages in some quite interesting parts of their anatomies. Later, in France, a girl courier I used blushingly told a story against herself. She had to travel by rail from one town to another to bring a verbal message to me. During the journey she went to the toilet and found that, like so many trains in wartime France, the lavatory was in a disgusting state. For hygiene's sake she spread newspaper on the toilet seat, and when she stood up found that the heat of her body had moistened the printers' ink enough for her bottom to reproduce the newspaper she sat on. She tried hard to remove the 'message' but could not, and spent the rest of the journey feeling very anxious. She thought that if she was thoroughly searched—as sometimes happened on trains—the Germans might believe she was carrying secret messages on her bottom. She got through all right, and the first thing she did was to have a bath.

We were also taught at Beaulieu how to survive in the open. Our instructor in this art had been a Royal gamekeeper at Sandringham, and he showed us how to poach birds and fish, how to build shelters of branches and leaves, and passed on all the lore of the countryside that had come to him through the years. He always said at the end of his lecture that he would not be sympathetic to anyone he caught after the war pinching the King's pheasants at Sandringham.

My last exercise, almost a passing out examination, was to Nottingham. I was told that I must go there in civvies, without any identity cards, get into a forbidden zone, garner what information I could, and return to Beaulieu. I invented a cover story, set off, and, without any trouble at all, evaded guards at the factory where I was to ferret out production details and so on.

Survival was the basis of all our training at Beaulieu. We were told: 'Keep your mouth shut and do not discuss any matters affecting your job. If you go into a public place, like a restaurant or bar, don't stay completely dumb, because that will attract the sort of attention you don't want.' We were taught to take a quick look round just in case there were Gestapo about or Germans, or Miliciens, the French equivalent of the Gestapo, and then to pick a table facing the door, or the foyer, so we could see what was going on, and who came and went. It was also necessary to sit with our backs to a wall—so that no one could creep up and shoot from behind. Even now, twenty years after, I still find myself doing it. Escape routes, in case of trouble, were also important. A window, the waiters' entrance to the kitchens, or some similar door, must be marked mentally within seconds of entering a strange building. We always had to have identity cards with us in case there was a sudden check in a bar or hotel.

Without them you drew attention to yourself, and had to accompany a policeman to your house or hotel to pick them up. If you had to do that it gave away more information—namely the place where you lived.

At Beaulieu they showed us that pipes normally had tiny flaws in them which were stopped up with putty, or something like it. A tiny message could be hidden in a small hole in a pipe and then cemented in. We were taught to search clothing carefully, to take out linings of suits or dresses, even cut open the heels of shoes, because all these were popular hiding-places.

Cover stories had to be repeated at least once a week, and I did this the whole time I was in France, so that I never had any trouble remembering small details.

It was important, too, to have ready a simple excuse for being in a particular place at a particular time, for it was easy to dry up during a snap police check, so that you could not explain where you were going, or why.

When I passed Beaulieu's last course André Simon sent for me and said he had no hesitation in telling 'them' that I was fully trained as an agent. I would shortly be sent as an 'organiser' to France.

This delighted me because, in my view, it was the most interesting assignment of them all. An organiser was a man who chose his own agents, couriers and commanders, was responsible for maintaining contact with London and for arranging that arms and stores were safely delivered by the RAF. It was the plum job. I left Beaulieu, stayed in London, and was in and out of Orchard Court several times a day, making the preparations for the drop into France. I found out that SOE—despite the bare room in which I was first interviewed—was certainly not run on a shoestring. Everything I needed I got. I was fitted with two good suits cut in the French style, with padded shoulders, and I lived up to my schooltime nickname of 'The Square Man' when I was wearing them. I wore them regularly on trips to London so that they would not look too new when I arrived in France. The labels of a well-known French tailor were sewn in, and I memorised the name of the tailor and the place where I was supposed to have bought them.

My French wardrobe was complete down to pants, vests, socks, shoes, ties, razor blades, pocket-knife, fountain-pen, and pencil. I was given French matches and lighter, cigarettes, and cigarette papers—essential for the smoker, for in France at that time you never threw away a dog-end. They were all stored away in a little box and re-rolled later.

Every article had to be reasonably well worn for new clothes would look suspicious as they were only available through the black market. I did not want to provoke police attention when I arrived in France because I looked like a dandy. I memorised a cover story, a new identity, and all the little details of my former fictitious life. My name was René Garrat, the son of a timber dealer, and I came from the port of Dakar. Dakar I chose because I remembered many details of the briefing for the raid that never took place—names of streets, hotels and the like. I chose the timber trade because I spent some time before the war in Siam working in the teak business. I repeated to myself details of where I was born, where the family lived, where I went to school, what jobs I had, the names of former bosses, the addresses of the firms, places I had been on holidays and stories to explain the scars on my body, like the crack on the leg I got in Scotland. An SOE interrogator spent hours with me in Orchard Court trying to fault my background. In the end I felt I had been Garrat all my life.

One morning an anxious girl secretary came in and said to my briefing officer: 'I'm a little worried about Raymond here. I've got all his forms but he can't produce a birth certificate—he says he has never had one. What shall I do, we must have it.'

The officer asked me to explain. That was easy. I had been born in Cierp in the Pyrénées, high up in the mountains. The local Mayor entered me in his register, but because I was British he did not send a copy to the central register in Paris as he should have done. A few years later an avalanche swept most of the hamlet away, including all the records and Le Maire as well.

'So you see,' I told the officer, 'officially I don't exist, I've never been born.'

He laughed, and the secretary walked away muttering: 'Doesn't exist, ridiculous—quite ridiculous.'

2

I hoped I was to leave for France almost immediately, so I was very disappointed when I was sent back to Beaulieu for yet another course, with Ely, Vladimir, and Roland. This time it was in another, much smaller, house, set in some woods. Here we were shown some particularly useful methods of opening handcuffs, picking locks, and breaking safes. All the instructors were in uniform, but I wondered once or twice whether their peacetime professions were entirely legal. There was a jolly little miniature train that ran through the grounds of the house, and we all practised methods of train wrecking, using plastic and the normal detonators. We were much more assured in their use at the end of the course, and we all enjoyed the bangs we made in that quiet part of Hampshire.

I got to know my companions very well during this time. I shared a room with Vladimir, whose real name was Grover Williams, a British racing driver. He was always cheerful, very philosophical, but impatient to rejoin his wife who was living in Paris. I met him later in France, where he worked very successfully for a time until Maurice Benoist, the brother of another racing driver, Robert Benoist, gave him away while he was being tortured. Vladimir was also tortured for long periods but never gave anything away. Then he was shot.

Ely, E. M. Wilkinson, was to become my great friend and we worked together in the south of France for some time, and later at Angers. His field name was Alexandre, or Alex, and he was captured with me on one occasion and imprisoned. The second time he was caught, the Germans made certain he would not escape again by shooting him at the concentration camp of Buchenwald.

Roland, R. M. (Bob) Sheppard, the youngest, was full of vitality and fun and managed to survive by watchfulness and luck. He had the misfortune to drop by parachute on top of a police station. He said later: 'It didn't matter how good a cover story I had, it was quite impossible to explain away my unorthodox method of dropping in.'

When we completed our course I was sent to a specialist to have my leg examined, and he told me there was nothing wrong with it. But when he saw my ankles he was not very optimistic. I had twisted them and weakened them several times over the years, tearing ligaments whilst running or climbing. 'I wouldn't give you twopence for your ankles, and one foot has lost all its spring. However I will allow you to parachute providing you stick carefully to the drill. Keep your feet well together on landing. In fact, I'd rather you parachute than run or walk long distances across open ground,' the doctor said. He bound both ankles tightly and ordered me to keep them bandaged until I had done my parachute drops.

I went to Ringway airfield, Manchester, for a course which lasted from five to fifteen days, depending on the weather. I joined other would-be jumpers at a house close to the airport, and everyone was very tense. Before our jumps we were taken to see the WAAFs who packed the parachutes, and the care they took was most reassuring. I only hoped they had not put on an act for us.

As I had never flown before, I was given a quick flip around to see if I belonged to the chronic airsick group. But I liked flying and was not sick, and as soon as we landed I was told that I was to make my first jump right away. My stomach knotted up. I became even more silent and tense as an instructor helped me on with my harness.

'How's that, sir, not too tight? Good. Remember, sir, if anything goes wrong and your 'chute doesn't open, let us know,

Xavier in 1944

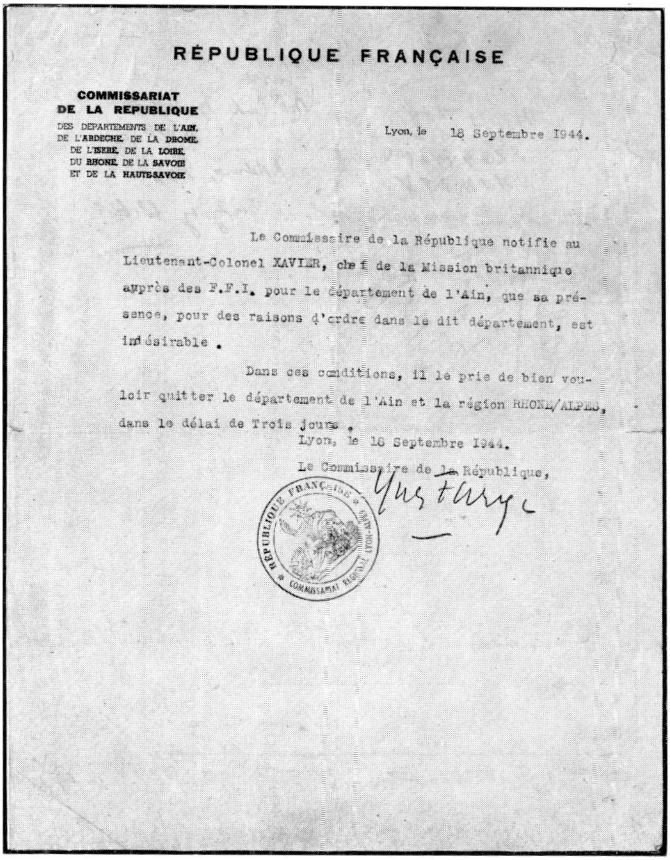

RÉPUBLIQUE FRANÇAISE

COMMISSARIAT
DE LA REPUBLIQUE
DES DEPARTEMENTS DE L'AIN,
DE L'ARDECHE, DE LA DROME,
DE L'ISERE, DE LA LOIRE,
DU RHONE, DE LA SAVOIE
ET DE LA HAUTESAVOIE

Lyon, le 18 Septembre 1944.

Le Commissaire de la République notifie au Lieutenant-Colonel XAVIER, chef de la Mission britannique auprès des F.F.I. pour le département de l'Ain, que sa présence, pour des raisons d'ordre dans le dit département, est indésirable .

Dans ces conditions, il le prie de bien vouloir quitter le département de l'Ain et la région RHONE/ALPES, dans le délai de Trois jours .

Lyon, le 18 Septembre 1944.

Le Commissaire de la République,

Xavier's order to leave the Ain

Above, Jean Saulnier of Annecy outside his Restaurant where the Maquis plotted

Above, The 'thieves kitchen' in the restaurant after a German search

Right, Mme Saulnier receiving the Legion d'Honneur from General Koenig

quoting the official number stamped on the back of the harness, and we'll issue you with another one. If you can't remember the number it doesn't matter—they're pretty decent about that sort of thing here.'

I thanked him most seriously for his advice. My mind was in such a state that some seconds passed before the penny dropped, and then we both had a damned good laugh, although I felt that mine was verging on the hysterical.

There were eleven of us in the Wellington bomber, the twin-engined aircraft used for training, an instructor, who would jump first, and ten learners. I was to be the last one out. The instructor swung himself on the edge of the hole in the middle of the fuselage, through which we were to drop, and although he had jumped something like thirty times before, I noticed that even he tensed up, just before the green light went on, and he disappeared.

The aircraft had to make nine circuits before my turn came. I hooked on my static line—the line that pulls open the chute as soon as you are clear of the aircraft—and dangled my feet in space. I gripped the edge of the hole, fearsome that I might tumble out before the green light. It blinked on; I pushed off . . . there was a flurry, confusion, noise, and suddenly, beautiful peace.

I glanced casually upwards and saw a pair of boots; then I realised that I was heading for the ground headfirst—not the recommended method—as my feet were entangled with the rigging lines. I was surprisingly calm, and methodically cleared away my feet until I was right way up. I looked around, and felt the exhilaration of parachuting I had read so much about.

As I neared the ground the instructor called up that I was doing well, that I did not need to touch the lines. 'Keep your feet together—that's it, fine.'

But just as the ground rushed up towards me, a gust of wind caught the 'chute and I landed flat on my back.

'Are you all right, Raymond?' the instructor asked as I struggled to my feet, a little dazed.

'Yes, thanks. I thought I'd do it that way to save my ankles.' Then we both grinned and it was over. He told me that when I left the aircraft I pushed off too hard. My head hit the opposite side of the hole, although I had felt nothing through my parachute helmet, and the knock flipped me upside down.

I managed the rest of my daylight jumps without trouble, but when my turn for a moonlight drop came it was too windy. To make up for it, they put me in a balloon the next morning, wearing dark glasses. I was petrified, for the balloon was winched up with me sitting in the basket, hanging on grimly. It was deadly quiet, which made the whole affair much more coldblooded than jumping from an aircraft, where there is noise, excitement, chatter. But I made it, although I turned one ankle on landing. At least I was entitled to wear a parachute badge on my sleeve from then on.

It was then early May, and I went back to Orchard Court to learn that I should be going into France in one month's time. The news of my weak ankles had reached them, and I was told I would not be parachuted in, but landed from the sea, probably in the south of France. There were also two more courses to attend. The first was on the Lysander, an odd-shaped aircraft, with a low landing speed, and capable of taking off from any fairly flat piece of ground. It was used many times to take agents in and out of wartime France. We went to yet another country house, near the airfield at Tempsford, where there were not only trainees but some tense gentlemen waiting for the time to come to leave for France. A group of FANYs helped to brighten things up. A well-stocked bar did the rest.

The Lysander is a small, two-seater plane. The passenger sits back to back with the pilot and speaks to him through an inter-com. Two passengers can be squeezed in if you wish to be very tight and uncomfortable. The aircraft carries no guns, is un-armoured, and the only chance of parachuting out is for the pilot to turn upside down and fall through the sliding roof. It is impossible to jump out of the door, as the tailplane will cut your head off. Briefings on the aircraft were given by the pilots themselves.

They taught us how to pick landing grounds and how to lay out a flare-path to guide the plane in to land at night. This was normally done by placing four hand torches, tied to stakes, in an extended line to give the pilot an opportunity of lining himself up for his approach and landing. I carried out day and night exercises with Lysanders, choosing grounds, laying out flare-paths and then flying in and out of the chosen grounds, as though I was an agent in France.

I had a great admiration for these pilots, who had no chance of escape at all if they were spotted in the air. Many of them were injured and there were dozens of narrow escapes. One pilot I met was about to land in enemy territory when he was greeted with a burst of tracer bullets. He turned his landing into a take-off and flew safely back to England, with a bullet lodged in his neck. Another one landed in a field in France and became bogged down in mud. It took a team of oxen to roll the aircraft clear before he could get off the ground again. The man who chose the ground got a great rollicking from London when the pilot reported.

We were also instructed in the use of the S-phone, a two-way R/T handset with a range of about twelve miles. I was to use the services of the Lysander and the S-phone with good effect in the future.

After this training, Roland and I and a man I named Fernandel were sent off to a naval course in Scotland. Fernandel really did look like the French comedian; his ugly face and his mannerisms were very similar. He was to be killed by Gestapo bullets.

We were based in a house overlooking a loch, on which floated a yacht commanded by a man named Christmas. He was responsible for teaching us the elementary rules of navigation and seamanship, how to set sails and furl them, how to tie knots and splice ropes. I was also, to my great joy, taught how to scull a small boat along by using a single scull in the stern. It is a good method of propulsion, as it is almost silent. We also learned to handle different types of canoes and rubber dinghies until finally we were allowed to sail the yacht, plot our course, and so on. And so came the end of this course and the end of training. June, and France, were only a few days away.

I returned to Orchard Court to put the final touches to my cover story and to be issued with false papers, ration cards, and clothing coupons—all freshly brought from France by another agent, and all of the current issue. I was also told to try and make the identity cards grubby, as though they had been handled many times.

I was still René Garrat, born in Dakar, and my father had been in the timber business in Dakar until he died in 1940. I was working with him before the war, but later worked in Marseilles for another timber firm. At the outbreak of war I joined the French Army, and was demobilised in August 1941 in Montpellier. I was then quite rich, as my father left me a reasonable fortune when he died. Since demobilisation I had just drifted around, as the firm I worked for in Marseilles had closed down. My mother had remarried and was now living in Lisbon. So I had no home or ties in France, and I was fed up with life. I had been made even sadder a few months before because the girl I loved had gone off with someone else.

This cover story was built up on facts, to help me to remember it. I knew as much about Dakar as anyone who had not been there since early youth. I had been to Marseilles a couple of times and I had studied the guidebooks and maps. My father really was dead, I had lived in Lisbon for two years, I had been in the timber business.

I also had a story about my army life, with a name for my officer and sergeant, and a history of operations, based on facts learned by SOE, of a real French Army unit.

I had documents by the handful. Military discharge papers, identity cards, ration cards, and so on, as well as a framed photograph of my 'lost girl friend'—my future wife, in fact—which, because it did not give anything away in hairstyle or dress, was safe to take.

I was as ready as I ever would be, trained by the finest instructors—and if I followed their rules for survival I would get through. Only once did I break one of those rules, and it cost me my freedom and very nearly my life.

They gave me a few days leave and said I might get a telephone call at any moment. 'Stay in touch, Raymond,' came the order. The call came only too soon and I reported again to one of the majors at Orchard Court.

'Well, Raymond, you're off tomorrow.' I felt a surge of excitement, and grinned like a schoolboy.

'You will not be parachuted in because of your ankles. Instead you will be flown to Gibraltar and pick up a submarine, which will put you ashore by dinghy on the south coast of France near Cannes.

'You will be met by Roger and a reception committee. On landing you will say "*Boulestin*", and they will answer with "*Écu de France*". You'll be taken to a safe house where you will meet another of our men, "Olive". You will give him a sealed envelope and a large sum of money and take your instructions from him. That's all there is to it. Repeat it back to me please—and remember, no written notes to remind you of anything.'

I repeated everything back.

'I want to tell you, Raymond, that once you are in France there is nothing we can do to help if you are captured—we have never heard of a Heslop or Raymond Hamilton. That's the way it is. Well, good luck. Go and be searched now,' and we shook hands.

I was thoroughly searched to see there was nothing on me or in my suitcase, which I had brought with me, to show any link with Britain; no bus tickets hidden in the bottom of a pocket;

no tobacco in my turn-ups, which could be analysed; no half-crown amongst my loose change.

I saw Vera Atkins, and she fitted me with a money belt to hold funds for Olive and myself. I was then told that the rest of the day was mine. 'But be here ready and packed at 9 a.m. tomorrow —and don't get too plastered tonight,' the Major said. 'Oh, you'll have to be searched again tomorrow.'

I went to a Spanish restaurant that night, my last night in England, and ate on my own. I drank a bottle of good wine, and savoured the security of this corner of London and the chatter of happy people, mostly servicemen out dining with their girl friends. I felt a little secretive and superior, and was not even upset by some of the officers, looking towards me in my padded French suit and long hair, obviously thinking that some people managed to avoid trouble.

But when I got back to one of the flats SOE had for agents and went to bed, the superiority disappeared. I was suddenly frightened, and fought with myself as I felt panic starting up. It was ridiculous to expect me to go into the middle of German occupied territory to wage a secret war. I was no hero, pain frightened me, and I would have no friends. I was still apprehensive the next morning when I arrived at Orchard Court, but finally the fear ebbed in the bustle and hustle of preparations.

I asked for a room to change in and was shown into the famous Black Bathroom. The décor was black, it had a bidet, and many agents were briefed in the Black Bathroom with the agent sitting on the bidet, the briefing officer on the edge of the bath, and the lavatory seat serving as a table. There was always a pretty secretary wandering about ready to help in the briefing. I often wondered what Gestapo men thought of British agents under torture who rambled on about bidets and secretaries in the Black Bathroom.

That morning I changed into another suit, I was searched again, my valuables were sealed in an envelope and left behind, and I was introduced to my travelling companion, a Frenchman named Leroy, a tough-looking man, with a slight cast in one eye, who spoke hardly any English. I met my Commanding Officer for the first time, Colonel Maurice Buckmaster, then still a major. He went through the briefing with me again and added one more thing. I was to be known in London as 'Fabien', and all radio messages would be sent to me in that name. I would also be known to other agents in France by that name.

He wished me well, and then handed me the traditional parting gift that he gave each agent—a pair of gold cufflinks. These were plain and simple, with nothing to show that they came from Britain. Apart from the gesture of sentiment, they could be sold, or pawned for quite a large sum, if an agent ran out of money. I kept mine.

Leroy and I, with Buckmaster and Major Bourne Paterson, went to Paddington Station to catch a train to Plymouth, from where a Catalina flying boat would take us to Gibraltar. We all shook hands, and we were ordered to report to the Security Officer in Plymouth on arrival. He knew we were coming and would tell us what to do next.

We settled in the train, but just as the whistle went and it started to move, the Railway Transport Officer shouted to me: 'Out, out, quickly.' I grabbed my bag and leapt, leaving poor Leroy, with his lack of English, on the train.

I was taken to another platform, and put on another train, where I found a great pile of mailbags, destined for the Governor of Malta, in a small compartment next to the guards van. I was told to guard them to Plymouth, which I did.

At the Grand Hotel in Plymouth I met up with a very relieved Leroy. We were told that if we did not hear by 10 p.m. we would not fly that night. We waited. At 10 p.m. Leroy and I had a farewell dinner, and that night I slept without fear in my mind. I hoped I would have no more self-doubting.

We had three more 'farewell' dinners in that hotel before the security officer came in and told us that we were off that night, by which time neither of us had any English money.

We flew for ten hours, making a wide detour over the Atlantic to avoid German aircraft, with me still sitting by the mail for Malta. We arrived at 8 a.m., to find the sea blue and the sun shining. It seemed a remote war on that balmy day in Gibraltar.

During the next few days I met many old friends for dinner or drinks, as our submarine had left without us, and we had to wait for a British manned trawler. We were given more money, and I enjoyed my holiday. So did Leroy. But he enjoyed it too well. One evening he had too much to drink in a bar and started to talk about his coming trip to France. A security officer overheard him, took him out, and brought him to me. Leroy was reported to the Intelligence Corps, who ordered him not to visit any more bars.

We were told to be ready every night at our hotel by 9 p.m., with bags packed and waiting in the hall out of sight. A security officer told me: 'I don't know which night it will be, but an officer in uniform will walk in dead on nine o'clock, look round the hotel bar, nod slightly to you, turn round and walk out. You and Leroy must follow him immediately.'

The next night I was drinking at the bar when Oliver, who had served in 52 Section with me, walked in with a Gibraltarian, and we started to drink. Dead on nine o'clock the officer in uniform nodded his head. My mind did not work for a minute. How the hell could I excuse myself to Oliver? In the end I stood up, looked at my watch and told him: 'God, I'm late—there's someone waiting for me at the bar at the end of the street. I'll go down and bring him back here. Hold on a minute.'

I walked out, picked up my bag, got into a car which was waiting outside, and was driven to the docks. I wondered how long Oliver had waited for me. After the war we met, and he told me he had realised something was up and had covered my absence with his friend.

Leroy and I boarded a small, grey-painted trawler run by British naval officers, and we were soon swapping tales in the tiny 'wardroom' as we drank their duty-free liquor.

Four more passengers came to join us later—Monsieur and Madame Dupont and two other men, Bernard, who had already been into France several times, and an objectionable Frenchman whom we nicknamed 'The Dunker' because he always dunked his thick slices of bread, butter and jam into his tea.

That night we were merry, happy and slightly tipsy with the strength of the navy's liquor. At eleven there were noises above our heads and shouted orders. The engine started up, and we all fell silent.

We were on our way, a tiny British ship heading out towards the sea and the ominous land now called 'German occupied territory'.

3

I slept heavily aboard the trawler, and after breakfast the Captain briefed us. The trawler had been disguised as a fishing boat with nets at the ready, he said, so that if anyone looked at her closely she was just about to shoot the nets, or had just hauled them. All the crew were in fishermen's gear, but were ready at any time to grab the machine-guns and cannon that were hidden away on board. We were told that if an aircraft were sighted we would have to dive out of sight and stay below until the danger was past.

'The real danger is if we are stopped by an Italian patrol craft,' the Captain said. 'If this happens I shall try to bluff our way through, but if they decide to board us then everything is up. I shall blow the ship up, so you will have to make up your minds whether to stay aboard and go up with her or take to the boats and be captured, tortured and probably shot. That decision is your own.' With these happy words he ended his briefing.

We were told, too, that the trip would take about twelve days, and that we would be transferred to a felucca for the last stage. I found our companions very interesting. Dupont wore dark glasses and a beard that he had quite obviously grown recently. His wife was much younger than he was—possibly in the late twenties—and when the weather got rough she would leave her husband and come and chat with the rest of us. We always felt that she liked to escape from him and was grateful to get away for these chats. Maybe he was jealous, or frightened that she would talk too much. Dupont was a very nervous man, and I thought he would have to pull himself together if he was going to survive in France.

Bernard was tall and thin and very pleasant, but 'The Dunker' was loathed by everyone from the Captain downwards. He was always complaining, and I wanted to tell him just what I thought of him, but I checked myself as I realised that I might meet him in France later on, and I did not want to make enemies.

He and Bernard were the first to leave us. We sailed close inshore off the French coast at some unknown point to drop them. We waited for a light signal from ashore but it did not come. 'The Dunker' was furious and told the Captain that he had made a mistake in navigation and had come to the wrong place. He got short shrift and the Captain told me later that he wanted to kick him off his bridge.

They were finally put ashore two nights later, but not before Bernard, who had five suitcases with him, asked me to take four of them and hand them on to Roger when I landed. I agreed but was annoyed to think that Bernard knew what I was up to. I asked Leroy if he had been talking again, and he admitted it. It was obvious that the man was a grave security risk. Thank God Bernard was on our side! But what was Leroy going to do when he reached the shore?

A little later an officer and three men went ashore at night by dinghy near the town of Sète, some ninety miles to the west of Marseilles. We waited for what seemed like hours, the trawler rolling and creaking in the swell. Finally the boat came alongside, and in it were a group of Polish soldiers who had escaped from a prisoner-of-war camp. They were in a pitiable state, starving, bedraggled, and in need of sleep.

The boat made two more trips, bringing off more men each time. When the third boatload came alongside, I was amazed to find André Simon aboard, my friend and conducting officer from Beaulieu, and the man who told SOE I was good enough to be an agent. He was with two RAF officers, one of whom was Squadron Leader Whitney Straight, the racing driver.

André explained that he had been on a mission, captured, put in jail, but had managed to bluff his way out. He thought it wiser to leave the country for a while, so was taking this exit route. Whitney Straight and the other pilot had escaped from a French POW camp and had been fortunate enough to join one of the escape routes. They were on their way back to England.

During the last day the Captain became anxious about the fuel situation and considered heading back to Gibraltar. Eventually, he decided to spend one more day waiting for the felucca to arrive, and when at last it did come he was making his final decision to turn about and head west again.

The felucca came close alongside, and I handed over my 'luggage', which consisted of six canisters of explosives, five suitcases, two packages, and the money for Roger. I shook hands with André Simon, handed him a letter to post when he reached England, and followed my bags over to the smaller craft. We stayed on board for several days, and took a heavy pounding from the seas and high winds. The Captain of the felucca was a very strong, very silent Pole, who had a fine reputation for landing and picking up agents in the Mediterranean. He was one man I expected to learn had been caught and shot by either the French or Germans. After the war, however, I found he had a reputation with the girls and he had been shot—by the Polish husband of a girl when he caught them both in bed. A strange end to a brave man.

The Duponts were the first to be sent ashore, and they went off without incident after a brief exchange of lights between ourselves and the reception committee. Then, a day or two later, it was our turn. We joined a small fleet of 'sister ships', all innocently fishing between Juan-les-Pins and Antibes, and under this cover we called the shore with a green light. There was no reply, so the Captain sailed farther round the coast and tried again. Still there was no reply. Finally, the Captain called me to the bridge and told me we would have to go in 'blind' or come back to Gibraltar with him and try again later.

I went below to get dressed in my white tropical suit, which had been made in Gibraltar. I decided, as I was carrying explosives, a British-made suit would not matter if I was caught going ashore.

We got into a small dinghy, Leroy, myself and Jock—a Scotsman on the way back to England—with Leroy sitting on the suitcases in the bows, Jock rowing, and myself squatting on the explosives in the stern. The green light was flashed occasionally from the felucca to guide us, but it was pitch dark. After twenty minutes we heard the sound of breakers and then saw the glow from two small lights. Was it our reception committee? On the still night air a voice carried to me: '*Mais mon vieux, qu'est-ce que tu veux que j'y fasse moi, hein?*'—'Well, old boy, what the hell can I do about it, eh?'

Obviously coastguards or gendarmes were patrolling the beach. Who else would be out at 3 a.m., smoking at the sea's edge?

I decided that the correct thing to do was to go back to the felucca. So we did, and the Captain radioed his headquarters later that morning to tell them what had happened, and asked for instructions.

'Roger standing by as from 10 July, try again,' came the message. It was now 12 July 1943, so we tried again that night, and we got an almost immediate red flash from the shore in reply to our green signal. Jock rowed towards the red flashes, until Leroy said that we were close to a rock. So I decided to swim, in my tropical kit, to meet the committee and see if I could get help to pull the dinghy in. Wading ashore, I came up to three men from the rear. I waited for them to flash a red light again, and then made quite a noise, on purpose, as I didn't want to be shot down within minutes of landing. They leaped round, I saw a glint of a gun before I got out my password: '*Boulestin*'. They replied '*Écu de France*'. They had been expecting the password to come from the sea, not the land, and were a little unhappy until I explained that the dinghy was offshore and we needed some assistance.

Soon the boat was ashore and unloaded. Jock shook hands and said goodbye, then rowed into the dark, leaving Leroy and myself on the shores of France.

Now there was a long argument (which I kept clear of) because there were not enough men to carry all the equipment to the 'safe house'. Roger, the leader, decided to hide the gear until it could be recovered later, and we set off walking to the hiding place.

I was a little despondent. No one seemed pleased to see us and their attitude implied that it was a nuisance having to turn out in the middle of the night. They were far more interested in whether I had brought them a present than in my presence. I was staggering along with a suitcase on my shoulders, when another argument started up, and now it was decided to row across the bay with the suitcases, as there was not enough time to walk to the hiding place.

A boat was found, and everything loaded into it—explosives, suitcases, Leroy, Roger and myself. The other men walked off. I rowed into the bay and asked Roger how far it was across. 'Only a kilometre,' he said. But once we were a hundred or so yards out, water started lapping over the side of the overladen boat, and I knew we would never make it.

I pulled hard towards the shore, and Leroy took over while I baled with Roger's hat. Suddenly I heard breakers.

'What's the land like here—is it sand or cliff?' I asked Roger. He didn't know. We got closer and, straining my eyes, I finally saw a rock as the boat, now out of control and sinking, swung round.

'Grab a suitcase and jump for that rock,' I shouted, and leaped over the side.

I heard a gurgle and despairing cry as I landed, and turned round in time to grab Leroy and haul him, suitcase and hat, on to the rock. After he spat out the seawater, he said he had a weak leg and could not swim.

Roger landed safely with a suitcase and found a way up the cliff. He went off to find his boys to help us take the gear back to the safe house. The main road was only a few yards away, and we decided to make directly to the house. We knew that if the dinghy was blown ashore and discovered with its explosive contents, the hunt would start immediately. It was broad daylight when we reached the house and climbed over a back wall to be greeted by the owners, a sculptor and his wife. They gave us dressing-gowns while our clothes dried, and produced hot coffee from the bag of 'goodies', brought with me for my reception committee, which included whisky, chocolate, and coffee. Then Leroy and I went thankfully to bed.

I was woken at 11 o'clock the same morning by a man dressed all in white—shoes, socks, shorts, and shirt. 'Don't worry, it's me, Olive,' he said and sat down. I gave him his sealed packet of orders from London, plus the money, and asked him what instructions he had for me, as I was expecting him to tell me where I should start my own underground organisation.

But he had no plans, and suggested I took a few days off to familiarise myself with the routine of living in France in wartime. We were in the unoccupied zone, so there were no Germans about, and Olive had arranged for me to go to another house in Cannes, where I could wait in peace for orders to come through.

Leroy was going to Marseilles that day. We shook hands and I wished him well. He had a stout heart, that one, even if he did drink and talk too much.

Georges, aged eighteen, the son of the family with whom I was going to live, arrived with two bicycles, and told me that he would pedal ahead. If he was stopped, I was to pass him and wait farther on. If I was stopped, he would come back and try to help, as he was well known in the area and all the policemen were friendly to him. He got on a lady's bicycle and strapped my suitcase on the back.

'Don't worry about the case—I often carry a radio transmitter on the back of this bike for a Resistance W/T operator, and that is much heavier than this. It'll be all right,' Georges said. And he set off, shouting over his shoulders: 'Don't forget to ride on the right, and look out for one-way streets.'

All went well, and soon we arrived at Chalet Charles-Edith, near the Hotel Windsor, in Cannes, the home Georges shared with his parents, Monsieur and Madame Audouard, and his sixteen-year-old brother Edouard.

I told them that my name was René Garrat, and we made a plausible cover story to explain my reasons for staying with them. Immediately after we worked this out, Madame showed me the rear exit, which I could use in an emergency, and warned me not to keep anything incriminating in the house. She showed me a cache in the garden where I could hide money, documents, or a revolver, if I wanted to.

She also told me that her sons would escort me round the town for a day or two, so I should know what areas to avoid and get a general idea of routes out of Cannes. Finally, she showed me to my room, and said that because of the shortage of food, she could only provide breakfast and dinner. I would have to use my ration cards to get a midday meal.

In my room I gathered my thoughts. There was no doubt about it, the organisation here was chaotic, and Leroy and I were very lucky still to be free. No provision had been made for a cache near the reception spot, and because of this we could have been in 'the bag' within a few minutes. Roger's men seemed completely undisciplined, and argued loudly against his plans. The decision to take to the sea, instead of hiding our equipment, had resulted in the loss of valuable explosives, and might have ended in three deaths.

The Audouards, however, were obviously very security conscious and took their job seriously. They were pleased to have me with them, though the others, apart from Roger and Olive, were indifferent to my arrival. A little enthusiasm, I felt, would not have been amiss. I made up my mind not to lapse into complacency, and went through my cover story as René Garrat. I did this once a week during all my time in France, first as Fabien and later as Xavier.

For the next few days I was happy to soak up the sun and swim off the beautiful town in the warm Mediterranean. I learned to pay for my meals, using the correct ration cards, and even to slip the waitress extra at the beginning of a meal, asking for the 'supplementary dish'—a black-market dish for which you paid heavily. I kept clear of the fashionable bars and restaurants, but went to the cinema occasionally, and once to the theatre at the Casino. It was there that I was startled to see Major Bodington, whom I had last talked with when he was briefing officer at Orchard Court. He looked straight through me and I made no sign that I knew him. I guessed that he was the Jean Paul whom Olive mentioned was coming into the area.

The following day I had another surprise. I was sitting on the veranda of the chalet when I saw a man I knew but could not place, limping past. He looked up, saw me, and peered closely. I ducked in through the window and listened as he came to the front door.

Madame came in and said that the man knew me and wanted help. He told her he had parachuted into France two days earlier and had damaged his ankle. He recognised me because we had been on the same parachute course together. I watched him through a glass door, and finally it came to me. It was Clement; his real name was de Baissac and we *had* been on the same course.

He explained that he (under the field name of David) and Harry Peulève had jumped together. Peulève had broken his leg and was still lying where he had fallen. They had jumped 'blind', with no reception committee to meet them.

Monsieur Audouard decided to look after my visitor and then went to find Peulève to decide what could be done to help him. I moved out of the chalet and went to share a flat with another

Englishman, Julian (Newman), a radio operator with whom I had become friends during my holiday in Cannes.

The following day Julian and I went to meet Jean Paul (Major Bodington), and I told him about the two agents and their troubles. He agreed to try to help.

He also brought some more exciting news. I was to leave for Lyons on Sunday night, by train. In Lyons I was to meet Phillippe de Vomecour, whose field name was Gauthier, in a square in the centre of the city, beneath the fourth tree on the right, at 10 a.m. on Monday. This was in the best tradition of cloak and dagger, and I thought the instructions were very melodramatic. Jean Paul told me that I would be given details of my mission by Gauthier.

'Do you know what this mission is?' I asked him.

'Yes—I can give you the broad picture. You've got to contact ten former French officers, all very tough and determined men, and you'll have to lead them on a raid into the Occupied Zone. Gauthier will show you how and where to cross the demarcation line between Vichy France and the Occupied part. That's the outline and you'll learn the details in Lyons,' he said.

This was exciting, but not what I came to France for—my job was to organise an area, not to lead commando raids. But no doubt London knew what they were about. I left to make arrangements for my journey of more than two hundred miles.

On the Monday I met Gauthier as arranged, and he told me the operation would have to be delayed as there had been several arrests in the Lyons area recently, and they all feared it to be the work of a traitor. He could not give me the addresses of the ten officers, and said it was too dangerous to cross the demarcation line into occupied France.

'Well at least tell me what I'm supposed to do with these damned officers when I finally get at them,' I said irritably.

'Haven't they told you? You are going to raid the prison where they've got my brother a prisoner, and get him out.'

I just looked at him blankly. 'Did you say raid a prison?' I asked him. 'A German controlled prison? Well I'm damned.'

I agreed to wait because I could see Gauthier set great store on the attempt to get his brother out. I knew how I would have felt if I had a brother in jail, possibly being tortured. The raid, however, was not just a sentimental affair to save a brother's life. The man was an important agent with important contacts. As Gauthier had no idea where I could stay, I wandered from hotel to hotel, trying to find a room for myself. Finally, tired with walking around in the heat, I sat down at an open-air café to have a drink.

And the first person I saw was Wilkinson, from SOE, grinning at me from behind a newspaper. Jacques, Gauthier's second-in-command, was with me, and I asked him if he knew the man behind the newspaper.

'Yes, do you?'

'Very well indeed,' I told him.

'He's the man who can help if he will. He can get you over the demarcation line and fix up the operation for you. I'll arrange for you to see him later. Don't acknowledge him in the street.'

Later Jacques took me to a very gloomy flat. The door was opened by a girl, who looked at me with suspicion, but at a nod from Jacques, she showed us in, and there was Wilkinson, the pipe-smoking, hawk-eyed, slim man who was my friend.

'Hello, how are you? You don't look too happy,' he said.

'Hello—it's good to see you. Very good to see you.'

He introduced me to the girl, Mary (Virginia Hall)—a very brave American girl—and they carried on with their conversation. 'Don't forget Cuthbert, it may not be all that easy if you forget him,' she was saying. Two or three times in as many minutes the name of Cuthbert (who seemed to be a real fly in the ointment) cropped up, and I could stand it no longer. 'Who's this damn man Cuthbert?' I asked.

Mary simply banged one of her legs against the table, and it gave out a hollow sound. 'That's Cuthbert,' she said. 'He's wooden.'

Alex and I then had a long talk. He said he had been operating in the Angers area for the past few months building up Resistance groups, but was hamstrung because he had no radio operator. Without one he could not get arms or stores dropped, and his men were beginning to lose faith in him. 'You remember Vladimir—you know, Grover Williams the racing driver—well he's been in Paris for about the same time as I've been in Angers and he hasn't got an operator yet either,' said Alex. 'I went to Cannes because I heard they had more than they needed. I can understand this. If you're caught in the unoccupied zone there's a chance of buying yourself out and not being handed over to the Germans. But if you're caught in the German zone, it's curtains.'

In fact, I found the opposite later on. In the occupied zone nearly everyone hated the Germans, and so there was less treachery. But in the unoccupied zone many a traitor was tempted by the high prices offered for turning over an agent to the authorities.

Alex had finally managed to persuade an operator to join him, and they were leaving the following day. 'Would you like to join us?'

'Fine. I'll take you over the demarcation zone at Limoges and then I'll put you into a "safe house" until Gauthier contacts you again. I'll then take Rake—he's my radio operator—on to Angers.

'Come and meet him. He was in the theatrical business, and he's a bit of a clown really, and as frightened as hell. He was caught crossing the demarcation line recently and put in jail, but managed to get out. His nerves are all to pieces, but he's the best I can get. We'll have to put up with him best we can.'

I met Rake later that evening, and it was obvious that he was a badly scared man. But it takes real courage to admit one is frightened, and then carry on, especially after you have already had one taste of prison. We arranged, the three of us, to catch the morning train to Limoges, and parted for the night.

On the way to the station I went through my cover story, for I was about to go through my first police identity check. Naturally I was frightened. Would the documents, prepared in London, be good enough? Were the official stamps the right ones? Was the paper the right kind? My stomach tightened up, and I could feel sweat come into the palms of my hands. As I walked with a great crowd of travellers towards the entrance to the platform, I could see one gendarme demanding identity cards and checking each one. With my suitcase in my hand I handed my card over. He looked at it in a cursory manner, looked straight into my eyes with that world-over look of a policeman, 'ah-ah-what-have-you-been-up-to', which made me feel even more nervous, and then muttered '*Bon*', and waved me through.

Later on, of course, I got more used to these checks and could tell before I went through how thorough the investigation would be. If there was only one man on in uniform, it generally meant a routine check with the gendarme as bored as the travellers. If there were several uniformed men and some plainclothes men, it was certain they were hunting for someone. I was posing as a rich man about town and decided my best reason for visiting Limoges was to buy some pottery—should anyone ask.

The three of us had arranged to meet on board the train, and I soon saw Rake standing on the platform looking very, very anxious. When he saw me he looked pleased.

'Have you seen Alex—where is he?' he demanded.

'Relax, I haven't seen him yet, but he'll be along in a minute.'

Rake put his bag on a seat, and as the time to leave came closer he started hopping on and off like a fussy grandmother, trying to decide whether to catch the train and leave her grandchild behind, or wait for the next one. People were beginning to notice him. Mind you, I was a little anxious too, as there was no point in going to Limoges without Alex. We were both relieved when he finally appeared, lugging a large suitcase, just before the train left. Later in the journey I met up with him and asked: 'Where's your suitcase, left it somewhere?'

'What suitcase? I haven't got a suitcase,' and he winked.

Later I found out that the 'suitcase' was Rake's radio transmitter, and I learned not to ask questions about people's luggage. The wise man dumped his case in one part of a train, and disowned it if a check was made on luggage.

We reached Limoges at 5 p.m. and left the station separately, meeting again in the road outside. Then we started searching for a hotel room. Alex tried the Café des Faisans, where he knew the proprietress, but there were no rooms. However he did manage to leave the radio in a dark store cupboard, without her knowing. We found one room, gave it to the anxious Rake, and finally found another to share in the annex of a small hotel. Then we talked about the methods Alex planned to get us into the occupied zone. 'I have a railwayman friend who drives expresses from here to Paris, where he lives. He has agreed to hide us and get us over. He'll slow his train so we can clamber aboard, then we'll stay in a little hideout on the engine by a fusebox. We'll be smothered in electric sparks, which look dangerous but aren't. He'll slow down at a given point for us to drop off. It's quite simple really. Tomorrow I'm meeting him in town. This will mean a pub crawl with him, as he always drinks steadily on his day off. With a bit of luck we should be on our way the day after tomorrow.'

We met Rake for dinner, and for security reasons did not tell him where we were staying. We agreed to meet him at 11 o'clock the next morning, outside the Café des Faisans.

That evening Alex brought out a revolver and oiled it. He reckoned that as he would be carrying a radio transmitter it did not matter if he carried a revolver as well—and a gun might save the day if we were stopped. We concocted a story about our relationship in case there was a check. My name was René Garrat, as usual, while he was Jean Montfort. Rake was a friend of Montfort's, and I had met him for the first time on the train.

That should be enough for a brief check. Just before we went to bed the old lady of the house brought up the forms every traveller had to fill. We completed them, Alex wrapped his revolver in brown paper, and we slept.

Next morning I was up early and wandered in the sunshine around the town, looking at the shops, which were half empty—very different from Cannes where they were well filled. Alex left the hotel before me, after tucking his paper-wrapped revolver under his armpit. Dead on eleven o'clock I met up with him a few yards from the Café des Faisans, and we strolled up to it, paused outside waiting for Rake to come out and join us. But he did not.

So we walked on, both worried. Alex, puffing away at his old pipe said: 'You know what Rake is like; he's so nervy. He'll probably be late. We'll come by again in a few minutes.'

We both knew that this was the wrong thing to do. It had been drummed into us that an agent never hung around when an appointment was not kept. The drill was to come back for the second appointment—for one always fixed two appointments in case the first one could not be kept. A train might be late, or a car have a puncture or, of course, the agent arrested. We talked about the risk but we did not want to leave Rake, as we considered him the sort of person likely to miss appointments. We decided to stroll round the block and re-pass the café. If he hadn't turned up then, we would leave.

We approached the café very slowly, both apprehensive, paused outside—and were immediately surrounded by five men in civilian clothes. One produced an official police identity card with the tricolour in the corner.

'We're police—your papers, please.'

We had broken a rule and suffered the penalty. We were caught.

4

Firstly I felt fear, and then my mind ran wildly ahead, thinking in terms of trying to get free. Before the next demand came—'Your papers, please'—I'd already dismissed the idea of hitting and running. There were too many of them for that. I thought the best thing to do was to sit it out and hope that we could bluff our way through. After all, we had good papers and nothing was known against us. But how the devil did they know we were going to be at the café? It could only be Rake, he must have told them.

'Your papers, please!' I handed mine over. The policeman looked at them and put them in his pocket. All five were smiling and outwardly friendly, but I guessed this was because they did not want to cause any trouble in the street. They looked at Alex, who was standing saying nothing, with a book under his arm, still enjoying his morning pipe of tobacco.

'Papers, please,' came the more insistent request. Alex produced his and protested that a Frenchman should not be stopped in the street and subjected to ignominy like this. They ignored him, took his cards, and asked us to go with them to the police station. 'I believe that Monsieur le Commissaire would like to talk to you both,' we were told.

Inside the police station in Limoges, the smiling attitude of the five men changed to downright bullying. We were searched by uniformed men, while Alex was continually protesting that we could not be searched until a charge had been made against us. They searched me thoroughly. I thought I might get away with 2,000 francs, rolled in some toilet paper as a hiding-place, which

I kept as emergency money, but the police took the toilet paper sheet by sheet to examine it—I presume they thought there were messages on it—and unravelled my money. I turned to Alex to give a sign that my reserve had been discovered, and was just in time to see another pantomime. He took out his revolver, still wrapped in brown paper, and held it out to an inspector—a very smooth and nasty character—who ordered Alex to unwrap the parcel. He did so in such a way that the butt of the gun fell into his hand with the muzzle pointing at the inspector. I thought the inspector was going to pass out. He went noticeably whiter and made a gurgling noise at the back of his throat. The other police grabbed their guns and shouted: 'Look out, look out, he's going to shoot.'

But Alex raised his eyebrows mockingly, opened the breech, showed the police the gun was unloaded, and tossed it contemptuously on the table. This was typical of Alex. He was the only man I ever met who seemed mocking, contemptuous, and above all, cool, and unaffected by alarming events. He made the police look fools, which they did not like. They shouted and ranted and threatened him with horrible prison penalties. They were, of course, just frightened—as I would have been if a man had suddenly pointed a gun at me in the middle of an apparently normal interrogation. They then took our ties, shoe laces and belts, in case we tried to hang ourselves, and ordered us to be taken to the cells. Just as we were walking out we were called back, shown a photograph, and asked if we knew the man on it. We looked hard, both shook our heads and said 'No'. They laughed, and took the picture away. The picture was of Rake.

There were five cells in a row facing the latrines. I was put in the end one, and Alex in the next one. Although it was well past lunch, I was not hungry and walked up and down the tiny cell. It had no window, a stone bed with a thin straw mattress on top, one blanket which stank, and the police latrines, only ten feet away, smelled even worse than the blanket.

They took Alex away for interrogation after an hour and whilst he was away I went through my cover story time and time again to be prepared for the interrogation which awaited me. I was worried how Alex was going to explain away his gun, and I was beginning to think that he would never rejoin me when the door of the cell next to mine was opened, there were footsteps, then a whisper. 'Raymond, Raymond,' Alex's voice came through using the code name that I had used under training. 'Raymond, it's Rake. That's how they got on to us. He gave us away. But I have told them nothing at all.'

I was bloody furious, and paced my cell angrily. That man had been a nuisance from the very first time I saw him, always frightened, always twittering away like an anxious sparrow. As I paced, I became more and more tired and lay on my bed and waited for the French to take me away for questioning. I waited an hour or two, while my anger died away to be replaced by fear. I could not lie still, just waiting for the footsteps and the key in the cell door. I started pacing again, up and down, up and down, while my mind dwelt on Germans, Gestapo and torture. Torture, I had realised before, might be inflicted on me, but this had been an academic thought. Now I was faced with the real, naked terror of it. I had read enough and been told enough of the tortures used on agents, to make me doubt my ability to withstand them without compromising myself, my friends, and the workings of SOE. Three in the morning is not the best time to think on these things especially as, on top of the fear, I was tired, unshaven, and could not get away from the stench of sweat and urinals.

But the real reason for my sleepless night was remorse. I had been trained for months by SOE, and on my first operation I broke one of the commandments which had been drilled into me so many times. All I had achieved in my time in France was to have a fine holiday on the taxpayers' money on the Riviera, and then put myself in a position where, under torture, I might reveal who was operating in Cannes, where to find the family Audouard, Julian, and all the rest. I did not like myself that night, and I did not hold out much hope for myself in the future.

Next morning I was taken before Inspector Morel, a man I did not like. On his right stood another inspector, toying with a revolver, and behind me were two more inspectors. I sat in a chair facing Morel as they questioned me and I told them of my life as René Garrat. They listened, smiled, and said: 'Come, come, we know that you are a British officer.' But I stuck to my story, and they got angry. One pushed a gun in my ribs and another made as though to punch me—but did not. Then they changed their line and soft pedalled a little, saying that they did not want to hurt me but they knew I was British, as my friend Montfort had admitted we were both British officers. Then they tried the hard line again, shooting questions one after another. They still could not break my cover story. I insisted I was René Garrat. In the end they gave up and sent me back to my cell, where I collapsed on the stone bed. I hardly noticed the stink from the blanket as I pulled it over me. I whispered to Alex, who was still in the next cell, that I had said nothing, but that they obviously knew quite a lot.

They took Alex away again later, and he did not come back that night, but by then I was so exhausted, dirty, unshaven, that I did not care what happened. To hell with SOE, to hell with the clandestine life, to hell with these days and nights as an agent. What was the point of all the troubles and anxieties that Alex and I and all the other agents went through? Were they to try to improve the future for men like the frightened French policemen, who were only determined to stay on the winning side; were we there just to provide a few hours sport for the Gestapo, a training body for teeth pulling, testicle twisting and kidney punching experiments; were we there just to give power to some career-making politician back in Whitehall, to enable him to pull an extra string in the game of power?

In the morning they hauled me off for another interrogation. We went over the same old ground and I kept saying: 'If you know everything, why the hell question me?'

Suddenly I made up my mind. I would give them the

'confession' they wanted, but it would be completely false. 'All right, I'm a British officer. I parachuted into France a few days ago, and you caught me as I was about to make my first contact.'

'Ah, *mon brave*, we knew all the time,' and suddenly they were all smiles.

I told them that I had dropped into the Drôme near Montpellier, that I had caught a train to Marseilles. I was able to give them train arrival and departure times because I had helped Audouard look them up only a short time before. This impressed them enormously. I told them I met one man in Marseilles called Charles and he gave me instructions to come to Limoges and contact a woman called Jacqueline, in the Café des Faisans near where we had been arrested.

I described Charles and Jacqueline. They helped me with Jacqueline, asking whether she was wearing a black hat with flowers on it and so on. I said 'yes' and Morel turned to one of his men and said: 'I told you we should have picked her up at the café. By now she will be miles away.'

They asked me where I stayed in Marseilles, and I gave them the name of the Hôtel du Paradis, a place where no one signed the register. I knew this from reading guide-books and talking with SOE executives in London. In very good humour, they sent me back to my cell, where I immediately wondered if I had said too much. What if Jacqueline, a complete figment of my imagination, was a regular at the café and they arrested her? They left me alone for the rest of the day, but the following morning I was shown into another room, where I found Alex, still smoking his pipe, and Rake, who looked very sheepish. There was a Belgian there called Charles, who said he had been arrested on his eleventh trip from Belgium to the South of France, where he had been taking details of the Belgian coast defences. He was a fine man, and I knew we had an ally in him. This room was much better than the cell. It had four beds with mattresses, clean blankets, two or three benches, and a cupboard.

Unfortunately a policeman sat in the doorway watching us for twenty-four hours a day, whether we were asleep or not. I noticed that Alex was not talking to Rake, and would not talk to me at all if he thought Rake was within earshot. He kept looking at Rake as though he would like to kill him. I found out why. Alex learned that Rake was arrested at his hotel at 8 a.m.—three hours before we were picked up at the café. He had been interrogated at the police station without violence, and suddenly admitted he was due to meet two British officers at the café at 11 a.m. If he had not cracked we would have been in the clear.

After another day Alex decided to adopt the story I had already given, and said that he, too, had been on his way to meet Jacqueline. The police were delighted. They beamed. We briefed Rake on the new story, and he helped us with our cover the next time the police talked with him.

It was not until later that I discovered that the police had already established a link between Alex and Rake, for they found that both of them were carrying bundles of new, 1,000 franc notes—and those in Alex's pocket were consecutively numbered with those in Rake's. So are agents trapped. I also learned later that our capture was the result of an astute hotel manager at the place where Rake had stayed the night. Rake had talked incautiously, not giving away any secrets, but enough to give a hint to the manager that Rake was not all he seemed to be. This, coupled with the Briton's obvious anxiety, was enough to give the police the tip when they called to make the routine 5 a.m. check on the hotel documents. The police came back at 8 a.m., saw Rake, and he told them immediately that he was meeting two friends at 11 a.m. While we were in prison later on, Rake told me that he did this because he was 'het up' and he thought he would have a better chance of survival if he was with Alex and me.

We then saw the Commissaire of the 'Surveillance du Territoire'—roughly the equivalent of the British Special Branch—and although he seemed sympathetic, he warned us not to try to escape. Alex, in the meantime, had become quite friendly with the Commissaire and several times in the next few days, walking on his own through the streets, he went to see him at his office. The two discussed our problem and Alex tried to bargain with him. He offered to help the Commissaire and his family to escape from France if, in return, he would look the other way for enough time for the three of us to get free of the town. He did consider this and was on the point of agreeing, when he remembered Gerry Morel, another British agent. '*Non, monsieur,*' he told Alex, 'it just cannot be done,' and told Alex that Morel had been in hospital after a major stomach operation. With the stitches still in the wound, he had stolen a doctor's white coat and just walked out of the front door of the hospital, leaving an astonished medical staff and bringing a heavy reprimand on the Commissaire. The effect of that reprimand was still uppermost in his mind and he would not agree to help at all.

During these visits, Alex met Caesar, the Commissaire's Corsican cousin, and he was a very different person. Caesar was disgusted at the Commissaire's reluctance and then refusal to help, but he promised to do everything in his power to get us free.

The Commissaire, perhaps out of remorse, did his utmost to try to make our lives comfortable. He allowed good food and wine to be brought in, saw that we were supplied with books, and once let Alex and me out of jail for an afternoon. He demanded my parole—Alex had already pledged that he would not try to escape—which I gave, and sent us off with Inspector Imar. He led us down to the river bank where the inspector met his wife or his mistress, and as the two lay together talking, Alex and I lazed in the sun, walked about, and enjoyed the fresh air. I said to Alex: 'Wouldn't it be easy,' and nodded towards the couple. 'A quick crack on his head and a gag in her mouth and we would be away.' But we had given our word. I often wondered whether the Commissaire was disappointed when we walked back to jail that day.

Extraordinary things happened in that police station and its cells. Three Jews were brought in. They were terrified, and every time a policeman or an officer in uniform walked into the buildings, they would leap to their feet, click their heels together, and give the Hitler salute. Black marketeers were caught regularly, and we always benefited from their arrival. When one was about to be arrested, a gendarme would come and tell us and say: 'Good food tonight, right?' For the marketeers always demanded luxurious food and wine to be brought in, but as soon as they had the meals laid in front of them, they always lost appetite. They would look at the food, smell it, look at each other, shrug, and push it away. I do not know what made this happen time after time, perhaps it was the smell of the sweat and the urine in the building—smells we had become accustomed to—or whether the sight of luxury brought to mind all the good things they were missing outside. We did not care what put them off their grub, we always looked forward to those evenings.

Another regular customer at the jail was a little rat of a man. He would come in, stay an hour, and then scuttle away. Alex found out from a friendly guard that the 'rat' was an informer on black marketeers, for which he was well paid by the police. We disliked him more than the black marketeers. A little old lady, quiet and gentle, was brought in one night, and we wondered why she had been arrested. We found out later that she was an abortionist who had been caught practising her trade.

I decided to have a good inspection of the cell to see if there was a way we could escape. It was, after all, a police station and not a top security prison we were in. I found that our room had a second door, sealed off by three metal clamps, which led straight out into the street. I talked with Alex about this, and he agreed to have a look at the outside of this door the next time he went off to see the Commissaire. When he came back, he said that the outside of the door was protected by wire and railings—but that these ended eighteen inches from the bottom of the door. As the door opened inwards, it meant that all we would have to do would be to crawl under the wire—an easy job. We decided all we needed to break out was a chisel to cut through the metal clamps. But how to get it? Alex could not walk into a shop and ask for one, as he passed no shops on his way to the Commissaire's office. The only thing to do was ask for one. We did. We picked on Inspector Imar, who had seemed so friendly by bringing us extra food and razor blades. The next time he came into our cell we said bluntly: 'We need a chisel, can you get us one, please?' He looked at the clamps on the door, grinned, and said he would, 'tomorrow'. And the next day he came in with one, and gave it to Alex.

It was obvious that Imar knew what we were up to, but despite all his offers of help, for which we offered large sums of money, we were not certain that we could trust him fully. He did return some of the money that was taken off us when we arrived in jail, so I sewed some into the turn-ups of my trousers, and hid a 1,000 franc note in a packet of cigarette papers. Imar also gave us the name of a doctor in the city who would help us, the same man who had helped Gerry Morel earlier. Things were going quite well.

But now Rake took to his bed and became quieter and quieter. Charles and I did our best to cheer him up but nothing we did could bring a smile to his face. Alex continued to ignore him, and I think the thought that he had betrayed his friends worked on Rake's conscience. One day he was so ill that he was taken to hospital. It was a relief, really, for although I did not think he would volunteer information, he was unreliable under stress.

We started to work on the clamps. One of us chipped away, while the other two leaned on the bars with their backs to the clamps, making a lot of noise to cover up the scrapings and bangs that came from the chisel at work. We sang, too, and I even taught Charles 'I've got sixpence, jolly, jolly, sixpence,' and he would sing this, in very bad English, which was the most effective

Andrés, head of the Spanish group in the Haute Savoie. He was shot down by German checkpoint

Elizabeth Devereaux-Rochester, Xavier's courier

Bayard, his British sabotage officer

Capitaine Montréal

Lt Louison – La Brosse

Jo Grosfillet of 'les yeux verts', a courier

Colonel Chabot

Dr Touillon, who brought medical aid to the Maquis

Marius Chavan, Mayor of Mont-griffon, co-founder of the Maquis de l'Ain, who was shot by Germans

Colonel Romans

(4th from left) Mimile, Romans, Chabot, Montréal, Plutarque

Below, Train sabotaged by one of Chabot's groups in June 1944

way of drowning the noise. After a few days we had broken two of the three clamps, but the last one was tough and we decided that it would have to be broken forcibly with a tyre lever another guard had given us.

Two things then happened rapidly. Firstly, three prostitutes were brought in one night. It was the first time I had seen a girl close to for a long time so I chatted up the youngest and blondest of the three, who was complaining at being picked up on the street. When I told her I was a British officer she nearly cried. 'Ah, an Englishman. I will help you all I can. You must get away. They won't keep me here long, so when I go home I will leave my door on the catch every night so you can just walk in any time. No one will find you there—and I do not charge my friends.' We really were getting organised—two addresses to go to, money, Alex's compass hidden in a tin of coffee, and the door to our freedom hanging on one metal clamp.

The second incident forced us to make our bid. The Commissaire said to me one morning: 'The Gestapo are interested in you and your friends and they are coming to see you. We know that they should not come into the unoccupied zone, but as they are in civilian clothes they create no stir, and anyway there is nothing we can do to stop them. But I will give you some warning. If I come in and say you are wanted and I'm not wearing a handkerchief in my top pocket, it will mean that the Gestapo have arrived and are waiting to interrogate you.'

A day or two later the Commissaire walked in—and there was no handkerchief showing. I felt very frightened as I followed him into a small room where two stern-looking men in civilian clothes were sitting on plain chairs at a wooden table. The Gestapo. The real toughs in Hitler's Europe, my heart thumped and my guts tightened with fear.

'Sit please,' one said. The Commissaire stood behind me after I chose another simple chair facing the two men, but he took no part in the interrogation which followed.

'So—you are a British officer,' one said coldly. 'Kindly tell me how you come to be in France in wartime.'

I had realised, before, that it would be useless telling the Gestapo the false 'confession' story I had given the French police as there were too many holes in it to survive a detailed investigation, so I had decided to give my 'true' confession, prepared for me in London before I left.

'I was the navigator of a Mosquito (a twin-engined, high flying, fast, reconnaissance plane of the day) and was shot down,' I told them. I told them the name of the village near which the aircraft had crashed, the name of my pilot, my false name, the date of the crash. This story was a true one. A Mosquito had crashed on that day, the pilot had been killed, and the Red Cross in Geneva had the name of the navigator—the name I was using—listed as 'Missing in Action' in their records. I gave the Gestapo the details of the flights that aircraft had made over enemy territory, again all true, all taken from the squadron records by SOE.

'What is the cockpit of a Mosquito like—and what instruments did you have to use?' I was asked.

These boys are thorough, I thought to myself, and a flash of panic hit me. But I pulled myself together and told them, for my story had even included these details. The Gestapo man snapped question after question at me based on the Mosquito, but although I was very frightened, I remembered all the details that had been drummed into me by SOE and I did not falter.

During the interrogation the second man had been leafing through page after page of a big book and after each page looked up into my face. It was upsetting, for I realised he was checking my face against known agents, and it was possible that my picture had been taken in the south of France while, say, I was with Olive or other British agents.

At the end of an hour the book was closed, the two stood up and told the Commissaire to take me back to my cell. The Commissaire walked back with me, and then quizzed me about the new story he had just heard. 'You were lucky I had not taken down your old story and that the Gestapo did not demand your records. So which story do I believe?' he asked me.

'You must make up your own mind,' I told him. 'The facts are still the same—I'm an escaped British officer and I'm still your prisoner.'

He did not press me on this, but he did make me very worried, a little later in the day, when he said that the Gestapo were not satisfied with my story and the chances were that they were going to demand my release to a German controlled prison. That news decided me—we must make our escape bid immediately.

Before we did this, Alex felt that he had to withdraw his parole. Honour came first with Alex. I had not given my parole, except for the brief trip we made to the river. So Alex told the Commissaire he was withdrawing his parole, and within minutes there was bedlam. Gendarmes rushed into our cell, they shouted, tossed clothes and bedclothes about, inspected the doors and found the two broken clamps. We were ordered to be searched. Alex went first, leaving the chisel in his windcheater. They found nothing on him. Then it was my turn, and they went through everything, although I said I had nothing to hide. When the searching gendarme came to a suspicious bump in my turn-ups, he looked up at me and asked again if I had anything to hide. 'Of course not,' I told him, but with a jerk he split open the linings and found my wad of notes. He screamed at me, but I told him that they had been there a long time and I had forgotten all about it. Strangely, he believed me and quietened down. They did not find the chisel.

The Commissaire was livid. He gave us a severe lecture on the penalty of escape and increased the number of guards by putting two more inside the room, two just outside and two patrolling. It gave a little boost to our morale to see all the care they were taking to look after us. The clamps, of course, were renewed and, outside, the gap was wired, making it impossible to wriggle through. The escape was off for the time being.

Two days later we received very bad news. The Commissaire told us that we were to be removed and taken to a real prison in the south of France, as we had tried to escape and he no longer wanted to take the responsibility for us. This, of course, upset Alex, Charles and me, and we approached Caesar and told him he must work out some plan to make certain we were freed. Caesar came back to us after a few hours and said that we were to be taken that night. 'But do not worry, 'he said, 'I have arranged for a gang of toughs to jump your guards and set you free and I shall then escort you to a safe address.' We felt much better then.

We were given a good meal that evening and then, just before we were to be taken off, the Commissaire came to visit us. He looked distraught, and his face was sweating. 'Messieurs,' he whispered, 'the escape is off. Caesar told me about the bid, but unfortunately he cannot get enough men together to get rid of your escort. There's nothing more he or I can do to help you. I should have liked to have helped but I cannot—it is the family; I fear for them.'

Alex and I were very, very sad, and paid little attention as we were handed some of our possessions. I was allowed a small suitcase, in which I packed a shirt, spare socks, briefs, a face towel, soap, shaving kit, a box of matches, the cigarette papers with a 1,000 franc note inside, the tin of coffee in which the compass was hidden, and Buckmaster's cufflinks. We were also given two days' ration of bread—half of one of those long French loaves—and we also took along two bottles of wine.

Our escort arrived just after midnight, and we were chained together, my right wrist to Alex's left. Charles was left behind. Alex made a terrible fuss over the shackles but no one paid any attention, and we were marched through the main office of the police station. A dozen or more policemen on duty all leapt to their feet and called in chorus as though they had rehearsed it: '*Bon voyage et bonne chance.*'

'Words, just words—that's all one ever gets from you brave patriots,' Alex shouted loudly back at them as we were pushed through the main entrance into the dark night.

The two guards were uneasy and very alert that night and they kept one on each side of us, just out of reach, so even if we tried to jump them we could only tackle one at a time, as our chains kept us together. We found the railway station was packed, and everyone looked at us as we were escorted in. Some observed us pityingly, others as though we were bearded ladies at a funfair. One of the watchers caught Alex's eye. 'Look,' he said, as he nudged me, 'there's Caesar—over there in the fawn mac. Something might be on yet, so be prepared.' The sight of the little, energetic Corsican cheered us both up considerably.

When the train drew in, we had to stand in the corridor of a first-class carriage as no seats had been reserved for us. An elegantly dressed woman forced her way past us, sat in an empty seat in one of the compartments, and said in a loud voice to the gendarmes: 'Surely, criminals should travel in the guard's van or third class,' and to give them their due the two apologised to us for her rudeness. A few minutes later she got up, passed us again, and returned with a suitcase a few minutes after that. And behind her came Caesar, with an even bigger one, which became jammed in the corridor as he tried to pass me. I suddenly felt cold steel in my hand and for one glorious moment I thought it was a gun, but I found it was a rough file about eighteen inches long. I tucked it up my sleeve as Caesar winked at me and passed on, and put it in my right trouser pocket after he had gone. I whispered to Alex and showed him it, and he grimaced as he saw the length of file sticking out of the top of my pocket and edged closer to me so that it was concealed between the pair of us. Later we found seats in a third-class compartment. One gendarme sat in one window seat facing us, and on our side was the other gendarme, then me, Alex, and a woman. A few minutes later Caesar stuck his head inside, grinned, and went on when he found the compartment full. The gendarmes were still uneasy and barked at us every time Alex and I talked, which made the poor woman in the corner cringe.

After a while the two guards nodded off and Alex and I decided it was worth while trying to get the file into his windcheater pocket where it would be hidden. I inched the file out of my pocket and on to the seat between us. Every time we moved the chains clinked, and the woman next to Alex realised that something was going on and became very restless. When Alex started to work the file into his windcheater it clanked against one of the bottles of our wine he already had there and we had to rattle our chains to cover the noise. The situation tickled our sense of humour, and every time the file clanked and we rattled our chains we burst into giggles like a couple of twelve-year-old schoolgirls.

We finally got it stowed away, and then decided we would ask to go to the lavatory in case they unshackled us. But they were wise to that trick, and all four of us piled into the smelly compartment. So we decided to get a little rest, too, and nodded off. We woke as the train pulled into Toulouse and as we climbed down Caesar made his last appearance, waved and shrugged his shoulders. We had a warm spot for him, and his presence had given us some hope and the knowledge that we were not entirely friendless. We had a long wait at Toulouse and the gendarmes pushed the pair of us into the darkest corner of the buffet while they sat a little way off drinking coffee. We wondered where we could hide the file, and suddenly I remembered the French loaf. I told Alex who, with his back to the guards, pulled the file out and pushed it firmly into the centre of the loaf. The guards took no notice, and Alex and I grinned when he got it safely back into his windcheater.

I was very depressed as we sat drinking some very poor coffee. I wondered how everyone was back at home. No one knew where we were and SOE did not know if we were dead or alive. Later I found out that we had been given up for dead, and my mother received a letter saying that I was missing and a second one saying that there was little hope that I was still alive. We were at our lowest ebb, that early morning, with no friends, no hope, and the threat of a prison only a few miles away. But somehow Alex and I bucked up, and we even persuaded the guards to go and buy us some grapes in the town. One of them went shopping for us and we had to pay an enormous price for this little luxury. But it was worth it.

Our train finally came in and took us to Castres, where we got out. We were shepherded out of the station and after a few minutes' walk we turned a corner and there was the blank, thirty-foot high wall of a prison. We skirted this, turned another corner, and saw an iron gate with an iron handle for the bell. Three times the guards tolled this, before we heard shuffling feet, the clink of keys, and the gate was swung open by two men, in blue uniforms, wearing berets. We walked down a long, dark corridor into the prison office, where the Chief Warder immediately screamed abuse at Alex for not taking his beret off in his presence. I never felt more despondent than when I walked in through that iron gate and faced this horrible man.

We filled up forms, told our cover stories briefly, and the phrase 'British officers' brought no reaction from the warder. I was allowed to keep a handkerchief, a box of matches with some money hidden in it, my cigarette papers hiding a 1,000 franc note, a pencil, and some lavatory paper. The Chief Warder told us that we would be in separate cells and must divide the food between us. While he was saying this he was examining Alex's pipe on the table next to the bread and grapes, and I was bracing myself for the explosion which would come when he felt the loaf. But Alex, self-assured and confident as usual, bent over in front of him and picked up the loaf. 'I'll have the bread, you can have the grapes,' he told me, and pushed the fruit towards me. Quick thinking.

We were at last unchained, and Alex was led off to his cell saying in farewell, so typically: '*Merde.*' I looked around as he was being locked in and saw a huge, empty hall, three storeys high, with galleries running round it. On each gallery there were rows and rows of cell doors with eyeholes, through which the guards peeped at the prisoners by flicking back the Judas gates. At the end of each gallery was a warder, dressed in blue and wearing felt slippers, sitting on a chair. I could hear no sounds, except for the shuffle of the slippered warders and the echo of Alex's steel-tipped shoes pacing his cell. Then I was led up to the third floor and locked in. I sat on the bed for a long time without moving, without even taking in my surroundings. I felt abandoned and without hope, as I gazed at my feet and thought that this *must* be the worst that could happen to anyone—to be cast in a cell unknown to one's friends, without hope, without knowledge of the length of sentence, without knowledge of the next move. Would that be to a firing squad, suddenly one morning? I was in despair, and did not even look up when the Judas gate was flipped open, and a guard peered in and clicked it shut again.

Some while later—it may have been two or three hours—the door was flung open and a guard brought in a tin, leaking at the bottom, holding thin, green liquid. This was supper. Seeing that I was not paying attention, the guard told me that when the whistle went, I must get into bed immediately and not get out until another whistle went in the morning. I must not lie down on the bed during the daytime, he ordered. Then he went out. The soup, green muck though it was, and a handful of grapes, made me feel a little better, and I took stock of my cell. It was about fifteen feet long, by ten feet wide, with clean, whitewashed walls and a brick floor. The bed was an iron frame, with a thin mattress, two blankets, and a highly coloured quilt, but no pillow. There was also a wooden chair, a shelf, and a bucket. A window was set high in one wall and protected by a wooden hoarding that leaned into the room. It let the air in but it prevented one from looking out. Over the door was a powerful electric light bulb, let into the wall and protected by heavy glass.

As soon as the whistle went I got into bed and dropped off to sleep immediately. But two hours later the powerful light, which had gone out as the whistle went, came on again, and the Judas window was clicked aside. The guard was making certain that I was there and not getting up to any mischief. This happened every two hours throughout the night. If I covered my head with the blanket to keep the light out of my eyes, the guard would scream at me to wake up so he could be sure that the blanket did not hide a dummy.

It went on like this for weeks. I saw no one to talk to from one week's end to another. My main interest in life was in whether the soup of the day was going to be brown or green—not that it mattered for they both tasted the same—or whether I might get twenty-two minutes solitary exercise in the prison yard, instead of the regulation twenty. I went to the barber once a week for a shave—a painful business as he used a blunt, cut-throat razor and no lather. There might be one or two other prisoners waiting for a shave, but they were kept with their faces to the wall and were not allowed to talk. I lost all track of time, and I never knew the date or whether it was Monday or Friday. I was just an animal, mute, uncaring, and despairing. I talked to myself occasionally, just to hear a voice and partly to make certain that I could still talk.

This misery ended one morning, when the guard ordered me to pick up my belongings and follow him. I was shown into another cell—and there was Alex. We clasped arms, and I knew I was not far from tears at seeing the face of a friend again. We were both drawn, and we had both lost weight.

When the first excitement was overcome, our first thought was on escape. 'What do you think—can we get out of here?' Alex asked me.

'Not a hope. These walls are thirty feet high. There're no projections and even if we managed to get a rope, we'd still have to get over the outside walls, and they are thirty feet high as well. The only way out is with inside help, and there'll be little enough of that,' I said, and Alex reluctantly agreed. 'I've still got the file, though. We might be able to hack our way through some bars with that, and get out. But God knows where.'

I told him he should bury this in the exercise yard until the time we would need it, as if it was discovered it could only cause us trouble. He agreed, but decided to hang it out of the cell on a thread taken from a blanket.

Five or six days later we were joined by Rake, who had been well looked after in hospital and seemed much better. Three in a cell was a little cramped, but it meant more company. But Alex's mistrust of Rake continued and he still refused to talk to him.

It was a lovely autumn in 1942 and the three of us, who were taken out to exercise together, decided we must try to get fit again. We started to do exercises in the prison yard—knees bend, push ups, and so on. But as the food got poorer, we had to stop, for we became so weak that we could hardly climb the three flights of stairs to our cells at the end of twenty minutes in the sun. But life inside did improve in other ways. Some of the warders whispered scraps of news they had heard on the BBC and we were allowed to receive apples from the prison canteen, brought round to us by warders every three weeks. We could also buy matches from the canteen, and every time we were allowed goods I would ask a warder for matches. I had quite a stockpile after a bit. God knows what I thought I could do with them, but one never knew.

Alex had two visitors one day when I was out of the cell for some reason or other—the barber probably. One was Inspector Imar and the other a man from the Deuxième Bureau, whom we had seen briefly in our police-cell days. They offered to get us out of jail. They said that they had arranged to arrive at the prison gates with four men, two of whom would have false papers giving their occupation as police inspectors. They would carry forged documents ordering the Chief Warder to release us to their care for transport to Vichy. The other two would be dressed as gendarmes and would be our 'escort'.

'Our only trouble is that we don't have a car or petrol, and these cost a lot of money,' Imar told Alex. 'If you can arrange for us to get some money, we can buy these on the black market, and you'll be out within a few days. Can you fix this?'

Alex told me later that he was very tempted by this offer, but, when he considered, he realised there was a great flaw in their conversation. If they could forge documents, including one from the Vichy Government, they would have no trouble in commandeering a car with other forged documents. Sadly, he turned the offer down. We talked it over, and I agreed with him that he had made the right decision, for the only way we could have got money would be by putting them in touch with our SOE contacts and we would not have done that.

Three days later, Rake and I were ordered out of our cell and locked into separate cells. The Chief Warder and the local chief of police walked into my cell and ordered me to strip. They searched me thoroughly, tore the linings out of my clothes, the heels from my shoes. They found my stockpile of matchboxes, and the Chief Warder nearly went berserk and screamed in rage at me. They took all the boxes, including the one with my money in, but allowed me to keep the cigarette papers with the hidden 1,000 franc note. I was allowed to keep my underpants and shoved into another solitary cell. Later my clothes, with the linings roughly sewn back and my shoes with the heels nailed on, were given back. Although I did not know it at the time, the uproar was over our famous file, which had been found dangling from the cell. Alex had been taken out and repeatedly beaten across the face by the Chief Warder. He took the beatings without murmuring, but at the end turned to him, spat on the ground, and said: '*Vous n'êtes pas un Français—vous n'êtes qu'un salaud.*' When the two of us were together again later, Alex asked me to swear that, after the war, we would search out Chief Warder Andrieu, and kill him. I solemnly swore.

Alex was dead when it all ended. But I remembered the vow

and returned to the prison at Castres to pull the clanging entrance bell outside the main gates. When a warder arrived, I asked to see Andrieu.

'Andrieu, il est parti,' was the answer. No one knew where he was. I do not think I would have shot him, but at least I would have made it very clear what Alex and I felt about his inhumanity.

We were put in solitary confinement again. No more canteen food, no more fresh fruit. Food became the usual round of snails in green soup. Sometimes, on a Sunday, the soup had a particle of gristle in it. My main distraction was hunting fleas and bedbugs in my cell. My record haul was seventeen fleas in one morning. Bed became a happy relief, despite the two-hourly lights on and snapping of the Judas gate. I did everything possible to try and bring some interest into my life, some human contact. I even looked forward to the regular interrogations, which were kept up over the months by the Chief Warder. I had a little game there, by trying to prolong the interrogation, just to keep the sound of a human voice going as long as possible.

Loneliness. This was true loneliness. I can imagine the old-age pensioner sitting alone in a small room. Lonely, yes. But by opening a window at least the sound of a voice, a distant radio, a passing train, the clicking of a girl's heels on a pavement, even the lowing of a cow, can be used to break the monotony. At least there's a morning paper, the milkman, the weekly visit by a friendly welfare officer. We had nothing. The prison seemed to be without sound, apart from shuffling slippers, the clang of a door, the click of the Judas gates, or the shouts of a Chief Warder. There was no friendliness, no communal life. Nothing. I kept my sanity by little things. I found one day that there was a small hole in the hoarding over my window and, peering through it, I found I could see the exercise yard. After a while I saw Alex, bent and stumbling, walking slowly round it. I prised out two or three pieces of mortar and flicked them through the open window towards him. He looked up at the third piece—not that he could see me—and smiled that wonderful smile of his. I got a piece of lavatory paper, wrote that I was okay, and threw that out. I saw him pick it up, read it and he waved back at me. At least he was still alive.

Another time, through the same small hole, I saw Rake, and risked whistling a couple of bars of 'I've got sixpence'. He looked up, waved and smiled. It all seems very trivial, twenty-five years after, but at the time it was important.

On 7 November 1942 we had been in the wretched jail for nearly three months. I was very weak, every move was an effort, and I had constant headaches. I had lost a great deal of weight, and each little set-back grew into enormous proportions in my mind. On that day I sat in my cell, my head in my hands, not far from tears, appalled that I had been brought to this state by Frenchmen—the people of the country where I had been born and raised. In France I had found courtesy and kindness, valour and dignity. The French were my blood brothers, and yet they had been overbearing, aggressive, violent and deceitful. The men who imprisoned us were not much better than their German masters.

As I was sitting, one of the kinder guards slipped back the Judas and whispered: 'They've come to fetch you. You're leaving this afternoon.' I'm sure he meant to be kind, but the news made my heart pump. I knew fear, real fear. Were they coming to take me to an execution ground?

Half an hour later I was taken to the prison office and handed my small suitcase, with the tin of coffee and its hidden compass. A few minutes later Alex and Rake were brought in, both looking very ill and very thin.

I must have looked the same, because Alex did not recognise me at first, and when he did he murmured: 'My God, what have they done to you?'

'Not only to me, but to all of us, Alex. I don't care where we go now, providing we can all be together,' I told him.

A few minutes later we were led back along the dark corridors to the main gate. This time there was no need for an alert guard or chains—we could not have run away if the whole of the escort had dropped dead at our feet. We did not have the strength.

The main gate was opened, and we were shown out. I turned to look at the thirty-feet high walls as we stumbled away, and I swore that I would never go inside another prison as long as I lived. Once was enough.

5

Just to be outside was enough for the moment, to see people and children again, cars and bicycles, the greenery in the trees and grass in the parks. The three of us, each handcuffed to a gendarme, looked around and smelled air that was fresh, air that did not contain the prison odour of urine, sweat, and bad food. We even managed to smile.

We were taken by train to Toulouse, then on to Lyons, where we were put in a black maria and driven to the police headquarters. Our escort was kind, and when we reached Lyons they sent out to a local restaurant for us. When the woman proprietor heard that we were British officers, she brought us the finest meal we had had for months, complete with magnificent wines. She refused to take our money, so I gave her a small ivory horse, which I had bought in Gibraltar on my farewell dinner with 52 Section. She was delighted, but I thought it was small payment for the fine food she brought us. Alex and I ate well, but we were sensible enough to remember that our stomachs would not take vast quantities of rich food, after what we had been used to for the past three months, so we ate carefully. I felt quite tight on a couple of glasses of wine and suddenly life was magnificent.

In the Gendarmerie Nationale four RAF NCOs were shown in after we had settled, and they were all swearing at 'those bloody French traitors'. They had crossed out of the German zone but had been turned in by a Frenchman who, no doubt, wanted the reward. We were delighted to see them, as we felt we might be on our way to a prisoner-of-war camp. We were. In the afternoon, the seven of us were driven in a coach to Chambaran, in the Isère, where we arrived late at night. The camp interpreter met us and shouted: 'Welcome, welcome. There's great news just come over the BBC—we've landed in North Africa.' We all cheered and shouted, which brought guards out with fixed bayonets. But they quietened down when they heard the reason for our joy.

We found that the camp was full of British officers and men from all three services and was commanded by a Frenchman with French guards. We were among friends and found that life was a paradise compared with Castres. The food, mainly from Red Cross parcels, was filled with luxuries like marmalade, corned beef, and sugar. The three of us lived with the eighteen other officers in the camp whose senior officer was a Lieutenant-Commander in the Royal Navy, known as Smoky Joe. He had been caught ashore during the Dieppe Raid and he always delighted in answering the question: 'But what was a seaman doing ashore?'

'Well, I laid a smokescreen from my ship, which was very successful, so I thought I'd nip ashore and have a shot or two at some Jerries—which I did. But when I tried to find my ships, I couldn't—the smokescreen was too good. So they put me in the bag.' That was his story, anyway.

I gained strength daily with the better food, fresh air and the friendliness of the 'natives', but when I tried to instruct some of the lads in boxing, I found that my heart pumped madly after only a few seconds sparring. I was still far from fit.

We knew that it was likely the Germans would take over the whole of France, now that they had the enemy facing them across the Mediterranean, and I was not surprised to hear that they had marched into Marseilles. It was obvious that it was only a matter of time before they took over our camp, so we set up a guard system, under which one man was awake at all times during the night to give warning of the arrival of Germans.

One morning the parade was taken by a new French Commandant, a well built, thickset major with a beard, called Boucher.

He made the normal sort of morning address, but his general attitude gave a feeling of confidence. I felt he was on our side. The next morning, Alex and I, together with three or four other prisoners, were called before the Commandant. 'Messieurs,' he told us, 'I know from my records who you are. I know from reports that the Germans are coming here soon, and they've already given orders that you are to be shot.'

My heart jumped with fear, and I saw that the hand holding Alex's pipe had tightened, so that the knuckles showed white.

'But, gentlemen, I cannot allow that to happen. So I'm going to set you free. The rest of the genuine prisoners will have to take their chance.'

That speech had the most extraordinary effect on me. My legs started to shake, and I thought I would have to sit down. All we could do then was to shake the Commandant by the hand and say 'Thank you.' It was, I felt, a feeble way of showing gratitude for our lives.

We were told a coach would take us to Roybon, drop us there, and from then on we would have to make our own way to safety. We would be given money and ration tickets before we left. Alex and I decided to go with a Captain Cooper, a man who had served for twelve years in the Foreign Legion, and who had been an agent in North Africa before capture. We talked about going with Rake, but Alex was adamant. 'That man is unreliable. Anyway, he may crack up and we can't afford passengers on this trip.'

I packed biscuits, bread, bully beef, cheese, socks, underpants, lint, elastoplast, and boracic powder. I dressed in civilian clothes, except for British army boots, which were all I had. I put the lot into a small suitcase, including our compass, Buckmaster's cuff-links, and a map which the escape committee had let me have. Alex and Cooper packed similar gear into rucksacks.

Freedom was around the corner—if we could evade all patrols and checkpoints and keep out of the way of German groups, who would seek us out once they took over the camp and found we were missing. Alex and I discussed our plans and decided we would make for Le Puy, a small town about 150 kilometres from Roybon. 'We'll walk,' I said. 'That's the only safe way. I know we've still got our original papers, but they are useless now—we are known, they've got our photographs. Once we go through a checkpoint we are lost. The only way of avoiding them is walking.'

Alex was dubious. It was November, there was already snow in the passes, and he and I were far from fit. But Cooper agreed with me, and Alex shrugged and fell in with the plans.

'We'll do it in three days—right. Fifty kilometres a day. If we take longer than three days the Germans will have too much time to find us,' I said, and checked again that I had the lint and bandages.

Over lunch, we told our friends that we were being transferred to another camp, but one or two of the brighter ones came over to us before we left and wished us luck. 'It's only right that people like you should get a chance—we'll be all right.' And they meant it.

We got into the coach just after lunch and, just before Roybon, Alex, Cooper and I, got down and made for the nearest woods. It was 3 p.m. on 27 November 1942 when we sat down in the cover of the trees to smoke a cigarette and savour freedom. It was a great feeling, sitting there in the pale November sunshine, gazing contentedly at the fields, and listening to the distant sound of cattle. As we relaxed for half an hour I thought, with great admiration, of Commandant Boucher, who had behaved so courageously in releasing us. I learned later that he had left the camp at Chambaran before the Germans arrived and reached safety in England.

I then studied our map, and traced the route we wanted to take through Hauterives and Serrières, where we had to cross the greatest natural barrier between us and our goal—the River Rhône. We would then climb up into the mountains, through high passes to Saint Bonnet-le-Froid, then to Yssingeaux, and finally Le Puy, where Alex had friends with whom we would be safe. I found that my calculations had been wrong; there were 160 kilometres to go, not 150. So I stood up, picked up my suit-case, and said: 'Right, away we go.' We set off at a good pace, as I was determined to cross the Rhône that night, otherwise we might be forced to lie low all the following day and thus lose time on our tight schedule. At first we chattered like magpies, but slowly we fell silent as the unaccustomed exercise started to take effect. I plodded away, feeling the muscles in my calves beginning to tighten and slowly those in my thighs became sore at the steady, plod, plod, plod along the hard road. We passed a few people on the road but no one paid us any attention except for a nod and a 'good evening'. At dusk we were on the edge of a small town and we decided to take an hour's break in a barn until it got dark, and then walk through the town. This would save us fighting our way through hedges and fields to skirt the buildings, and also save some of our energy. We ate a little, rubbed our sore muscles, and relaxed. But Cooper developed a feeling about the barn, and wanted to get out of it and on our way again. We respected his feeling—we had been in the game long enough now to know that one always respected 'feelings'—gathered up our gear and pushed on. We split and went through the town singly, but none of us saw any gendarmes or Germans, and when we regrouped, the other side, we continued to walk on towards Hauterives. Cooper got the first blister, and swore as he felt the rawness in his heel. We stopped and I used the lint and sticky tape for the first time, bound his heel, and we went on again. After only three hours I was walking like a machine, not thinking about anything, not hearing anything, just concentrating on setting one leg after another, as the unused muscles became more and more tired, and more and more painful. At nine o'clock the three of us decided to stop for a time, and we broke out a little food, which we chewed listlessly as we sprawled in a hedgerow. There was no conversation, and I was sure everyone felt as I did—exhausted.

We got under way again and slogged on towards the town,

which we reached after curfew. I had blisters on my heels then, so I tidied those up, and we tried to work out the best approach to the town—through it or round it? We decided through it—I believe that we were almost reaching the point where we did not care if we were captured again, so agonising was our progress. Alex went first and I followed him five minutes afterwards. The town was absolutely silent and I could only hear the thunder of my army boots on the pavement as I went down the main, winding street. I turned a corner and saw a light streaming across the road from an open doorway, only a few yards ahead. Over the door was a blue lamp with the inscription in white letters 'Police'. It was useless turning back, as the sound of my boots must have heralded my coming, so I just strode on into the blazing light. I screwed up my eyes at the brightness and tensed myself to hear the command: 'Halt'. But nothing happened and I walked on, out of the town, and met up with Alex. He laughed as he heard my panting voice, but he admitted that he, too, had been shaken by the light. We waited for Cooper and the pair of us laughed at the tough, ex-Legionnaire, when he exclaimed: '*Merde*, that bloody light.' We had been lucky to get away with it, but in one way it had been a good experience, for it certainly snapped me out of the lethargy I had been feeling that it would not matter if I were recaptured. I cared now. At midnight Alex and Cooper wanted me to stop for the night, but I was obsessed with the idea of crossing the Rhône. I agreed to stop for an hour, when we catnapped, changed the bandages on our blisters, and rubbed our muscles. At the end of the hour I was very cold. I had not noticed the cold before, but I realised how important it was to either keep moving or keep warm. We were in no state to be freezing—our health would not take it. On we went again, but in a few minutes we heard the roar of motor cycle engines and saw the glow of lights coming towards us. 'Quick, into the ditch, and keep your heads down so your white faces don't show up,' I shouted, and flung myself into the edge of the road. I counted seven motor bikes and a car pass us. We started again and kept going for the rest of the night, a painful, agonised night of hell, broken only once by a halt at a roadside fountain for a drink of ice-cold water. At 6.30 a.m. we reached Serrières and the River Rhône. We turned upstream, still on the main road, and, as dawn broke, we saw the bridge and the river shrouded in morning mist. We had a muttered talk in a doorway and decided to cross the river by the bridge rather than by trying to find a boat and rowing it. I agreed to have a look at both ends of the bridge and come back if all was clear. I walked down the street, my boots making a hell of a noise, but I saw no one on the west bank. I walked across the bridge and saw no guards on the other bank. I waved my friends on and the three of us set off over the bridge. One man came out of the mist on a bicycle, stared at us, but said nothing. And then, at last, we were across the river. I was relieved, as we headed clear of the town into the country again.

We stopped off the road for some breakfast, and then pushed on again, tired, unshaven, and with Cooper now limping badly from blisters on both heels. Within minutes we ran into a group of German soldiers marching towards the bridge. They were the first enemies in uniform I had ever seen, and I felt very scared as they came towards us. I held my breath, watching them approach. But they did not question us, and we went quietly on, sighing with relief. We now entered the Ardèche, a very steep, mountainous area, with cliffs rising sheer on one side of the road, and a precipice on the other. There was no hedge or haystack to hide behind on this sector. We kept going, but Cooper was walking more and more slowly and Alex and I, although very tired, frequently had to wait for him to catch us up. We climbed that rugged road all morning and arrived at the summit of the pass, some 4,000 feet high, at midday. There we found a small village. We had been walking—apart from the two hours of resting in barns—for just about eighteen hours, and I was amazed that we had been able to keep going. I felt that we deserved some rest and refreshment, so we walked into the village café.

I ordered a couple of bottles of wine and asked if they had any food. There was only soup. I said we would have a drink and then some soup. When we had finished the second bottle, Cooper pushed his chair back and walked into the back of the café. Ten minutes later he came back, grinning. 'I always knew I was lucky. Monsieur le Patron was in the Legion, and he's asked us all to join his family for a meal. Come along.' We ate an enormous meal, drank more wine and paid very little. We waved the family goodbye, and got on the road again.

The first half-hour was agonising. The rest had given our muscles time to seize up and mine just creaked and pained until I hit the right rhythm again, the deadened cadence of the marching soldier, who sees and feels and senses nothing for mile after mile. We kept going, Cooper still limping, and Alex uncomplaining, although I knew he was as weak as I was and in just as much pain. Once, a passing gendarme stopped us and asked who we were. I told him that we were just three friends heading into the next town for a few drinks. He accepted that, without much enthusiasm, and we walked on. We kept on, it became dark, the wind rose and screamed coldly, as we limped and stumbled our way towards Le Puy and the hopes of succour and sanctuary. By 8 p.m. we were finished, so we turned into a farm and asked the farmer if we might sleep in his barn. He looked at the drawn, tired, near exhausted faces of the unshaved trio, and nodded. Cooper managed to get us some hot soup and some thin wine. We warmed outselves at the great kitchen fire, in the farmhouse, before we went out into the barn. We carefully took our boots off, I changed the bandages on Cooper's heels, where I found the flesh was red, inflamed and badly puffed, and helped Alex to dress his blisters. We then wrapped outselves in sacks, buried ourselves in the sweet-smelling hay, and slept like the dead. It was our first sleep, apart from one catnap, for forty-eight hours.

We were up at first light. The farmer, thankfully, came over with a bowl of soup each and a glass of cognac. He wished us '*bonne chance*', and we were on our way again. Cooper was almost completely crippled by the blisters, which were now inflamed and must have caused him untold agonies. On top of these, an old wound in one of his legs was aching with a dull pain. Alex, however, was the person I was worried about. He rarely said a word. The confidence that was so much a part of him had gone. He was a machine, a hobbling, white-faced machine, kept going by courage and doggedness alone. He was obviously far from well, and I remembered that he had only been released from the prison camp hospital a few days before, where he had been treated for exhaustion following his stay in Castres. But I knew our only hope was to keep going. Delay would give the Germans the chance to organise a major search.

But Cooper walked more and more slowly, and even Alex managed to keep ahead of him. Cooper sat on the edge of the road and told me that he could not go on. 'I've got friends in the south of France, I'll head there and lie up for a few days, to regain my strength and to get rid of these damn blisters,' he told me. I agreed, and he walked off. I was sorry to see him go but it was obvious that he only had a couple of kilometres left in his feet. In any case, he knew how to look after himself.

Alex and I walked on alone until 11.30 a.m., when we came to a small town. As we had seen no Germans or gendarmes we decided to stop for lunch at a hotel. We had a good meal, and were at the dessert stage, when *le patron* came over and said that two gentlemen were waiting for us in his office and would like to see us after we had finished our meal.

I thanked him and then silently cursed, for I knew it must be the police. I remembered Castres, chains, cells, cross examination, confinement. We could not run for it, because every step brought agony. We decided to say that we were British RAF officers, escaping, and hope that the 'gentlemen' would be good enough to let us go. Alex was to talk in French; I was to pretend I knew no French.

In the office we found two gendarmes leaning against a desk, one elderly, one young. 'We would like to see your papers, please,' said the older one.

'I'm sorry, we don't have any papers,' Alex said. 'We're escaping British pilots,' and he told them the same story I had told the Gestapo earlier.

The gendarmes were astonished, and only believed him when he showed the WD mark on the underpants he had obtained in the prisoner-of-war camp, and when they inspected my British army boots and saw the tin of English tobacco Alex had received from a Red Cross parcel. Then we had to wait. What were they going to do?

The old one suddenly laughed. He laughed long and loud. He clapped us on the back, shook us by the hand, opened his pocket book, and asked us how much money we needed. 'You can go as soon as you've finished your coffee,' he told us, to our complete astonishment. We thanked them and Alex gave him some of his tobacco, but we refused his money.

The young one had not looked very happy and asked his comrade: 'But what are we going to tell our boss about these two?'

'That's easy—we'll tell him their papers were in order,' and he gave a great belly rumble of a laugh. 'Don't linger on the road and don't let yourselves be seen too much,' was the advice he gave Alex. 'Finish your coffee, there's time.'

We finished our coffee, and a brandy to get over our shock, and went on our way. We were climbing again and the wind became more savage and more biting as we struggled on our way up the twisting road towards the snowline. We stopped in the dark at about 8 p.m. for a snack from our rations, and by then we were frozen. Alex was so cold and numbed that I had to take his haversack off, cut up bread and cheese for him, and feed him piece by piece. His hands were so cold there was no feeling in them. I chafed them between mine, and we did a little arm swinging to try to get the blood going, but it took too much energy out of us and we stopped before the tingling reached our fingers. We started off again and I hoped to make Saint Bonnet-le-Froid—how aptly named—and the highest point of our climb that night and risk sleeping in the village inn. But Alex was in such a bad way I decided to take him off the road, out of the wind, and into a barn. An old farmer grudgingly allowed us to use his barn for the price of fifteen francs, and once again we snuggled into hay. I slept immediately, but woke after about two hours to find myself frozen, despite the layers of hay. Alex had been awake for some time but had let me sleep on.

At 1 a.m. we set out again on a beautiful, icy, starlit night, with the snow crunching under foot and stretching on all sides as far as one could see. We struggled for another two hours upwards, ever upwards, through the snow-covered road, slipping, cursing, freezing. Only fools and the hunted were out on a night like that. We eventually reached Saint Bonnet-le-Froid, looked with longing at the shuttered village inn, and began our descent. This was very dangerous, as the traffic to the summit had made the surface glacier-hard and ice-rink slippery. Once Alex fell on his back. He struggled to get up, but all he did was slither. I edged him into the side of the road, where the snow was soft and gave a better foothold. We laughed and laughed as he wriggled on his back like a stranded beetle and I fought to stop myself joining him in the snow. We were not far from hysteria and I think we must have been suffering a little from exposure.

From then on we walked in the soft snow, which was harder work but safer, until we reached a section of the road which had not been swept by a snowplough. Now we waded, thigh deep at times, and once nearly got lost, as we wandered away from the road towards the mountains. And all the time we were frozen, our legs ached, our heels, bloody and bandaged, sent shooting pains into the legs at every step. We fought on, hour after hour through the Arctic-like night, through the snow, the frost, the wind, until at last the snow thinned and we were again on a paved road in the valley. At dawn we reached Tence, another small town, and as the light brightened we walked into farms, asking for some soup or drink. But all the people were sour and shook their heads. I swore at some of them, in a croaked, cracked voice, but it made no difference. I cursed them for not being patriots, and it was only later that I considered that they probably thought we were a couple of ruffians, for we were unshaved, our clothes were battered, our faces lined and weary. But a little farther on we came to a tiny, lorry drivers' café, and here a young girl took pity on us. She gave each of us a bowl of piping-hot milk and some hot, freshly baked, bread. The drink was marvellous—it was the first milk we had drunk for months. We thanked her, and went back to the road, which now started to climb up into the snow again.

Again we plodded, one foot after another. It seemed I had been walking all my life and that I was to spend the rest of it with pain in my feet, my legs, and my thighs. It seemed as though I would never be warm again, never experience joy, or happiness, or pleasure, or comfort, ever again. I slumped to the ground, defeated and weary. I felt Alex put my head between my knees, and the world was steady once more. We walked off again, scrambling and stumbling towards that magic name of Le Puy. We reached the snowline again at Yssingeaux where, at midday, we stopped at a small café for a snack, soup, and bread. We had coffee, and nearly fell asleep over it, for the room was warm and the lack of sleep, apart from the physical effort, was nearly too much for us. But when we left, we knew there were only twenty-eight kilometres to Le Puy—only eighteen miles to go. First, though, we had to climb up to 4,000 feet again, over the Col du Pertuis. We had done two passes, one more would not kill us. Half-way up, we heard the sound of an engine behind us and, looking back, we saw a coach climbing slowly towards us. We looked at each other.

'It's a temptation,' said Alex.

'Yes, but we're nearly there now, so don't let's take any unnecessary risks,' I replied.

'Well, if we took it only a dozen kilometres we should be all right, as there's not much chance of a checkpoint in the mountains,' Alex said.

We stopped talking just as we reached a coach stop—and the coach pulled in beside us. We both got in, without looking at each other.

It was good to sit in the warmth and watch the kilometre stones flick by, but the dozen kilometres we had talked about were soon over, and we got out, leaving just twelve kilometres to go.

I began worrying Alex about his friend Joulian, the man we were heading for. Was he safe? What if he was no longer there? What then? He kept telling me not to worry, Joulian would be there. And if he was not he had another friend forty kilometres away in the mountains, and we could go there. But the thought of another night in the snows did not bear thinking about. So we just kept on plodding, heads down, aching in every limb, until we walked into Le Puy, just three days and three nights after leaving the POW coach. We had kept our schedule.

'Here we are,' said Alex, and pointed out a medium-sized building with a flat roof, which was a combined home and factory. On the front a large sign said: '*Véritables Lentils du Puy.*'

'And there's Joulian—come on, it's all right now.' We went up the front steps and into the first floor offices. A small man, thick set and wearing pebbly spectacles, got up from a desk and peered at Alex. He peered for several seconds into the unshaved, white-faced friend of mine, before he exclaimed: '*Mon Dieu*—it's Alex. What have they done to you? Where have you been? We heard you'd been arrested and we thought you dead—I must tell my wife.'

I sat on a stool until the wife came in, kissed me on both cheeks, and made me welcome. We were both taken to their lounge, where Madame pulled off our boots and socks, and put our feet into slippers, as we warmed in front of a fire. In the distance we heard hot water being run for the bath they had promised us, and the couple rushed around finding clean clothes for us and laying them out on the beds we were to use. Then the bath. I lay in it until the hot water soaked into every pore. I felt myself get cleaner every second and my aches disappear. When I got out I was just tired, and the only pain left was in my raw heels.

Joulian had been a chef in the Savoy Hotel in London at one time, and he had prepared dinner as we bathed and shaved. He also produced a bottle of white wine from 'Porquerolles' and a red 'Hermitage', but not until he had poured a pre-war Pernod for the two of us and his wife. The food was marvellous, and simply to see cutlery, good glasses, and white serviettes was an immense pleasure. The beds after dinner were soft and warm and I slept like a dead man, worn out after the terrible voyage.

6

The next day I got up and discussed Alex with Joulian, and he brought a doctor in to see him. He shook his head when he saw Alex, but took him under his care. With the good food, medical care, and rest, Alex was soon back on his feet, but it took several weeks for him to throw off the effects of the prison and the long walk. The two of us pottered around the house and the factory, and we were soon ready to think about our purpose for being in France—Resistance. We had, of course, checked our escape route out of the house, which was through a piggery at the back and underneath the factory.

Joulian was in charge of a small Resistance group and had a few arms and explosives dropped to him by the RAF. These were buried in his garden. We asked him for ration cards and identity papers, which he provided, but when we asked if he had any contact with London he shook his head. He said that his immediate chief, Lieutenant Chas of the French Air Force, would contact us and try to arrange a radio link.

So started our long fight to get in touch with London, as we wanted not only to let Buckmaster know we were operating and get instructions from him, but to inform our families we were still alive. Chas sent two men from Lyons to see us, and they promised to let London know if they could get in contact. The days passed and Alex became much stronger. He at last decided to go to Angers, to join his French wife, and also to contact Vladimir, who might have a radio operator in Paris. We arranged a simple postcard code, to pass on any news of contact with London, or whether I should join him, or him me.

Alex left. There was nothing for me to do except wander round the area, keep my eyes and ears open, and pray that Chas would raise London. I walked round Le Puy a lot, and one of my great entertainments was to watch German troops—the town was a divisional headquarters for the Russian front—going through their drills. I was always amused to see troops goose-stepping past an imaginary saluting base. A soldier who did not do it properly was screamed at, and the instructor would make him crawl back on his hands and knees to the starting place and do it all over again. In mid-January, Lieutenant Chas's brother was arrested in Lyons, and another Le Puy Resister was caught by the Germans. This news worried the local group and it was decided to move me to Langogne, in the Lozère, a village with two saw mills and a railway station. I shared a room in a flat, owned by an elderly woman who hated Germans, with Henri Picolo, a chemist, who was wanted for his Resistance work in Carcassonne. I met some of the local group, who were all very pleasant and earnest. But I felt I was wasting time, and decided to move back to Cannes and see if I could get a message back to London.

I got a ticket to Marseilles and slipped away without telling anyone, bar Picolo, where I was going. I went through the normal railway check, but it was a cursory one, for which I was grateful. It was the first checkpoint I had been through since our escape and I had been nervous about it.

Back in Cannes I rejoined the Audouards, and was very well received. Normally one treated a man who seemed to come back from the dead with a certain amount of suspicion, for sometimes they were released so they could be followed to the other members of an organisation. Others had been known to turn traitor to save their own skin. I mentioned this to Audouard, but he laughed and said: 'That you would turn traitor impossible. And you are much too fly to give anything away involuntarily. We saw all the precautions you used to take so you would not compromise us.' I took this as a great compliment, not only to myself, but to the SOE instructors who had trained me.

He told me that Olive, Roger, and one or two others had been caught and arrested. Julian had left, but there was a new organisation and he knew Paul, the new radioman. I met him, a Russo-Egyptian Jew called Rabinovitch, the following day, and he promised to tell his chief about me. The day after, I was taken to a delightful flat overlooking the Mediterranean, and there sat Peter Churchill and his assistant, Odette Sansom, both of whom seemed very jumpy and on edge.

They regarded me, quite properly, with suspicion, as they had no orders to meet me, and for all they knew I was a traitor trying to break their cover. They asked me a string of questions, so many, in fact, that I began to think that *they* might not be who they were supposed to be. But finally we were both satisfied, and Raoul—as Churchill was known—agreed to call London.

Later, he said that there was a message from London to say that money, clothes, and instructions would arrive 'next month' for both Alex and me. They would come through a contact I was to meet outside the Church of Saint Sauvin in Toulouse, and I was to be there, according to Raoul, twice daily, at 10 a.m. and 3 p.m., from 8 March 1943 for twelve days, until we met up. I was not told who the contact was, but he knew me.

This was a relief, but still exasperating, as I still had to wait nearly a month to make contact. Finally, I set off for Toulouse, a city too close to my old home at Castres to be comfortable, and stayed with Madame Aubain, the wife of a rich industrialist, her daughter Zizi, who was about twenty-one, and their cousin, Jean, who was about twenty-eight. All were strong Gaullists, and the younger members of the family were active in the local Resistance movement.

On 8 March 1943, promptly at 10 a.m., I walked up to the church, strolled round it twice, as though studying its architecture, and then had a brief look inside. I was not approached.

did this twice a day for fifteen days, growing more and more annoyed. I began to think that Churchill had sent me on a wild-goose chase, to get me out of the way.

Once I thought I had made it, when a well-dressed woman, wearing little make up, hovered near me. I walked close to give her the chance of using the password. Then I heard: 'Hello, *chéri*—are you coming home with me?' It was only 10 in the morning!

Later, on the Place President Wilson, I came face to face with a man with his hand outstretched. He came forward and said: 'But what are you doing wandering around here?', and I remembered where I had seen him last—as part of the prison escort that took me to Lyons on the way to the prisoner-of-war camp.

'Hello,' I said. 'It's nice to see you again.' My heart started to pound at the thought of Castres prison.

'Did they let you go? They couldn't have let you go just like that,' he said.

'Of course they let me go, they had nothing on me, anyway. I wouldn't be walking around here in broad daylight if I hadn't been released, would I?'

'Monsieur—you are not telling the truth,' he said.

'No, I'm not.'

He put his hand out again, shook mine firmly, and said: 'Monsieur, carry on, and may the best of luck go with you.' He turned and went away.

I walked in the opposite direction, thoroughly shaken. For half an hour I used every trick in the book to make certain I was not followed. I went into stores and came out of back doors. I hopped on buses and dodged down sidestreets, just to make certain that no one would have a chance of finding out where I was staying.

I left Toulouse the next morning, and headed back towards Langogne. I bought a ticket to Nîmes, for if I was arrested it was better they did not know the real place I was heading for, and went up to the ticket barrier. I handed over my papers, the gendarme looked at them briefly and handed them back. At least they were not looking for me yet. But I was not happy until I had changed at Nîmes and was heading back to Langogne. When I got there, Henri Picolo told me that there was a message waiting for me from Alex with Joulian at Le Puy. So I set off two days later by bus.

As this rumbled through the country lanes, I had time to review my position. Cannes was out of the question at the moment, and I still could not decide whether Peter Churchill had purposely wanted me out of the way. Lyons was rather a vague set-up with only a faint chance of success at the time. Which left Alex at Angers, with the nucleus of an organisation in that part of France. I had good contacts with the Resistance at Le Puy, Langogne and Villefranche—a small village to the south of Langogne, where I had spent many hours with the local leaders—as well as in Toulouse, and I knew I could extend this chain of resistance into the Ardèche through the Audouards.

But I was powerless without a link to London, as I could not organise supply drops, or set up training schools on sabotage and weapons, and within a few weeks would be regarded as a man of little worth. I was important, in French eyes, only if I had a link with London. My only hope lay in Alex, and if he had no contact, then I decided I must get into the escape pipeline, go back to London, and start again.

In Le Puy, the Joulians greeted me warmly, and Madame's sister, who had just arrived from Paris, had seen Alex there. His message was that I should join him in Angers as soon as possible. The Joulians also said that there were two other men who they heard had links with London, and that Chas knew about them. So I met Chas and went to Lyons to meet the first of the two. Alex might not have made contact yet, and anyway, two London links were better than one. But Chas's friend said bluntly that he could do nothing to help me. To soften the blow, he gave me an enormous black-market lunch—only to be obtained in the town of Lyons, famous for its '*bon manger*'. I met, too, Madame

Paulette Giraud, who was visiting her husband in the jail only a few yards from where we lunched. She agreed to take me to Tournus, where the other man who was supposed to have a link, was living. He was her cousin, but when we met him the follow-day, he, too, was not optimistic. He told me that on two occasions RAF aircraft had landed near Tournus and picked people up for London. But he did not know when the next plane was coming—if at all. That left Alex and Angers.

We were delayed for two more days, waiting for 'reserved seat tickets', without which one could not travel on the crowded, Paris-bound trains. I finally left Tournus on the express, with a nasty 'beginning of term' feeling, which lasted until I had gone through the major checkpoint at Dijon, controlled that day by French police and a French-speaking German.

The train reached Paris at 6 p.m. I found a small hotel for the night and then had a walk around depressing, wartime Paris, with its bare windows, holding nothing but posters of Pétain and exhortations to join the Waffen SS. There were few cars, many bicycles, and tandems with a bathchair trailer for one passenger. There were Germans everywhere. The meal I got was dreadful, just indifferent vegetables, with no meat or fish. I was glad to go to bed early, and left the next morning before anyone was up, and without filling in any of the necessary forms, which meant there was no record of my visit to the city.

That evening, after dark, I found Alex's home, and was shown in by his wife, to find my friend in his study-cum-drawing-room. He was looking much fitter, and said that he had fully recovered from his ill-treatment at Castres and the walk over the mountains. He also had good news. He had seen Vladimir (Grover Williams) and Prosper, who was head of another organisation, and received a message from London that he was to run the Angers area. I was to help him, for the time being, until I was sent to open up the Dijon area.

'I'm not very happy here in Angers,' Alex said, as he puffed at his pipe, 'I'm too well known. As it is, I can't go out until it's dark, and even then I daren't go into the centre of the town. I may suggest that you take over Angers and I take Dijon—it would be safer for me, and you would benefit from the organisation that we're building up here.'

I did not mind Angers. I was just aching to do something constructive after all the weeks of frustration, so Alex introduced me to his second-in-command, a young ex-artillery lieutenant, who was full of fire and energy. He told me that the organisation was growing rapidly in numbers and, although no arms had been dropped yet, the RAF had accepted a zone suggested by Alex, and they were expecting a drop soon. The BBC announcement that the drop was coming was to be: 'Jim and Vic are two fine retrievers', in honour of Alex's lovely dogs.

I went out to inspect the dropping zone, but was not very impressed with it. It was two small fields with some tall trees at one end, and it was only three miles from the centre of the town, which was teeming with Germans, and protected by batteries of anti-aircraft weapons. There were also a lot of farms nearby, some of which might alert the Germans, who would be on the scene in minutes. And it was bordered on two sides by rivers, the Mayenne and the Loire, which formed two sides of a trap if the reception committee was raided. I talked to Alex about this, and he agreed that the site should be changed. I looked around, and found a perfect place, some thirty kilometres outside the city. This was much more isolated and inaccessible to the Germans. I told Alex of the new ground and he went to Paris to contact Vladimir or Prosper, so that London could be told of the new site of the dropping zone. I took over in his absence.

I felt much more content now that I had something to do, and despite the number of Germans in the cafés and roaming the streets, the first tension I felt disappeared. I felt I had been living in ancient Angers for years. Every evening I listened in to the BBC broadcasts, just in case Alex did not manage to get his message through before the RAF left for Angers, remembering always to twist the dial to a French station after the transmission had ended. Men and women had been caught through ignoring this simple rule, as the first thing a Gestapo raider did on entering a house was to check the radio to see if a family had tuned in to the BBC.

I set out to gain as much local knowledge as possible, and walked round the streets to find the locations of the German units in the town and on the outskirts, and the site of the Gestapo headquarters. I found that the dungeons of the old castle were ammunition dumps, well protected from air attack. A raid on the castle could only bring huge civilian casualties, as it was near the town centre, and if the dumps went up, many would die. I also inspected the bridges and pondered the tactical problems which would have to be faced when the Allies invaded. Should they be blown to trap the Germans in that section where the two rivers merged, or should we fight to keep them in one piece so that the armour could flow without hindrance?

One night I heard on the BBC: 'Jim and Vic are two fine retrievers.' The RAF was coming that night. I decided the drop should go ahead, even though it meant using the old dropping zone, because this was the first to be attempted in the area, which meant that the Germans would not be perturbed at low-flying aircraft. Most important of all, it would be a great boost to morale to the Resistance fighters if at least some of them had guns in their hands.

I asked for Henri, Alex's deputy, the man who knew the arrangements for a drop. Annette, Alex's teenage daughter, said that he was out of town and no one knew how to contact him. I was furious. Only he and Alex knew the group who had been recruited to handle supply drops and without a group of men the parachutes and their containers could not be carried away and hidden.

Alex's former wife—she had divorced him at the beginning of the war to escape being rounded up as the wife of a Briton—was also furious. She agreed to try to find a handful of trustworthy men to bring the arms in. In the end she could only find Monsieur

Bruges and Boris Tourganief. Monsieur Bruges was a small, almost undersized man, who was living in Alex's house. Boris Tourganief, Russian by birth, who had spent all his life in France and was married to a French girl, was a big man, tall and strong.

When I left Alex's house, at 10.30 p.m., they were my only helpers. I could only hope that they would not get fainthearted and could evade the strict curfew as they left after me to head for the dropping zone.

I hoped to God that my operations in France in the future would not be so badly arranged as the first supply drop I faced that night.

7

I left the house at half past ten, taking with me the torches I needed to mark out the flare-path, hoping that my two helpers would join me before the aircraft passed overhead at midnight. It was, of course, after curfew and although I did not have to pass through the centre of the city, it was not all that easy to escape being challenged by patrolling police and German soldiery. As it was a still night, with a moon, I was able to hear the heavy-footed guards in sufficient time to dodge down side-streets to avoid them, but my main problem, when I finally reached the dropping zone—which seemed tiny in the moonlight with the trees appearing to be so high—was where to hide the equipment if the RAF managed to find my field. I walked round the area and decided my only hope was to store the goods in a wooded estate, which was bordered by a high wall about a kilometre from the edge of the field. But I found this too late to climb the wall and investigate, and had to run back to the field to prepare the torches for the RAF.

During my training I had been shown how to put down torches to lead the aircraft into the wind, in the shape of a half arrow. The aircraft flew down the arrow and dropped the parachutes when it passed over the last marker. As there was no wind, I laid out the torches, with red glass over the lamps, in the shape of an arrow. This would allow the containers to drop farthest away from the trees. But I could not switch them on until I saw the aircraft and signalled to it, so I sat down in some bushes to wait for the big man, the little man, and midnight. It was a peaceful night, and all I heard, as I sat, was the croaking of frogs in the marshes, the call of an occasional duck, and some far-off voices, which I preferred to think belonged to a pair of lovers and not a ranging patrol. The moon was high, and through the trees I could see it glinting on the River Loire. All very peaceful, until the silence was destroyed by the wail of the air raid sirens in Angers, which probably meant that my aircraft was on the way. As the noise died away, I heard the ducks start cackling furiously and then I saw two figures, one big and one small. My helpers had made it, but I waited until they were only a few feet away from me before showing myself, just in case they were not friends. I told them where the torches were, positioned them so each could switch on half of them when they saw one quick flash of my white torch, and told them to return the torches to me when the operation was over.

By the time they were in position, I heard the drone of a distant aircraft. It was midnight. The RAF was on time. It seemed a small miracle that this one aircraft had come from England, to find a tiny field in France and be there on time. I ran into the centre of the field, flashed my torch at Boris and Monsieur Bruges, and stared into the night as the engines droned louder and louder. Then I saw it, dark in the moonlight, and very low. I flashed the code letter at the sky once, twice, and then the right code letter flashed back to me.

The aircraft flew off, circuited, and flew the length of the field, letting go its cargo as it reached the last marker, in as precise an operation anyone could wish for. The containers floated down and seemed as though they must hit us. Monsieur Bruges dived into a ditch to get out of the way, but Boris and I stood our ground until we, too, decided that a tree was a wise place to shelter under. We saw four containers drop within a hundred yard radius, in the middle of the lamps, and a crash in the branches of the tree under which we were sheltering told us where the fifth had ended up.

The aircraft came back and flashed us a goodbye. It did me good to see that plane. I did not feel so alone. I stood in the middle of the field and waved at them, although I was pretty certain they could not see me, even though the moon was high. As the aircraft banked and headed north, I felt a wave of homesickness and wished that I was aboard and heading for England with the crew. I fancied I could smell the bacon and eggs they would have for breakfast. Then I saw the lights were still showing in the field, so I ran and picked the torches up. Action restored my equilibrium.

I ordered Monsieur Bruges and Boris into the trees for twenty minutes, just in case some nosy farmer had seen the torches, the aircraft, and the parachutes. After a while the all-clear sounded and, once again, all was quiet except for the night noises. I waved my helpers on and we walked into the middle of the field, where I showed them how to lever open the containers, which was a noisy business, and remove the cells.

After each one was opened we lay still and listened for a minute or two in case we had been heard, straining for the sounds of patrols on motorbikes or afoot. But everything remained quiet and we rolled the silk parachutes, lovely to feel in the night, and stuffed them into the containers. Then I took the containers to a small pond and sank them.

Boris did very well, for he was a big man and broad, but poor Monsieur Bruges found the work of carrying the separate cells to the hiding of a near-by hedge a tiring one, and I watched him stagger as he carted one off. We stored all the cells away in their temporary place, and I went to check on the container that had fallen into the tree. I saw it was hopeless to get it down without a ladder and an axe and, unfortunately, the only white parachute in the group was now folded completely over the tree like a white counterpane on a newly made bed. It would show up for miles around in the morning, and the Germans would be sure to start a search for the other goods as soon as it was reported. So I was forced to move the twelve cells from the hedge right away if I was to stop the Germans from seizing the lot.

I told my helpers that we would have to carry them more than a kilometre to the estate. They were not very enthusiastic and I could not blame them, for each cell weighed 40 lbs, and was shaped like a drum, with sharp edges which cut into the shoulders. I was glad when I reached the estate, as my cell seemed to weigh *400 lbs*, and poor Monsieur Bruges collapsed on the ground after a few minutes walk with his, and said he was going home, and to hell with it. Boris and I left him and trudged the kilometre to the wall, which Boris climbed to report that, although there were many trees, all the undergrowth had been cleared and there was nowhere to hide our goods. Worse, the grounds were in full view of a large house. This was a serious setback and I wondered what was the best thing to do. In the end I decided to hide the stores under the shrubs and blackberry bushes, which grew thickly at the base of the wall. We tucked the first two cells away and walked back to see if we could help Monsieur Bruges. Luckily, I had brought a flask of brandy with me, and after a few nips he felt much better. Boris and I managed to make him laugh a couple of times, and persuaded him to complete the journey with his load. In fact, he made two more journeys, by sheer will-power rather than the strength of the brandy flask, which he emptied on his own.

I was trembling, and my knees were knocking by the time I had carried my fourth load and hidden it away. Monsieur Bruges was worse off than I was, and I thanked God for the tall, tough Russian, who not only carried his four cells but also managed to walk more than half a kilometre with Monsieur Bruges's fourth. But at least we had stored them, and unless the search was very thorough, I felt the Germans would not stumble on our cache. By now it was five o'clock in the morning, so we set off, very tired but very pleased, back to the house, to find both Madame Keller, Alex's wife, and Madame Bruges exhausted with worry. They had heard the sirens and the aircraft and waited for hours, boosting each other's morale by saying that we were too careful to be caught. But a bottle of wine, an omelette, bread and cheese restored us all. Monsieur Bruges was exhausted, and after his meal he went straight to bed—where he stayed for nearly a week.

Madame Keller suggested that the cells be stored in her garage, so I decided to go immediately to bring the goods in, using Alex's bicycle which had a small trailer attached. Boris would have come with me, but he had to go to the other side of town to reassure his wife, and to be on time for work at eight o'clock. It was just getting light when I set off, and by the time I had made my third trip, bringing in two cells each time, people were beginning to move around. The cache was in full view of a farmhouse and, apart from the anxiety that an unfriendly farmer might spot me, I was worried that I might be stopped by a policeman on my way into town. He would, of course, be searching for black-market food, but I could imagine his outrage if he found British war material. I decided to stop after three trips and pick the rest up when it got dark.

I was too tired and overwrought to sleep, so Madame Keller and I decided to open up the packages. It was like Christmas, and we both laughed light-heartedly as we opened up our presents from the Royal Air Force. I had to keep a beady eye on Alex's wife, for she was apt to handle safe things as though they might blow up in her face, and handle dangerous things as though they were pounds of butter. Madame Keller worked hard with me, but I always felt that she was not a true patriot. I sensed that she worked only because Alex was involved, and because her help would enable them to obtain advancement in later years. She was so unlike Alex, who was devoted to duty and who had no thoughts for himself.

When I got to bed that morning I felt well satisfied. At last I had achieved something and Henri, who had arrived back at the pension by now, would have a good store of arms, explosives, and detonators hidden away at our proper cache within the next few hours. We were in business.

During the next few days I set out to get a better cover for myself, and was given a job in a machine-tool factory run by one of the young men staying at the pension with me. It was a wonderful cover to be genuinely and regularly employed, to have a proper work permit from the labour exchange, and to be on the firm's books in the correct manner. I was taken on as a learner, with a view to my becoming a salesman. This enabled me to be absent at any time, without other workmen talking about me, when I had to go to neighbouring towns on my subversive activities. It also meant that I could cover up my real reason for visiting another town by calling in on one of my clients and so providing a cast-iron alibi for my journey. As a further safeguard, I obtained from a Resistance doctor a certificate to say that I was recovering from pneumonia and was not fit enough to work a normal day. The traces of my prison stay were still visible, so this fitted in very well also.

I put on blue overalls and went to work like any other person. I even found the work of making drills from tungsten quite absorbing, and I became quite proud of my skill with different lathes. By a happy coincidence, Boris, who was a dental mechanic, used to visit the factory frequently to order drills. He was a good man and helped me a lot in the weeks ahead, as did his wife. She was a little person who worked for the gas company, and she 'cooked' several gasmeters in homes where the weekly allowance of gas had been exceeded, saving these people from big fines. They used to ride a tandem (with her on the back) towing a small trailer, and tour the countryside, looking for black-market food to help out with their rations. Boris bought me a bicycle for the outrageous price of £40, and I used to join them on their week-end hunts—except that I was looking for other landing grounds for the RAF and good places to store arms.

The couple would also bring back food for their relatives, one of whom was very anti-British and very pro-Pétain. I, of course, was introduced to him as a Frenchman, and I always laughed at the way big Boris would tease this man. He would bully him about his pro-German tendencies, and refuse to hand over the food unless the relative stood up and shouted '*Vive Churchill*'. The wretched man would eye the food, look around apprehensively, open the door of his flat to see if there was anyone listening on the landing, and then say with a sickly look: '*Vive Churchill.*' Boris would roar with laughter, slap him on the back, and leave.

I was to take over Angers, and Alex was going to run the area around Nantes where he already had friends. Better still, we were to get our own radio operator. This was important, for we would at last be certain that our messages got through, instead of hoping that another group would pass them on. Other groups were more interested in clearing their own messages than those of outsiders. Even more important, so far as our morale was concerned, was that London would be attributing to us our fair share of success.

We were not looking for praise, simply acknowledgement of our efforts, but we knew second-hand messages might well leave out the fact that Alex or myself were responsible for a job, and London might feel that we were not worth sending supplies to. This could lead to a group dying; our own radio operator made certain we would stay in business.

We also got news that another stores operation would take place in April, and that the RAF would use the new ground I had chosen. The BBC message announcing the drop was chosen by me in honour of my friend Picolo, in Langogne—'*Après la soupe un verre de vin*'. If he heard it, I was sure he would know I was thanking him.

Before I made plans to receive these stores, I met the foreman of a French labour gang, conscripted by the German Agence Todt, who had some very interesting information about the Château de Pigneroles, just outside Angers. We had known for some time that it was being used by the Germans as a Naval Headquarters for controlling submarines and surface craft from the major bases at Lorient, Saint Nazaire and Nantes, and we signalled the RAF that it was a perfect bombing target, as it was outside the town and could be attacked without danger to civilians. But my foreman produced plans which showed that the Château was just a blind, and that the real HQ was hidden underground, three-quarters of a mile from the Château. My friend showed me the passage that led from the Château to the offices, mess, and sleeping quarters. I made scale drawings of the target and put them in an airtight fruit bottling jar, which I buried in the garden of the pension for safety until I had the opportunity of getting them to London. I also arranged for the RAF and SOE to be told the next time we managed to get a radio link about the underground HQ, and at one time a plan—later dropped—was drawn up to land British Commandos to clean up the place. I went out to the Château two or three times and strolled around the grounds, which were not difficult to get into, and I was never challenged. But I found that there were frequent patrols and booby traps, which I told London about.

It was now nearly time for our stores drop, and I travelled thirty kilometres to the chosen vineyard to make final arrangements to receive twelve containers of guns, ammunition and other stores. I found that there was nowhere suitable to hide all this equipment, so I decided, with the vineyard owner's permission, to dig pits in which to hide the stores. I took three men with me the following Sunday, and we dug two pits, branched them over, and then turfed them so they were almost impossible to detect. We needed ten more pits, but I thought I would test out the two, for a few days, to see if they were discovered.

They were. A gamekeeper put his foot through one of them and fell into the hole. His description of the pit caused enormous excitement, and the French and German police came out in force to examine it. They searched for miles around, looking for pits, and stumbled on to the other one. Both holes were carefully measured, examined a dozen times by detectives, and finally pronounced to be graves dug to receive the bodies of two people, who had been murdered or were going to be murdered. It was a reasonable guess, as my pits were six feet long and four feet deep. Their discovery, of course, meant that I had to think of some other scheme to hide the containers. But they had played a small part in the war by keeping dozens of police experts busy wasting time.

Alex was nearly ready to take over at Nantes. He had organised his group and was already working with them, so all that was left was to take his wife, Madame Keller, to their new home. He left with her one evening for Paris, to take some messages for London and to make arrangements for 'dead letter boxes' and couriers, which we would use to keep in contact. He also had some radio messages for Vladimir to send through his radio operator, as our own man had not yet arrived. This was a dangerous operation for both Vladimir and Alex, as any journey to Paris was fraught with checks, and Alex's face was well known to the Gestapo. It also meant that Vladimir's radio operator would be transmitting for twice as long as normal, thus doubling the chances of radio detection vans fixing his position.

The morning after they left, I dressed in my overalls to go to work at the factory, and stopped for five minutes to have a cup of coffee in the kitchen of the pension. I was sitting at a table, sipping, when the door burst open and a German officer came in followed by a civilian. The officer shouted at me in German, so I just looked at him blankly. The civilian then came over and asked me in French: 'You are Monsieur Wilkinson, aren't you?'

'Monsieur who?' I asked.

'Monsieur Wilkinson—the owner of this house.'

'You must have made a mistake. I am not Monsieur Wilkinson, nor do I own this house. It belongs to Madame Keller,' and I turned to Madame Bruges, who had walked into the kitchen after hearing the noise. 'Isn't that right, Madame Bruges—this isn't my house, is it.'

She told the Frenchman: 'This house did belong to Monsieur Wilkinson, but he has been in England since the start of the war, and now it is run by Madame Keller. But she's away at the moment.'

The man looked up as Anne-Marie, the kitchen maid, came in. He barked at her: 'Who is this man?' and pointed at me.

I saw her take a deep breath. Then: 'This gentleman is Monsieur Chanbaran, one of our boarders who has come to have his cup of coffee as he does every morning.'

The German officer put out his hand and shouted in French: 'Papers!' I gave them to him. He and the civilian studied them very carefully. Then I was asked: 'Where do you work?' I told them.

'You're late for work—it's nearly nine o'clock. Why is that?'

'Well,' I said, 'we find it very difficult to work full time. We have plenty of orders, but we cannot get the material to fulfil them, and there's only a limited amount of electricity to work the machines. It is all very difficult with this war going on. But my patron doesn't mind if I come in late. Anyway I have this doctor's certificate which says I'm not to work full time yet as I've been ill.' And I showed him my certificate. This seemed to satisfy them, and they told me I could go. They searched the house, as I drank my coffee with a very shaky hand, but without undue haste. When I finished I walked across the road to my room to fetch my revolver, which I had brought to clean as it was covered in grease. I cursed myself for this, as I had broken another of my rules—never take anything incriminating into the house where you are staying. I hoped to God that no one would follow me, but I put the gun in my pocket and walked off to work unchallenged. The Germans were too busy searching the building to worry about a sick lathe operator. I longed to walk in, to see what was going on, but that would have been foolish. I had to act naturally, do my morning's work, and then go back for lunch as though nothing had happened.

Henri, the man who had not turned up for the parachute drop, came up to the factory and told me that the Gestapo was turning the pension inside out. I did not think that they would find anything, for I knew how careful Alex was. There was the fruit bottle buried in the garden with the plans of the German Naval HQ in it, but only Alex, his wife and I knew where they were buried. Henri, however, solved one riddle for me. Who, I asked him, was this Monsieur Wilkinson the Germans were asking about? Henri grinned: 'That's Alex's real name, didn't you know?' This made me really anxious, for the Gestapo was obviously looking for Alex, and I was grateful he had left the night before.

I went back to the pension at lunchtime and found Madame Bruges, white-faced and worried, just finishing the task of putting the house in order after the Gestapo had taken it apart. The searchers had moved all the furniture, lifted all the carpets, kneaded all the cushions, mattresses and pillows, and checked the two radios to see if they were tuned to London. They were not, as we always switched them back to a French station after listening to the BBC. The men also searched Madame Keller's writing desk, and found a typed copy of a coded message, which made them search even more diligently. They asked where Madame Keller was and when she was returning. They were not satisfied with Madame Bruges telling them: 'She's gone to Paris and we don't know when she's coming back.' They questioned boarders and the staff, but none of them could help. They finally left, taking the typewriter, the coded letter, and a photograph of Alex—Monsieur Wilkinson—and ordered Madame Keller to report to Gestapo headquarters the instant she reached home.

Alex and his wife had to be warned, but not one of us knew how to contact them. I decided that every train from Paris must be met, not, of course, at the station, in case the Gestapo had any of us under surveillance, but somewhere between the station and the pension. I decided to keep watch in a street they had to walk down from the station, and Henri was to conceal himself in a place where he could watch Alex and Madame Keller without being seen, and so find out if they were being followed. I would meet them, and if they were being followed he would pass on his bicycle and ring his bell three times. If they were not being followed, he would pass without ringing his bell.

It was also decided I must leave the pension. Up to then I was not a suspect, but one never knew with the Gestapo. They might come round at any time to ask more questions, and it was better for everyone at the pension that I was not there, in case they discovered my real identity. I packed immediately, and told everyone that I was going to Rouen for my firm. If the Gestapo came back, my boss would confirm this for them. I did not tell them where I was moving to but arranged places in Angers for them to leave messages for me, or receive messages from me. I cycled off, taking various precautions in case I was being followed, and arrived at the house of my friend Boris, the Russian, and his wife. I told them what had happened at the pension and they readily gave me shelter, offering to put up Alex and his wife as well if I managed to contact them. Boris was leaving within a few hours for Le Mans, to stay for three days, and during his stay he promised to search all the Paris trains, to try to find Alex and his wife. This was a fine gesture, but I knew that I could not rely on the couple being spotted, for the trains were always packed.

I took another chance that night by going back to the garden at the pension, after curfew, to dig up the precious plans of the Naval Headquarters. At the time it seemed a reasonable risk, and I had a good look round the house in case the Gestapo had hidden watchers in the area to check on visitors. It was important not only to get the plans but to protect the people in the house. They would have been in big trouble if the Gestapo dug up the grounds—as happened in some places—and found the bottle. I discovered that Alex had put one more item in the hiding-place—a fresh set of false identity papers for himself with his photograph on.

I took the documents through the town to a dilapidated house I had discovered on the outskirts. It was empty, the roof leaked, it needed a lot of decorating, and the rent was very high. I had approached the estate agent and put in a bid to lease it 'on behalf of relatives who have been bombed out on the coast'. The high rent would not bother me, as I could always get money from SOE to meet that, but the important thing was that I could use it as a headquarters and permanent hideout. I took my bottle of plans there that night and hid it away alongside some incriminating papers, a small arsenal of personal weapons, sabotage equipment, and a set of torches for use on parachute drops. Then I made my way back through the curfew to the Tourganiefs' house.

For the next three days I met the three daily trains from Paris, with Henri tucked up a back street to watch Alex's tail, but it was not until the afternoon of the fourth day that I saw Madame Keller walking down the street carrying a suitcase. I strolled towards her, greeted her, took her suitcase as though it was a normal meeting between landlady and boarder, and said, conversationally: 'You cannot go back to the pension, the Gestapo has been there. Is Alex on the train with you, for we must warn him too?' She and Alex never walked together in Angers.

'Of course I'm going back to the pension,' she told me. 'It's not the first time I've had the Gestapo call, and I don't suppose it'll be the last. They know I was married to an Englishman, and they're always trying to check up on me. It's just a routine visit.'

Quietly I told her that it was no routine visit, that they were definitely looking for Alex. 'They have searched your house and they've found a coded letter. They've told you to report to Gestapo headquarters the instant you return to Angers.'

She said nothing for a moment. Then her face went white, and she stumbled as though the strength had gone from her legs, obviously more shaken than her brave reply suggested. Just then Henri rode by on his bicycle, without ringing his bell. At least there was no one following her. I asked again if Alex was on the same train as I walked her away from the direction of the pension. He was not, so he was safe for the moment. Slowly the colour came back into her face, but Madame Keller at that moment was far from the strong-minded woman I had known. She seemed to have lost her independent spirit. Such was the power of the Gestapo in the war years. She said she had nowhere to go and knew no friends who could put her up, so I decided to take her to Boris—reluctantly, as I did not like the idea of having too many eggs in one basket. Boris and his wife greeted her most sympathetically and, after a few minutes, she regained her spirit and answered my questions about Alex. He was still in Paris, and I said that I would go to the capital and warn him myself.

That was one problem out of the way, but what of Madame Keller? I told her I did not think anything would happen for a week or so, but then the Gestapo would begin to wonder what had happened to her, and might turn very nasty with Madame Bruges and the rest of the staff. I suggested she wrote a letter to Madame Bruges, with an address a long way from Angers, saying that she would not be returning for some weeks, as she had slipped and broken a leg, and asking Madame Bruges to run the pension until her return. She thought this was a good idea, and I gave her the name and address of a French collaborator in Saint-Etienne to use, hoping he would have a lot of trouble at a later date when the Gestapo came to call on him. I arranged for someone in Paris to go to Saint-Etienne to post the letter for her, warned Madame Bruges about it, and saw that Alex's daughter, Annette, went to her grandparents in Normandy. I also promised that I would try to get some of Madame Keller's jewellery and valuables from her home.

I left her, to catch the 2 a.m. train to Paris, which meant I had to be at the station before the 11 p.m. curfew and sit in the waiting-room until it came in. The normal check went without incident and, once in Paris, I found Alex at the first address I had been given. He was shaken by the news, but soon recovered, and started to make plans to get his wife to safety and warn others who might be involved. He and I spent most of the day visiting friends and contacts in bars, cafés and houses, passing on the news.

I asked him how a copy of a coded letter had been found in his wife's writing table.

'A simple story, but it's the simple mistake which costs a life,' he said, as he lit up his pipe. 'I coded this in December to send to London and to report that we were alive and ready to go on working. The copy was to have been handed to a courier, but he did not turn up. It became mislaid, muddled with the bills, and that was that. Bloody careless.'

We caught a train together that evening. I was going to Angers, and he was going to Nantes to take over control of his area. On the train, we decided that I should accompany Madame Keller, by bicycle, to a farmhouse 115 kilometres from Angers and thirty kilometres from Nantes, where we could lie low for a while. 'You'll have to do the journey in one day,' Alex told me, and when I doubted whether his wife could survive a ride of just over seventy miles, he snapped: 'She'll have to.' That was that.

I left Alex at Angers station and went back to the Tourganiefs, to find Madame Keller in a bad state of nerves. Originally she had been excited by the idea of a clandestine life with her husband and made plans to dye her long, golden hair black. But she had been alone all day and had not been outside the house on my orders. She had been thinking about the Gestapo, and was sad at being forced to leave the home she had fought to keep going for Alex since the war began.

I told her about our bicycle ride and, surprisingly, she cheered up immediately. We agreed to leave at eight the next morning, and I got in several hours sleep to make up for the night I spent standing in a packed train for Paris. She didn't sleep at all, but she was still eager to leave for the farmhouse, so I scouted around the Tourganiefs' first, waved to the house that everything was clear, and rode slowly down the road. In a few minutes Madame Keller passed me, as I had instructed, and I followed her for a kilometre or so to make certain she was not being followed, before catching up to ride along beside her. She was very jumpy, and saw a policeman behind every hedge and a Gestapo chief on every bicycle. Once she wanted to ride off the road when she spotted two specks approaching. I persuaded her not to, as it was a local curé and an elderly parishioner. However she kept a very good pace, and by lunchtime we had covered many kilometres. I insisted on stopping, but she refused, so I got off my bike, threw it in a hedge, and sat down on the grass verge with a bottle of wine and some bread and cheese. She had to stop, and I managed to persuade her to take a little food. We pedalled all afternoon and she did not complain once, although she must have been very saddle sore.

We walked up the steep hills, but the last hour was nearly too much for her. Even on the flat she was hardly crawling along, and I repeatedly fell off my high-geared bicycle because the pace was too slow. At seven, after eleven hours of cycling (apart from the one lunch break), we reached the farm, and were greeted by the youngest seventy-year-old grandfather I have ever met—Papa Jules, who had just married his third wife.

He brought wine and cheese, and drew off a jug of the special cider he knew Madame Keller liked. But she was in a state of near collapse, and refused to eat or drink. Fortunately, she had a good long cry, and when Alex arrived she sat down with us to an excellent meal of steaks, grilled over a wood fire of vine cuttings.

Alex asked me to stay for a few days, as he had a parachute drop planned and was short of men to handle the stores. I agreed, and with Alex and Papa Jules spent some memorable hours. Papa told me how he once bought a piglet at the local market and was so proud of his bargain that he stopped at the houses of all his friends to have a glass of wine with them and to tell them about it. At the sixth house his friend asked to see the piglet, and the pair walked out to Papa Jules's horse and cart. But there was no piglet. So Papa Jules drove his cart round all the houses he visited asking: 'Has anyone seen my piglet?' No one had. But the episode started a Papa Jules tradition, and the three of us spent several days 'looking for my piglet', which led to some very heavy wine drinking and, on one occasion, Papa Jules falling off his bicycle twice in half a mile. It made a break for Alex and myself, and we were all the more ready for work.

On the Monday Alex heard that his stores operation had been cancelled, so I decided to return to Angers, as I was anxious to get Annette away to her grandparents and to retrieve some of

Madame Keller's clothes and valuables. I took some false identity papers for Madame Keller, which needed stamping in Angers—a job for Henri—and rode off on the Tuesday morning, a drizzly, cold day, with seventy miles of road ahead. To give me heart, Alex rode with me for a few kilometres, puffing at his pipe and cheering me with his chatter. He stopped at a milestone, we shook hands, and I thanked him for the days we spent with Papa Jules. He cycled off, smiling, towards the farm. It was the last time I saw him.

8

The rain poured down, and by the time I reached Angers, after six hours of cycling, I was wet through. But my coldness did not stop me making a cautious approach to the Tourganiefs' flat. There was no one hanging around, however, so I went up the first two flights of stairs, carrying my bicycle with me, and paused at the second flight to make certain that the stairs down to the back door were clear, as it was my only escape route. The Tourganiefs lived on the third floor, so there was not even a roof to get on to. I climbed on up, and saw a notice pinned to the door. It read: 'Will the owners of this flat call at once at the Kommandatur on their return. We have called twice today and received no reply.' It was signed by an officer, and bore the official stamp of the German headquarters.

My heart gave a great thump when I read this, and I swore softly out loud. I decided that as they had already called twice it was unlikely that they would call again, so I went in, changed clothes, and started to read a book to help me wait for the return of Madame Tourganief. I dropped off to sleep, but woke up with a start when I heard voices, and the sound of a key opening an outer door. I crept into the next room so that I could hear what was being said. I recognized Madame Tourganief's voice, coming from the kitchen, but could not make out the other voice. I stepped farther into the sitting-room, to hear better, and as I did so the kitchen door was thrown open roughly and the German Gestapo officer, who had seen me at the pension ten days earlier, almost ran into the room. When he saw me, he pulled up, peered closely at me, and called over his shoulder. His civilian, French-speaking friend came in, and they held a quick conversation in German.

The civilian turned to me and said: 'We saw you at the pension a few days ago—isn't that right?'

I agreed, somewhat relieved that they seemed to be surprised to see me there, as it meant that they had not come to look for me.

'What are you doing here?' he snapped.

'Visiting friends,' I told him.

'Come here, empty your pockets. Take off your coat.'

They searched my coat and felt through my trouser pockets. I thanked God that I had called at my empty house on the way into town and left the false identity cards for Madame Keller there.

'Take off your shoes,' was the next order. These were examined as well.

'Sit down.' I sat.

The two then drew up chairs. The German officer, who spoke a few words of French, brought his so close that our knees were almost touching, and his eyes were only a couple of feet from mine as he leaned forward and questioned me.

He spat out his questions, some in German, some in French, and I boiled as his spittle sprayed my face, but sat as calmly as possible under the barrage. The civilian interrupted to translate questions in German, so I was turning from one man to the other, rather like someone watching a tennis match. They had all my papers and took me through each step of my life story, making me very thankful I had kept to the rule of repeating my cover story in full to myself each week. Then, they took Madame Tourganief—who had watched my interrogation—outside, and questioned her, and again I was lucky, for I had spent some time with Boris and his wife drilling them on our joint story in case we were ever asked. Both had taken the drill very seriously, and now it was paying off. I was feeling very uneasy at the persistence of the Gestapo men, and when I did pause to search my mind, I found I was taking more and more time to recall details. All the time he was watching my face, searching for relief or anxiety. On one occasion I was saved by Madame Tourganief. They were asking me about my military service, and I had a completely true story which had been given me at Le Puy by Lieutenant Chas. When Chas first gave me this history, he could not remember one fact, the name of my platoon commander, so he invented one. Later he remembered the right name, and I memorised that. But as the Gestapo asked me the name of the platoon commander, all I could remember was the false name. I hesitated, and Madame saw it.

'A fine lot of gentlemen you are—letting a lady stand while you sit there and talk, talk, talk. You move into my house, turn it upside down, take my chairs and leave me standing. You haven't even told me why you are here. I have just about had enough,' and she stamped her feet in anger.

Both men got to their feet and offered her a chair, brought another in from the next room, and restarted the interrogation. The break had been enough, and I was able to give the platoon commander's name right away.

They left me, to search the house, and went through my room and the rest of the flat, but found nothing. Just as I was beginning to breathe again, they both shouted at me: 'Sit down.' The interrogation began all over again, and they asked the same questions four or five times. My head began to split with the strain and, looking down at my hands, which lay in my lap, I saw my left thumb was twitching. I quickly put my other hand over it, for I remembered a police inspector at Limoges, when I was first questioned, telling me later that the only emotion I showed throughout hours of grilling was the twitching of my left thumb. The officer then put all my papers in one of his pockets, which made me think he was going to take me off to the Gestapo headquarters for more treatment. I was not very optimistic of surviving further interrogation. So I made a mental plan to leap out of the second-floor window on the way down in the street, and chance that the two would not have time to shoot before I ducked round a corner. Also I hoped there was not another armed man waiting in a car downstairs.

They let me stand up and suggested that I accompany them round the house whilst they had another look round. Instead of the barking, spitting questions, they used bland, quiet, and seemingly friendly remarks, and I was more frightened by this gentle approach than I had been by the shouting. They walked around picking up this object and that, carefully putting them back from where they had moved them. The civilian picked up the book I had been reading before I dozed off to sleep earlier, and casually said: 'Do you know anything about codes?'

'Codes? What are codes—I'm afraid I don't understand what you mean,' I replied.

'You know—codes. Words made into a code so you can pass a message without the true meaning showing,' he said impatiently.

'I'm sorry—I just don't understand what you mean,' I replied. I was astonished when he shrugged and turned away.

Suddenly the officer turned to me, took my papers out of his pocket, handed them back to me and, using his spitting voice again, barked out a couple of sentences in German. I turned to his accomplice, who translated: 'Your papers are all in order, and we can find nothing wrong with them or with your answers. But there is something not quite right about you, Monsieur Chanbaran.' He turned to Madame Tourganief and said: 'When your husband returns, tell him to report to my headquarters.'

With that, both men walked out of the flat, closing the door behind them, quite quietly for Germans. As it shut I turned to Madame and put my fingers to my lips, for I saw she was bursting with indignation, and the chances were that the two were listening outside waiting for an indiscretion. I went through to the kitchen for a glass of water, as I was parched with thirst, and I had only taken one sip when the front door was thrown open again and my two Gestapo friends were inside once more. I could have thrown the glass in their faces. They started all over again, but this time they asked one question for which I was not prepared.

'Why did you leave the pension, Monsieur Chanbaran?' the civilian said quietly, and I saw that this was the important question. I had no ready answer, so I decided to tell the truth.

'I left, gentlemen, because you had called there,' I told them.

'Why? Are you frightened of us?' he snapped back.

'No, it was not because I was frightened of you. I have just been very ill, as you saw from my medical certificate, and all the turmoil and worry your visit brought to the pension was not good for me. I have been away on a journey for my firm, and when I got back today Madame Tourganief suggested I might like to stay here quietly for a few days, until the people at the pension have got over the shock of your visit and things are back to normal.'

Both men grunted, looked at each other, shrugged, and walked out of the flat, saying over their shoulders that Boris must not forget to report to their headquarters. I watched at the window, and this time I saw them walk away down the street. The two of us sat down, and said nothing for several minutes. I felt exhausted, and my whole body seemed to be quivering with reaction to my fright. The affair had lasted about three hours. Madame had been magnificent, and backed me up when she saw I was in trouble.

I turned to her, held out my hand, and said simply: 'Thank you, Madame,' as I shook hers. In those sort of circumstances long speeches were unnecessary. It was all that had been said by Leroy when I pulled him out of the sea at Antibes, it was all I had said when the Commandant at the prisoner-of-war camp let us go. It was all Alex said when I brought his wife safely to Papa Jules. It was enough.

She told me that the Gestapo had picked her up at her office and forced her to walk through the streets with them to her home. She felt ashamed at being seen with them and tried to walk a few yards ahead, as though she was on her own. When she reached the flat and saw my bicycle on the second floor, she talked as loudly as possible, to try to give me some warning of her arrival with her escort. She believed that they had come on a routine check of foreign nationals, as Boris was a White Russian and had been questioned several times over the months in a desultory way.

Boris arrived shortly afterwards, and we explained what had happened. He, like his wife, believed that the Gestapo were on a routine check. He also thought they checked the pension only because it had been owned by an Englishman. We decided I would move out, because my cover story had been stretched to the limit and any further, intense, interrogation would probably break it. I went over our story with him, as he would be seeing the Gestapo the next morning, and told him to emphasise that I was a sick man and, as I had told the Gestapo, a law-abiding one. Boris laughed at that and went to a cupboard, from which he brought out a special bottle of wine and three glasses.

'In view of your sickly condition, Monsieur, I think it is our duty to give you a tonic,' the big man guffawed. He raised his glass and in a loud voice he shouted: '*Vive Churchill.*' I toasted Madame for her bravery in helping me during the Gestapo visit.

Boris went to the Gestapo the next morning, answered the routine political questions he had been asked many times before, and was allowed to go. So ended that brush with fear.

We arranged to rendezvous in a day or two at the home of another foreign national, Vandaluski, who lived with his French-born wife out in the country, to the south-west of Angers. When we met with Boris at Vanda's—it was easier than calling him Vandaluski all the time—I found him to be very pro-allies and a quiet, thoughtful man, who dealt with matters in a cautious way.

I suggested, towards the end of a pleasant day, that he might like to consider finding fields which could be used for dropping stores from the air. He looked at me very hard, and said he would discuss the matter with his wife and let me know. I was delighted at the caution he showed. We met again two days later at Boris's flat. I told Vanda and his wife that I was a British officer on a mission to build up Resistance and sabotage groups in the Angers area. I said that the group, run by Henri, was now much too big, and that it was inevitable someone would be incautious, which would lead to arrests. I suggested that Boris and he ran a small group acting independently, though obeying my overall orders, which were centralised from London.

The fact that I had spent a whole day at Vanda's house without them suspecting that I was a British officer spoke much for Boris's discretion. Vanda was astonished at my news, but readily agreed to help, as I knew he would.

By now I had moved from Boris's flat and was living with the Blandeau family, who had a small house in Angers. Monsieur Blandeau was an architect, Michelle, the eldest daughter, was a secretary, and Madeleine, the younger daughter, was a schoolteacher. Madame Blandeau, tall and angular, with iron grey hair, was very energetic and forthright. Her husband was much smaller, with bad teeth and a bad digestion. But he had a lot of nervous energy, and was always cheerful. All four were in the Resistance movement and thought that it was the natural thing to do. They took as a matter of course, the risk of having me under their roof. They all admitted they were afraid, and asked me not to say anything if they showed it at any time. They were very fine people. It takes real courage to pursue a course of danger when you are afraid every waking moment. Monsieur Blandeau was part of a large organisation whose eventual aims were the control of Angers. He kept his battleplan concealed in one of his drawing boards at the office.

During these few days, I went to the Keller pension twice and brought out a suitcase on each occasion, which I packed with valuables belonging to Madame Keller, and sent by a courier to Alex. I also collected my plan of the Naval Headquarters and sent it to Paris by another courier. It reached London, via another courier, two days later. Communications were better.

A few days later, Monsieur Blandeau, who was one of Henri's stores operation reception committee, ran through the house shouting: 'The message, the message, it's come through.' I had told him to listen to the BBC for the phrase: '*Après la soupe un verre de vin,*' and this was what he had heard. He calmed himself, collected the rest of the reception committee, and we all went out to the vineyard where I had earlier dug my two pits.

The problem of hiding the twelve containers, and three other packages which had been added to the original list, had been solved quite easily in the end. The farmer had a great pile of faggots cut in one field, and immediately behind it was a hedge and ditch. By covering over the ditch with dead branches, it had been simple to make a safe cache.

It was a fine, moonlight night as we all gathered in the vineyard. There seemed dozens of men about, as Henri had brought his own team to help with the recovery of the stores, and we had quite a party, drinking wine and eating sandwiches as we waited for the aircraft to appear. At first everyone stayed very quiet, talked in whispers, and tiptoed through the fields. One of the reception committee, Duval, was forced to take his boots off, as they squeaked. For two hours this went on, then they became fidgety, talked normally, and one of the sentries even lit up a cigarette. Henri saw to it that the cigarette was put out, and the talking was hushed.

Suddenly the sirens wailed in Angers, and I rubbed my hands together with the satisfaction of a salesman who sees his victim reaching for his wallet. Not long after, I heard the drone of an aircraft, and it appeared over the brow of a hill, flying parallel to my flare-path, but some distance to the south. I flashed my signal at it repeatedly, but it did not answer, and flew away. Then it appeared again, much closer, and immediately flashed back. I called for the flare-path to be lit, and one by one the signal torches flicked on. The plane banked and thundered low over the ground, dropping the containers as it reached the right marker. I heard the parachutes open with a 'thirripp', and all the containers sailed down gently, except for one, which hurtled down, whistling like a bomb, to bury itself in the field.

The aircraft flew away, and all my helpers rushed around

looking for the containers and the three smaller packages, which, being lighter, had drifted off. Everything was recovered. I opened the cells to see what had been dropped, and noticed that the men handled the revolvers and hand grenades lovingly, but ignored the sten-guns. I supposed they had never seen one before. I saw one or two examining the beautiful parachute silks, so repeated my orders that nothing was to be taken away from the spot, as there might be road checks on the way back to Angers. The stores were to be hidden, and distributed later.

But Henri and I were breaking the rules by taking away the three small packages. I was carrying on the back of my bicycle two radio receivers which were to be sent to Vladimir in Paris, and Henri was taking back the cell of provisions, which was included in every drop and shared between the reception committee. It usually contained cigarettes, coffee, tea, sugar, chocolate, soap, and tins of salad oil. Sometimes there was even a couple of bottles of whisky. We decided to take a very careful ride back to town and to hide our goods if we saw or heard anything suspicious.

The whole of the group, now in good humour, rode away from the vineyard together, but we soon split up and I was left with our guide and Henri. We pedalled for miles, and after an hour the guide admitted that he was lost, so we stopped, and I checked our position on my map before heading for a main road in the greyish light that precedes the dawn. My bicycle, with two R/T sets on the back, was very top-heavy, and I fell off twice as I hit potholes and ruts. I was pleased when we reached the main road where progress was much easier.

By the time we reached the outskirts of Angers it was broad daylight, but everything seemed normal. There were no extra checks out, so I decided to continue as Henri branched off towards his home. I reached the deserted town and suddenly, out of a side street, poured a company of German infantrymen on bicycles, riding in the loose formation of dockyard workers when they leave at clocking-off time. They were all going my way, so I had to ride along in the middle of them. They seemed mild and inoffensive, and I passed the time of day as one or two tried out their poor French, wondering what their reaction would have been if I told them what I had been doing all night. After ten minutes or so, they all swung off to the right and I was on my own again, much to my relief.

I reached the Blandeaus' house to find everyone up, but no Blandeau. The rest of the family were worried, but I told them he would be along in a few minutes, and he was. As he walked in I had to laugh, for he looked as though he was in the last stages of pregnancy. I shook my fist at him, for I guessed what he had done, and I was right. Like a naughty schoolboy who has been caught stealing apples, he said: 'Please don't be angry with me—but I've brought a parachute. It's for my daughters.' The parachute was quickly disposed of by the girls, who unpicked all the seams, dyed it, and had the panels converted into underclothes, which I saw only when they were blowing on the line on washdays.

I sent a report of the success of the operation to London, through Vladimir, and was told in reply that I could expect another drop shortly. Two operations in one month was progress indeed, and I was well content. I had selected another dropping zone near Vanda's home, and this had been accepted by the RAF. I warned Boris and Vanda of the drop and said that I wanted to bring along Blandeau, and our friend of the squeaking shoes, Duval, to give them experience. I realised that if things continued at this pace I could not control every drop. Others must be trained as well.

Two nights later the BBC came up with our message and I headed once again to a dropping zone, with Duval and Blandeau. It was a cloudy night, with a waning moon. In the direction of Saint-Nazaire I heard frequent explosions and the noises of aircraft. Obviously a big raid on the naval and submarine base. At two in the morning an aircraft came flying in quite low. It headed straight for us and, so far as I could see, it was British.

I signalled, lit up the flare-path and waited for a returning signal. I got one, but it was not the answer I was expecting, for as I watched, another plane came into view and the first plane opened up its throttles and fled. I was able to make out that the second aircraft was a German night fighter, before they both disappeared in the night.

Despite the protestations of the others, I decided to stay until four o'clock, which allowed me enough time to hide the containers. At ten to four, another aircraft came in high, and obviously very much in a hurry. It gave me the right reply to my signal, flew up the flare-path the wrong way, dropped my containers, and disappeared at speed. I counted twelve parachutes, but as they had been dropped from height they all drifted off. We could only find ten, which we hid in the roof of an old barn. Then all the team went back, with the exception of Boris—who did not have to clock in at a set time—and myself. Vanda would have stayed, but he had to be in bed before his servant girl—who knew nothing of his night-time operations—came to call him in the morning. Boris and I waited, and easily spotted the white parachutes as it got light. We hid them away with the others, for all the stores from this drop were to be collected by Monsieur Bremond, a dyer and cleaner who owned a plain van. He would bring his son, Maurice, and Duval, fully armed, and if they met any Feldgendarmes—who generally patrolled Angers in twos—they would shoot them, bundle them into the van, and burn the bodies in the enormous furnace which was always alight at their dye works. The stores were to be in a clever cache built in the roof of the factory. To get at it, a ladder had to be placed on top of their machinery and a trap door lifted. Each time the cache was used, Monsieur Bremond plastered the ceiling over to hide the trapdoor. They moved our stores a week later, without recourse to the furnace.

I was very busy, now that we had stores, lecturing group after group on methods of sabotage and the use of small arms. The sten-guns were no longer ignored, for the French fighters soon realised they were a very fine, close-range weapon. I also instructed groups to draw up plans of possible targets, like oil depots, engine depots, bridges, and factories, which I might be called upon to blow up later, and asked them to keep a check on German troop movements and concentrations. A division of troops in a couple of fields would make a fine target for the RAF.

The lectures brought immediate success. Monsieur Blandeau came to me with drawings of a top secret construction being built by the Germans at Watten, in northern France. None of us could work out what it was, for it looked like no other structure we had ever seen. Blandeau had been given the plan by one of the foremen on the job—an Alsatian—who thought it must be of great value as the Germans had gone to great trouble to check all the workmen on the project and had extra guards placed in the area to keep sightseers away. We did not know it then, but this was a drawing of the first flying-bomb site. I thought it must be important and hid it, with the plans for the take-over for Angers, in Monsieur Blandeau's drawing board.

I heard, also, that the pension had been closed down by the Gestapo, who asked many questions about those known to have used it. Henri, in particular, was interrogated by the Gestapo, and I thought it would be wise to see less of him and the Tourganiefs.

The Russian and his French wife knew where I lived, but I had asked them not to come near the house unless it was a matter of extreme urgency. They agreed, and I always met them at other rendezvous. I asked Henri to do the same, but he started to visit me two or three times a day, using the most footling excuses. Madame Tourganief gave me a further warning about the Gestapo's interest in Henri, so I told him that it would be wiser for him to take a business trip away from the area until things cooled down a little. He laughed at the idea, until I said I was moving again and that I would not give him my new address. He flew into a violent temper and shouted: 'Do you trust me, or don't you? There can be no half-way about this, and I insist you tell me where the hell you're going to be. I've got to be able to get you in a hurry from time to time and I shan't be able to do that unless you're honest with me.' Of course I trusted him, and I told him so. But I also told him that I did not trust the Gestapo. He could not swear not to give away secrets if he was arrested.

Henri pounded his chest and said: 'They can put me against a post and shoot me—but they will never learn a thing from me.'

I told him quietly that shooting was the last thing they did, and it was the interval between arrest and shooting which led to people talking. But Henri was past reason and said that unless I told him where I was going he would have nothing more to do with me. The threat left me cold, for although he had been useful, he was getting too lax on security and I could well do without his tantrums. Fortunately the Blandeaus agreed with me, as did others in the group.

Monsieur Bremond, the dyer and cleaner, sent me to stay fifteen kilometres outside Angers on the way to Le Mans, where his two aged parents lived. He drove me there in his old, plain van, and I arranged to keep in contact with him through his children, Maurice, Renée and André, or through the Tourganiefs or the Blandeaus.

I got a message from Paris saying that Vladimir was sending someone to collect the two radios and a suitcase of clothes, sent over in the last drop. I was given the number and description of his car, a meeting place near my house, and a password. I did not need the password, for Vladimir himself stepped out of the car. It was the first time we had met since we were training back in England a year earlier. Vladimir (Grover Williams) was a well-known peacetime racing driver. So was his second-in-command, Robert Benoist, whom he had brought with him. The two fitted the radios into a secret place in the car which just held the two sets. They felt the new clothes might compromise them if they were stopped, so they decided to send these by train.

Vladimir asked me to leave with him for Paris immediately as there was a British officer there who wanted to talk to me. 'You'll have to take off those old blue overalls and get properly dressed, because you would look very out of place with the bunch we're operating with,' he said. I changed into my old blue suit and pulled on my black army boots. I was hardly the well-dressed man.

We reached Paris just before curfew. The car, of course, was very powerful, and with Robert at the wheel belied its vanlike appearance, and I found that he did not keep all his *élan* for the race tracks. We were stopped once when guards checked the car's and Robert's papers, but that was all. They would have had a good haul if they had been a little more efficient—two British agents, two radios, and Robert.

The following afternoon I went to Vladimir's peacetime house, where his French wife was living, and met the officer from London, Renaud. He was a Mauritian business man, called J. F. Antelme, well known in banking circles in France. He was awarded the OBE for his work in Paris, but was caught and executed before the Liberation. I gave him a complete breakdown of all the people I had met, their usefulness, and the possibilities of future targets.

He then told me that London wanted me to go back to England for a rest, as the Gestapo were not far behind me at Angers and it would be a good thing for the groups to lie low for a while. I did not want to go, as my work was going well, and I was reluctant to leave my friends.

'I know how you feel, old boy, but just take a look at yourself in the mirror,' he said.

I knew what he meant. I still looked as though I had just come out of prison, in spite of the good food and kindness I had been given. Life, under the constant state of tension, trying to be brave for other people as well as myself, had left its stamp on my face, which was heavily lined and drawn. I never relaxed, never felt safe. I was on guard even in my sleep. The word 'England' was a great temptation, and I thought of the countryside, lunch in Soho, of saying 'hello' to a policeman without my stomach turning over, and beer in a pub. I nearly agreed to go, but then I remembered Blandeau and Bremond, Boris, Vanda, and Duval, their wives and their children. There were no holidays for them, and they needed me.

So I told Renaud I could not go. He said it was all right by him but it would be up to London to decide after he had reported back to Buckmaster.

We talked a lot about Alex, whom Renaud had seen. London wanted him back, too, but Alex would not go. With his wife and family in France and his incredible devotion to duty, I felt there would never be any argument strong enough to persuade him to return for a rest. He believed that as the Gestapo were looking for him in Angers, and not in Nantes, he was as safe as one ever could be in wartime France.

Renaud asked me if I knew an Inspector Imar.

'Yes, I know him. He's a policeman who had dealings with Alex and me in Limoges. He is not to be trusted at any cost. Why do you want to know?' I asked.

He told me that Imar had got in touch with Alex again, asking his assistance to help two of our agents, who were in serious trouble. A meeting had been arranged between Imar and Alex for the following day.

I was suddenly very worried for my friend.

'Renaud, you must stop Alex going. Find him for me and let me persuade him not to go. Alex gets a rush of blood to the head on occasions, and this is one of them. I can stop him—*if* you can find him.' I knew that Alex was in danger, deadly danger. Do not ask me how, but it was an instinct developed over the months. Asked what was wrong with a situation, all one could do was to touch one's nose with the forefinger and say: 'The *pifomètre* says that it smells.' The *pifomètre* was saying very loudly—'Save Alex'.

Renaud saw my anxiety and agreed to do his best to trace Alex. He was generous and loyal to his friends, as I found out so many times.

All was well when I arrived back at Angers, apart from another outburst from Henri, who made a scene because I had left the area without informing him. People were beginning to treat him like a bad joke, or with suspicion.

I now had as many dropping fields accepted by the RAF as I could manage for stores operations and two, level, even clearings big enough for landing parachutists, or even a Lysander or twin-engined Hudson aircraft. I also had three good, small groups operating, the best of them being that formed by Boris and Vanda. Duval, squeaky shoes and all, had formed another small group at Ancenis, where the next drop was expected, and at Châteauneuf a very level-headed man from Alsace, called Louis, led another group. A drop was planned for Châteauneuf at about the same time as the one at Ancenis.

It was now that I experienced, for the first time, the antipathy existing between the rival political groups in France. They were looking to the future and a new, free France, and each group wanted the newness to be provided by their own political party. I accepted men in the Resistance from any political group, provided they understood that they had a soldier's job to do first and that they would not be released by me to play at politics until after the liberation. Politics was of secondary importance, I thought, and I knew that too many good Frenchmen were executed and tortured after being denounced by political rivals for their own ends. I was not popular with the politicians, for two main reasons. Firstly I was British, and secondly I had no political axe to grind and would not involve myself with the wranglings of the day. In the early days of the war the party of the right held back from any strong military action, but towards the end it was the leftists, reserving themselves to seize power, who held back. It was an extremely difficult job for a military agent in the field to manœuvre his way through the various factions to get his mission accomplished. At times I felt that a couple of hand grenades thrown among the squabblers would make my life much easier, but a quiet drink would calm me down and I reverted to diplomatic language to get my own way.

I went out to Châteauneuf for a few days with Monsieur Louis and stayed at a mill run by an active Resister, François Berger. Duval visited me there, and I told him he would have to run his own parachute reception operation. He was very proud to be trusted with the job. It was obvious to me that the increasing number of drops by the RAF would overtax the military agents and that more and more Frenchmen must take control of them.

Whilst I was there, Madeleine, the Blandeaus' younger daughter, cycled over and told me that the Gestapo had questioned Henri, the Tourganiefs, and Madame Bruges about me, and that her father and Bremond, the dyer and cleaner, thought it wiser for me to stay with Louis for a few days.

We had a picnic that day, a sunny, pleasing spring day, and in the evening, as we sat round the fire, there was a knock at the door. Everyone stiffened—that was the effect of *any* knock on the door in those days—but when it opened we found Blandeau and one of Alex's couriers, called Charles. After the meal Charles took me aside and told me that I was to report to Renaud in Paris, in four days time, at Vladimir's flat. It seemed, although Charles did not say this, that I was to go home for a rest after all. I told Blandeau that I was going on a journey and might be away for a long time. I suggested that, as the Gestapo was so active in Angers, he and the other groups should do nothing for a few weeks. When I came back, I told him, the groups could start up again, and if I did not come back, then I would see that another agent was sent to work with them. Blandeau was upset by the news but all he did was shake my hand and say: 'Remember, we are counting on you.' He was a very gallant little man.

It was later that evening that Charles gave me the news about Alex, of Renaud watching him enter the café, and his failure to reappear.

I spent the next day or two training Louis on how to run a stores operation, as he had never been on one. He was relieved when I said Duval might be able to help him if his drop did not coincide with the one at Châteauneuf, but I felt that he was capable enough.

His second-in-command was a real old warrior from the 1914–18 war, who had served in the present war and, after demobilisation, had smuggled his Fusil Mitrailleur—a weapon like a bren-gun—home with him and hidden it on his farm. 'By Gad, if the Germans come I'll set that gun up and mow them down,' he would say. I heard many stories from Frenchmen of what they were going to do if the Germans came, so I did not think much of his boast, but he suggested I would like to see the gun later that evening. I expected a rusted piece, or the excuse: 'I'm sorry, it's too well hidden to disturb it just to satisfy your curiosity.' But no, the old gentleman asked myself and Louis to his farm that night at 8 o'clock, We were there on time and were introduced to his family with cakes, coffee, and *eau-de-vie*. After two drinks we were taken into a back room and there, in the middle of the floor, was the FM set up ready for action. It was in perfect working order and spotless. The old man and his great friend, also a 1914 veteran, stood to attention by the side of their gun, holding the three pans of ammunition which was all they had.

'Give us some more ammunition and then let them come,' the old boys said. I believe they meant it.

Just before I left, Blandeau handed me the plans of the mysterious construction at Watten, and I arranged to give it to Renaud when I reached Paris. I was concerned with finding a good hiding-place for these on my journey, in case I was stopped and searched, until I remembered Alex and the loaf in which we hid our file. I decided the best place would be inside a sandwich, so I handed the papers to Madame Louis and asked her to hide them for me. She did such a good job that I had to mark the sandwich in case I ate it by mistake.

I cycled to the station accompanied by Monsieur Louis and left my bicycle at a small inn ready for my return, with orders for it to be picked up if I did not return within ten days. I bought my ticket, went through the normal check at the station entrance, and swung aboard the Paris train, which was packed as usual. That was the last time I saw Angers. I have never been back, although I wanted to go there after the war. But SOE advised me that for 'political reasons' it would be wiser for me to keep clear. There were few of my friends left at that time, for many who had worked so well and loyally with me were dead. The Tourganiefs were arrested, and disappeared. Vanda was arrested, but later got away. Bremond, the dyer and cleaner, was arrested and died from his treatment in captivity a short time after he was released. Alex's wife, Madame Keller, was arrested, but came through. It was a long, sad list.

I met Vladimir at his flat and was taken to his wife's house, where I saw Renaud again. He came to the point at once. 'London wants you back and a plane will pick you up in about ten days' time.'

I expected this order, but London had seemed so far away for so long, and so much had happened, that it took quite a time for the news to sink in that I would soon be free, if only for a short time, of the strain of being an enemy agent.

Renaud promised to go to Angers and tell Blandeau and Louis that they were not being abandoned by London.

He also said he had heard that the Gestapo were on the verge of a big clean-up and that I was suspect at Angers. Alex had been arrested and he might talk under 'treatment', but we found after the war that Alex, as I would have expected, did not say one word. I asked him if he had any further news of my friend.

'I saw him go into the café after I tried to persuade him not to, but I didn't see him come out. I went to see his wife, and she told me that she and a friend were in the café when Alex walked in. He was to give her a prearranged signal if things were going well, and a different one if the opposite was the case. Alex sat for a long time talking with three men, one of whom Madame Keller recognised as Inspector Imar. Presently Alex and the other three got up and went towards the gentlemen's cloakroom, and as Alex, looking very cheerful, passed her, he gave her the "everything OK" signal. She sat waiting and waiting, but he never returned.'

We were silent for some time, each with our own thoughts, and both heavy at heart.

I put my hand in my jacket pocket to pull out a cigarette, and felt something soft. I pulled out my sandwich, which I had forgotten, and handed it to Renaud.

'Thanks, not now. Camembert and white bread, excellent, but I'm not hungry,' he said.

I explained, and showed him the plans. He studied them carefully and seemed impressed. He had a courier going to London in two days, and would dispatch them then.

These plans were to confirm for me the internal jealousies of SOE. On the corner of the plan I had written my code name for London, Fabien. When I was in London later on, I saw the plans again by pure chance, but this time the corner with my name on it had been snipped off with scissors. I asked why this had been done, and the officer I was talking to was astonished.

'How do you know about this, it's a top secret business?' he said.

'Well, I know about it because I got the plans to Paris and handed them over—that's how.'

'Well I'm damned—we've been told that another agent was responsible for getting this.'

This was pettiness, claiming credit where it was not due. We were all in the same war, but these little jealousies persisted all the time.

Two days later I was taken to the Austerlitz railway station to meet Prosper, head of the Paris circuit and the man I glimpsed many months earlier as he came out of the famous Black Bathroom at SOE headquarters. He introduced me to Claude and Auger, the men who were responsible for handling the reception of the Lysander which would be taking me out in a few days, and also to Phillip Miller. He was an Englishman, navigator of a Mosquito aircraft shot down a few days before. He was a fine man, but he did not speak one word of French and looked as English as roast beef.

Prosper and I parted, and I went off with the other three. I did not know it, but I had escaped capture by a very narrow margin. An hour or so after I left Prosper he and a large number of his group were arrested by the Gestapo—the operation that Renaud talked of. Prosper died, so did many others, and his organisation collapsed.

I briefed Phillip, who had good false papers, to go to sleep as soon as he got on the train with Claude, Auger and me for the four-hour journey to Amboise, as the travelling French are very friendly and chatty. I also told him to watch me carefully when any official came round so that he would not hand over his papers when his ticket was needed, or vice versa. The journey passed safely, but then came the identity check at the station. We planned to let Phillip and Claude go first with me, with Auger following immediately behind. If there was a hold-up at the barrier over Phillip's papers, we would push and hope Phillip and Claude could run away in the confusion.

The gendarme at the barrier took Phillip's papers and studied them for a long time, comparing the photograph with the fresh-faced young British airman beside him. Finally he looked straight at Phillip, grinned, winked, and waved him through.

We cycled to a small hotel, where we waited for the Lysander and tried to protect Phillip from the curious residents, who thought the poor boy so young to have been made deaf by an explosion during a raid by 'those beastly British'. When we were alone, Phillip told me of his remarkable luck since his aircraft had been shot down and his pilot killed.

After baling out, he landed safely by a road, and walked, still in his RAF uniform, to a small crossroads. The signpost there meant nothing to him, so he chose the road that led downhill because he thought the name of the village it was pointing to was 'charming'. He passed two women talking beside iron gates, and then heard them calling him. He turned, saw them beckoning and, being a fatalistic young man, he joined them. 'Eengleesh, veney queek,' they said, and hid him away. The brother of one of these ladies happened to be part of an escape-route organisation for British pilots. So, eight days after being shot down, Phillip waited to be picked up and taken home again.

We stayed three days at the hotel until a message came through that the Lysander was coming that night. We cycled out to the woods near the field where the plane was to land, waited until 1 a.m., then heard an aircraft droning in the distance.

A Lysander appeared, very low over the field, absolutely on time, and I marvelled at the navigation of the lone airman who had ferreted the right patch out of so many. We lit the flare-path, she landed safely. There was a bustle at the door, and a man, brandishing a revolver, climbed out and handed down eight suitcases. I felt for the reception committee, as carrying that load on two bicycles for several miles was not going to be much fun.

A quick handshake from Claude and Auger, and Phillip and I climbed into the Lysander, which still had its engine running. Less than two minutes after touch-down, the pilot prepared for take-off.

I adjusted the headphones and the pilot said: 'Do you speak English?'

'Yes, I'm British.'

'Good show, well you'll find two push buttons on the seats, one on the port side and one on the starboard. Got them?'

'Yes,' I told him.

'If you see any night fighters or flak, push the button on the appropriate side. Got it. There's a thermos of coffee at the bottom of the cockpit. Hold tight.'

I shouted to Phillip, and he took charge of one of the buttons. Then the Lysander taxied to the end of the field and we were airborne. Phillip and I found one parachute at the back but, because we were both big men, there was insufficient space for either of us to put it on. We decided that the chances of getting out, if anything went wrong, were very slim anyway.

I was very tense as the Lysander gained height. I had a feeling that I was going to die in this plane and I refused to believe England and safety were so near. Suddenly there were lights and flashes all round the plane, and Phillip and I pushed our buttons frantically, but the pilot was already taking action, weaving and diving to escape the flak that came at us. He swooped to the ground, only ten feet above the hedgerows, which flicked by like telegraph poles seen from a fast moving train. Then the bangings stopped and the pilot came on the intercom.

'There's the Channel, we're okay now. Sorry about the bit of a shake-up.'

I blessed the coolness of that pilot and I was delighted, a few years ago, to see the courage of the men of the Lysander Force recognised in a book called *Moon Squadron*. They flew unarmed under the most difficult conditions.

All the way over the Channel I twitched, seeing night fighters in every speck on the windows, but finally we crossed the coast and at last circled the airfield.

The pilot came on again. 'We are about to land . . .' he paused, then with a chuckle, finished his sentence, 'in England. Don't try to get out until the cockpit is opened. Here we go.'

We landed very sweetly, taxied for a few minutes, and stopped. He switched his engine off, and I was engulfed by the stillness of the English morning. My tension disappeared. It was a sensual experience, a feeling of getting into warm, clean sheets—and the security of the arms of a woman you loved. I savoured those moments. Then the cockpit opened and a voice I recognised said: 'Hello, Raymond, had a good trip?' It was Jean Paul, Major Bodington, whom I had last seen in France. With him were André Simon, my old conducting officer who was frequently in and out of France, and Gerry Morel, the agent who had escaped from Limoges dressed as a doctor, with stitches still in his stomach after a major operation. It was good to be met by friends.

Phillip and I were taken into the mess and given whisky and

sodas, bacon and eggs. I explained who Phillip was, as he had not been expected, and he was hailed as a fellow flier. I kept touch with him, but only a short time after he went back to operations he was shot down and killed.

After breakfast I was driven back to London and arrived, shortly after 7 a.m., at André's flat. 'Look, old boy,' he said, 'I'm going to grab a couple of hours sleep. You help yourself. There's a sofa, hot water, tea, and coffee, and here's the telephone.'

I could not sleep, so I got into a hot bath and started thinking, trying to realise that I was in England, attempting to get back my English personality. I wondered if my mother knew I was still alive, and whether Vi, the girl I wanted to marry, remembered I still existed. She had been on a bomber station as a WAAF when I left for France.

I got out of the bath and reached for the telephone.

9

Eventually I managed to sleep for a few hours. When I woke I began to think of the information I could give Buckmaster, and to consider the results of my first tour in the field as a British agent. Self-analysis, I felt, would benefit any future work in France.

I realised that the months had changed me. When I landed in France I had an almost Boy Scout attitude towards the work I would be doing, and considered life a big adventure of cowboys and Indians. A few days in France changed all that, and subsequent meetings with Gestapo agents turned me into a professional, able to hate, but hate with a coldness that kept my temper under control. I had discovered too, that I could kill, play the executioner, if the position warranted it, an 'ability' I did not know I had in me when I left England. I had taken unnecessary risks, and I swore to myself I would not take the same risks again. I remembered leaving the revolver in my house at Angers. If that had been found ... Never would I repeat the stupid mistake Alex and I made trying to contact Rake, by going back for a second look at a rendezvous. Certain risks were justified, but they had to be balanced against the possible gains.

I felt, too, that I had become too involved in the lives of some people who worked with me. The relationship between an organiser and his associates, I believed, should be roughly those between doctor and patients. If a doctor becomes too involved, or too close to his patients, he is likely to be swayed by emotion rather than logic, and may prescribe the wrong treatment. I had become close to some fine people in France—Madame Blandeau, the Audouards, Boris, couriers, and, of course, Alex, whom I thought of as a brother. His arrest had grieved me deeply. I realised this sort of relationship was dangerous, as I would have risked much to have saved him, and I know he would have done the same for me. But danger lay behind such an association, for in rushing to help Alex I doubt if I would have considered the people I might give away under torture if I failed. I decided that I must never get too close to anyone in the field again, otherwise my judgement might suffer.

I asked myself, too, whether my nerve had been affected by the long strain and whether Gestapo interrogations, imprisonment, and the arrest of friends, had made me too jittery to carry on with the job. I had always been frightened, but had managed to appear calm, and I reasoned that I was still capable of doing my job, for now I was more careful. A few days of relaxation would be enough for me, I felt; then I could be off again.

Over the next few days I was de-briefed in London, at either Orchard Court, the headquarters of SOE, or at a house in Baker Street. Experts in the French section wanted as much detail as possible about French wartime life. I had an incredible memory for detail, and the interrogators were astounded at some of the things I recalled. For instance, I could talk about the price of a pair of braces, and what types were usually worn by workmen. I could discuss the fashions of the day, not that there were many of them, but the little fads that crept into a community, like leaving a top button undone on a suit and so on.

I talked to an RAF officer about the landing fields I had mapped out, and we discussed whether improvements could be made in dropping heights or in the shape of flare-paths.

Although many messages had been sent back by me on troop movements and concentrations, there was never enough time to put down every detail I had seen of German troops and police. I discussed the morale of troops and said that—in the main—the French were accepting the Boche more and more and there seemed to be just as many French girls going out with German soldiers as there had been a year earlier. I was also able to pass on much more information about sabotage points which could be attacked now that explosive was being dropped into the country more frequently and, in particular, I drew maps and plans of bridges, railway cuttings, tunnels, oil depots, and engine sheds, where I believed a lot of damage could be caused for little risk.

Finally I was told I could go on leave for a few days, but that I would be needed to go back to France if I still wanted to. Of course I wanted to, and I said so.

Leave freshened me up a lot. I started to lose the drawn, tight look that had been my normal expression since I was first captured at Limoges, and when I finally reported back to SOE I was feeling extremely well. I was sent off on some refresher courses, including one on shooting. Bill Sykes was my instructor, a fine shot from the Hong Kong Police, who at one time had been one of the greatest marksmen in the world. He and I were very worried about my shooting, for I found I could not hit a thing. Day after day I banged away in the underground shooting ranges used by agents outside London, but some of my shots were so wild that he never did find where they ended up. I wondered if there was some mental block in me against straight shooting since I had killed the girl with a classic pistol shot. But after a while I improved and regained my normal aptitude with revolver, pistol, and automatic weapons, thanks to the patience and concern of Bill Sykes.

At the end of my courses—none of them very strenuous and most of them in the classrooms—I went back to the headquarters of SOE to be briefed for my next job, the destruction of a ball-bearing plant at Colombes, just outside Paris. I was handed detailed plans of the factory, together with on-the-spot reports on sentries, patrols, and so on. I discussed these for many days with various experts in SOE, including engineers, who told me the best places to put charges to cause the most damage. As an additional nuisance, I planned to turn on the sprinkler system over the whole of the factory, by heating up one of the sprinkler sprays and melting the wax which stopped the water coming out. Water spraying at force over several hours would cause a lot of damage, as well as rusting and corrosion of the plant. I was not far from completing my plans when the door of my office at Orchard Court opened one morning and Buckmaster said: 'Ah, drop that. I've got something bigger for you to handle.' He explained that a joint British–French–American mission was to operate in certain parts of France to organise the Maquis, and that I had been chosen to lead it. With me would be an American radio operator, Paul Johnson, and young Rosenthal, who was to be known as Cantinier.

Jean Rosenthal at this time was aged about thirty-two, just a little younger than I was, and only began to take control of the Rosenthal business of furs and jewellery from his famous father as the war started. His headquarters were in Paris, where he had a town house, but he was a playboy at heart and loved the beaches of southern France and the ski slopes of the Haute-Savoie, where he had yet another house. He was slim, with fair, almost gingery, hair, wore glasses, and was always as perfectly dressed as you would expect of a leading French businessman-cum-playboy. He was full of energy, impetuous, and, at times, rash. But he had a great desire to rid France of Germans. I was introduced to him in London just before I returned to France. I liked him.

Buckmaster told me he wanted me and Cantinier to fly to France in a twin-engined Hudson aircraft, land in the Saône-et-Loire area, and make a fourteen-day reconnaissance of the Provinces of the Ain, Isère, Savoie, Haute-Savoie and Jura.

'We want to know how many men are under arms, how well trained they are, what targets are available for sabotage, what stores are needed, what security is like. We need to know everything there is to know. This is an important area, and when we invade Europe your groups will have a major job to do to disrupt communications and delay German troop movements. But we won't build up the area until we know that the morale is right and that there are sufficient men to take it on,' Buck told me.

'You will report to me when you get back from this recce and, if you recommend that we go ahead, you will be in charge of the Resistance in all the Provinces.

'You will go out later with the American, Paul Johnson, as your radio operator, and Elizabeth, who will be your main courier.

'One more thing,' Buck said. 'Your field name will be Xavier. Good luck.'

I was not to leave England for fourteen days, as I had to meet Paul and Elizabeth and also go to a series of meetings with the Free French in London, to learn from them of their own set-up in south-west France. Some of these meetings were very tricky; any British officer was suspect as the French seemed to see a political venture behind every bush. I had to assure them that I only wanted their military co-operation, and this I got.

I met Paul Johnson at Orchard House. He was a handsome, black-haired American whom we filched from the American undercover organisation, OSS. He had worked in North Africa with OSS and was a highly-trained radio operator who understood the whole problem of security. He was one of the kindest men I ever met and later, in the Maquis, used to live in rags as he was always giving away his warm clothes to men worse off than himself.

I also met Elizabeth Devereaux-Rochester, who was about twenty-seven, and looked as English as her name—but was American. She was tall, with a prominent nose, and she did not walk, she *strode*. When you saw her coming towards you in the mountains, you automatically expected to see a couple of Labradors at her heels, and that her first words would be 'Had a bloody good walk, yer know, nothing like it for keeping fit.' I thought SOE were mad to send her to France, as she stuck out like a sore thumb, but when I raised the question they said she was a fully trained operative and knew the Savoie well. I liked her too, and my reluctance to take her was only based on her English looks. She did a fine job, for she had guts and imagination.

Before going on the recce, I had to have a completely new cover story, and SOE decided that I should be a traveller for a jewellery firm. They picked a firm in Marseilles, sufficiently far away from south-east France for me to avoid running into genuine travellers of the company.

I did a course at Hatton Garden with a diamond merchant, who instructed me on the customary methods of handling precious stones, and on how to value rings, brooches, and so on. I thoroughly enjoyed this course, which was of great use to me later. For instance, I learned that you never picked a diamond up in your fingers to examine it, but only in a pair of tweezers. You did not bend down towards it, but brought it up to the magnifying eyepiece. There was also a very delicate balance for weighing stones, and I learned that they were always put on the same side of the balance—it was a custom of the trade. I only had to put my knowledge on trial once, during my second trip to France. I went with Cantinier to Lyons (a place I hated, as it was filled with intrigue) where he and I were due to see two French officers. I was taken to a house and left alone, for a short time, with the wife of one of the officers, while Cantinier went off on some business. She asked what my business was and I told her I worked for a jewellery firm.

'Oh, you're just the man I'm looking for,' she said. She went away and came back with a brooch.

'I want to sell this and I'm sure the jeweller is trying to swindle me. How much do you think it is worth?'

I went through the proper routine, examined the setting, the quality of the stones. 'Eight thousand francs,' I said authoritatively.

She started to make muttering noises in her throat, and I thought I had dropped a frightful brick. Perhaps the damn thing was worth 25,000 francs.

'I knew it, I knew it,' she finally exclaimed. 'He's only offering 7,000 francs. Thank you very much, monsieur.'

I reckoned I could not have been far off its proper value, and I was rather pleased that the diamond merchant's training in Hatton Garden had been so thorough.

To add to my cover story, I carried about £250 worth of uncut diamonds in a wash-leather bag. This particular cover also allowed me to carry large sums of money about, forbidden in those days to the normal person, as anyone caught carrying a lot of money was immediately suspected of being either a black marketeer or involved in subversive work.

Cantinier and I finally left from Tempsford airfield, late one night, in a shuddering, lumbering Hudson of the FFI—the Force Française de L'Intérieur. The aircraft and others were run by an organisation of the FFI known as SAP who were Service d'Atterrissages et Parachutages and were responsible for dropping their own agents and supplies to Free Frenchmen, operating as agents in France. We had a quiet, uneventful ride, the only hazard being the cold draughts which swept through the aircraft in flight. We landed safely in the Saône-et-Loire—even now I do not know where we were put down—and were immediately driven to a farmhouse, where we stayed for a couple of days for talks with local Resistance leaders.

One thing that stands out in my mind of that stay was a prettv girl, one of the farmer's family, who in September 1943 was twenty years ahead of fashion, for she wore a mini skirt. Cantinier was in raptures every time she leaned over the well to haul up water and, I must admit, it was a pretty sight.

Cantinier, who was making his first trip to wartime France, nearly gave us both away in Annecy, the first lunchtime we were together. We had a very good meal at the Saulniers' hotel, a glass or two of wine with some of our contacts, and walked out into the street. Cantinier went first and when I came out a few seconds later, I found him standing in the gutter and shouting at the top of his voice: 'Taxi, Taxi.' I hastily shut him up—for there were no taxis in France at that stage of the war, and people were looking at us as though we were mad. We would have been in trouble if any French or German police agents had been at hand.

We started fourteen of the most exhausting days of my life. I had to try to cover a vast area of France—four Provinces—and attempt to assess the worth of the Resistance, to gauge the morale, and work out the needs of the districts. The local organisers had arranged a Cooks tour, planned almost to the minute, with cars picking me up at one place, and handing me on to another group. Selected camps were seen, men paraded, and hidden arms produced.

What saddened me most was the low morale of the men who had been hiding for months in the Maquis camps. They were depressed, lacked arms, food, and equipment. Warm clothing was at a premium. They were away from their wives and girl friends, and hunted by the Milice. I decided my main task was to try to bring some cheer to these patriots, to show them they were not forgotten, that Britain wanted their help, and to promise them aid. I saw camp after camp and always managed to praise the appearance and keenness of the men, even if in some instances they did not deserve much praise. But morale was the main thing. If the desire to fight was not there, then there would be no point in supplying them with weapons. I must have told a lot of lies to the groups, but one thing I told the truth about was their weapons. If they were not well looked after, well oiled, and ready for action, I blew like the wrath of God through the camp and everyone, from the leader to the newest recruit, was told just what I thought of his efficiency. During that fortnight I went to some extraordinary places and saw, for the first time, the area in which I would be operating. I travelled the Ain, the Savoie, the Haute-Savoie and the Isère. I had intended going into the Jura as well, but there was not enough time and I did not visit this area until after I began to run the groups later on. The Haute-Savoie and Savoie contain some of the most magnificent country in the world, with rolling meadows and rugged, jagged mountains, with peaks rising, like Mont Blanc, to more than 13,000 feet.

There are hidden lakes, pines, and hamlets, holding a few dozen people, and a few herds of alpine cattle. There are chamois, edelweiss and narcissi in the spring. The country is beautiful, but highly dangerous for guerrilla warfare.

In the mountains it was easy to hide a thousand men, but there were few escape routes. I saw camps on the top of wooded plateaus, hidden from the air, hidden from the ground. But there would be only two ways into the place, and they were death traps. There were, of course, no roads, only mountain tracks which had to be travelled on foot, and slowly, with care. For the mountains are precipitous and one slip means a fall of, perhaps, thousands of feet. I saw it would be impossible for a group, with both exits blocked by fighting troops, to have sufficient manœuvrability to fight their way out.

The Ain, on the other hand, was a very different matter. To the north, there is a great plateau of level ground, dotted with lakes and pools, ideal for parachute drops, or for Lysanders to operate. To the south, the country was rather like Sussex, rolling hills, valleys, plenty of woods and hiding-places, good roads. The Ain was real guerrilla country, I decided. It was there that I met Major Romans-Petit, a man who is now a legend in France for his activities in the Maquis. At that time he was about forty, of medium height, stocky, with a chin that jutted out, and a pronounced nose. His hair was slightly touched with grey, he looked you straight in the eyes, and possessed the sort of personal magnetism peculiar to natural leaders of men. He had fought in the First World War, when he won the Légion d'Honneur and was mentioned in dispatches. Between the wars, he organised publicity for various fashion houses in Paris, but he left the elegant salons, the comfortable life, and a high income, to join the Resistance after Pétain surrendered to the Germans. In December 1942, nine months before I met him, he formed the Maquis de l'Ain.

This was the man chosen by the French to form their part in the Anglo–French–American team to run that area of south-east France.

I had been told in London that I was to lead the organisation, but I gained the impression that it would be more politic, and would ease French pride, if I gave the impression that Romans was the leader.

As it turned out, we worked together very closely and our decisions were nearly always unanimous although, once or twice, I had to persuade him from a course he wanted to take. In other words, I led without appearing to lead.

He and I were very cautious at our first meeting, for we knew that we would be fighting together from that September of 1943 through to the end of the Battle of France, and one has to be very careful in assessing the man who will hold your life in his hands. I liked him immediately, so it was not necessary for me to pretend to, as Buckmaster had suggested might be diplomatic. He was to become my great friend, as Alex had before him.

I was first impressed with the security network he had drawn up in the area. For instance, on leaving the Haute-Savoie by road, we had to cross the River Rhône to enter the Ain by the solitary bridge at Seyssel, and on the outskirts of the town the car pulled off the road whilst the driver went to see the local veterinary surgeon. When he returned I asked him why we had to stop. 'Ah, the vet is one of us, and keeps a string of helpers who let him know what checks are on at the bridge. There are no special searches on today; just the routine checkpoint, which won't worry us.'

I used that vet, Dr Vuillard, many times in the months to come, and he never made a mistake on the state of alertness or on the type of search. I remember one early morning, just before curfew ended, calling at his home to ask if it was safe to go on. He warned me that there was a great scare on and that every car and person was being searched. I was in a hurry and had to get back to the Ain, so I elected to use the other method of crossing, by boat. Just at dawn, I climbed into the boat, some seventy-five yards from the bridge, in thick river-mist. I heard voices, muffled and distant, but felt very safe as I was rowed out on to the broad river. The mist suddenly lifted, however, to show both banks, the bridge, and guards pacing along it. Why didn't they spot us? Perhaps it was because alertness in a soldier disappears at first light and, anyway, it was a chilly morning, better suited to snuggling into a greatcoat than peering into the mist.

During that reconnaissance Cantinier was of great help as he knew many people in the Haute-Savoie and when cars were incapable of climbing the mountain tracks he was able to produce a farmer with a dog cart, or another with a pair of mules.

I met Jean Blanc, a famous Alpine guide, who took us high into the mountains to inspect one small camp. As most of our time was spent in the towns and villages in the plains, I was wearing my city suit and a smart pair of shoes, and so was not exactly dressed for mountain climbing. Blanc led us along several ledges, only inches wide, which overhung giddy drops to the valleys below. He walked along them as though they were pavements of Oxford Street, but I shuffled and sweated and prayed that my slick shoes would not slip on the ice and snow. Blanc was strong and fit and showed no tiredness, whilst I became faint and had giddy spells from the lack of oxygen.

At the end of the fortnight, Cantinier and I returned to the Saône-et-Loire, where another FFI Hudson waited to return us to London. We took off, and this time I was completely immune to the winds and the cold and the fear of night fighters as I was busily assessing the value of the trip and whether I could advise SOE to support this vast strategic area of south-east France. I thought of the tattered uniforms and not-so-well-looked-after weapons. Morale, to say the least, was low, but I believed that a few cargoes of new weapons, some boots, and one or two small successes in the field, would set the area afire. Before we landed, Cantinier nudged me out of my deep thought. 'What's wrong?' I asked.

'Nothing—you've hardly said a word all the trip. I wondered what you were thinking about.'

I grinned at him. 'Cantinier,' I said, 'It looks as though you and I are going back to France very soon. Who knows, you might be able to find the girl in the skirt again.'

'You mean it's on?'

'It must be. There are more than 1,000 men there. They want to fight for France. We can't let them rot.'

I went straight to Orchard Court and told Buckmaster that the French, given support, could be used to wreck communications, factories—and the Wehrmacht itself—if the operation was properly handled.

He listened as I detailed the men available in the various areas, the arms and supplies they would need, and the targets they could attack. He did not interrupt me and when I finished, he simply said: 'All right. It's on. Go out and get cracking. I'll fix a plane for you, Paul, Cantinier, and Elizabeth.' I was delighted, and when I told the other three they were as pleased as I was. They bubbled with enthusiasm and for an hour SOE headquarters seemed like the last day at school.

Forty-eight hours after arriving back from France we set off again in two Hudsons—the quickest ever turn-round, I believe, in the history of SOE. Again it was an untroubled night ride for me, and again we landed in a field somewhere in the Saône-et-Loire area, where a car was waiting. It was not, however, a pleasant journey for Elizabeth and Paul, for just as their aircraft was on its approach to land in the dark, one wing hit the belfry of a church. The aircraft lurched, but the pilot held it, landed safely, and took off, making England without any further trouble. Elizabeth and Paul were a little shaken, but recovered quickly. This time we were all taken to the village of Poncin in the Ain, where the Leopolds ran a small factory. The village, I saw when daylight came the next day, was typically French, with a small square on which stood the Mairie, about a dozen small shops, and a row of buvettes, or cafés. It was on the side of a hill, close by the River Ain, a peaceful, hard-working community of about 2,000.

Henri Leopold was a very valuable man. One of his contracts was to make the rubber stamps for the Postes et Télégraphes for the whole of France, and so we could rubber stamp any document or pass with a genuine mark. His stamps were used to help Romans, whose cover as an inspector of the PTT enabled him to travel without hindrance, run a car, and draw petrol. Leopold, his wife, and his daughters Janine and Danielle, were our close friends, and later Romans and I often used their home as a stop-over if we were in the area.

At the Leopolds, Romans told me a little more about his organisation in the Ain. It had started in a small village, perched up on a hill, called Montgriffon, where Romans arranged to hold a meeting of farmers in the area, together with the local Mayor, Marius Chavan, who was a determined man, violently opposed to the German occupation. At the meeting it was decided that the farmers would collect together all the young men destined for forced labour in Germany and harbour them on their farms. The farmers were enthusiastic. Like all farmers, they were highly independent and some of them, perhaps, took on the job not only for France but because they could break a law. They are that sort of people. Romans kept a list of all the men, and started to train them, a dozen at a time, in sabotage methods and use of weapons. They only had one gun, a sten, which was stripped down a hundred times a week until it wore out, and Romans had to make drawings to show the workings of the weapon. The hidden youngsters, of course, could draw no rations or clothing coupons, so they were soon very tattered and reliant on the farmers for food. Romans realised the dangers of this and organised two or three raids on the quartermaster's stores at the German head-quarters at Bourg, to snatch food and clothing for the founders of the Maquis d l'Ain.

When I arrived, the young men had been moved into camps, mostly of thirty to forty men, with one or two holding sixty men (the ideal number in my opinion, and later I tried to make certain that each camp held sixty). The camps were very rough, cold and draughty, with few amenities, and some were built by the men themselves, using felled trees, or wood taken from disused barns and farm buildings. Others lived in broken-down farm buildings. All the men were between the ages of eighteen to twenty-two, from which the forced labour gangs were recruited, and their false identity papers always gave their ages as either seventeen or over twenty-two, depending on the appearance of the boy. Only a handful had been given any military training; there was little or no discipline, and only the fear of being caught and shipped off to Germany kept them together at the beginning. But there were two things in their favour—they were young, they were fit. Any recruiting sergeant would have rubbed his hands with delight over the 1,000 men scattered throughout the Ain, and they were ideal material to mould into guerrilla fighters.

From this nucleus, and a smattering of older men, Romans and I built up a fighting force capable of beating the Germans, disrupting communications, sabotaging factories, and of ruling south-east France. Discipline, once arms, food, and clothing came in abundance, was as good as in any regular army unit. There were some chaps who went 'over the wall' to visit girl friends in the local villages, but they were quickly made to realise that they were risking the lives of their friends. Those who did not learn the lesson, or those who became 'bloody-minded', were sent to a special camp, not like an army glass-house, but a place where they were detained so they could not breach security. They were not given any corrective training, but simply kept 'inside'.

As the months went by, leaders were chosen from each camp and promoted officers. Some of the finest guerrilla leaders in the area were young boys, who were dedicated to fighting the Germans and held their troops in control by a mixture of fierceness tempered with gaiety. The groups were trained in the use of automatic weapons, sabotage, and guerrilla fighting. 'Mobility is your strength,' I told them, again and again and again. They were taught that their camps were not forts to be defended to the last man. If attacked, they slipped away into the forests and either fought a rearguard action or ran to a prearranged, new camp. My commander on the southern front of the Ain, Commandant Chabot, a former regular soldier in the French colonies, at first treated his command post like a fort, and once tried to swap static fire with the Germans when Romans and I were present. He changed his mind when a bullet went through one of his ears and—holding a handkerchief to the bloody ear—ordered his men to make a traditional rearguard fight, all to the merriment of Romans and myself, who laughed so much that we forgot the fighting for a minute or so. Chabot became one of the finest exponents of guerrilla tactics, after he learned the hard way. 'I decided it was wise to live to fight another day,' he said.

The security of the camps, of course, was of great importance. Everyone knew, Germans and French, that the Maquis were in camps in the hills and mountains, but they did not know the exact position of our fighters. For this reason, fires were forbidden in the camps if German troops, or GMR or Milice were in an area, which was upsetting as that meant no hot food or coffee. But it did mean safety. The huts were camouflaged against air reconnaissance, but more important was the system of guards who patrolled the camps to watch against surprise attacks. If troops or Milice were seen, the local commander of a camp would send a runner to the next camp, which might be fifteen or twenty miles away, to report the movement. A local commander would make the decision to fight or disappear, depending on the chances of beating the attacking force, or he could call on his neighbour for help to annihilate a German or French column. Each commander knew only the position of the next camp. That, again, was security.

The loyalty to the Resistance by the men of the Maquis is legendary, but I encountered one or two incidents of treachery.

The worst occurred when Romans and I set up our headquarters at Balvay in the northern area, commanded by Montreal, the Maquis leader in the north, a vigorous swashbuckling character. As usual we pitched tents for the handful of people with us, and it was then up to the local commandant to make certain the headquarters were free from attack. In this case a local camp had been used to obtain close guard—a sort of picket line—and other camps were alerted for a wide area around us to provide outposts. As soon as it became dark, one guard saw a series of small red flares shoot up from the trees near his position. He crept up to the woods and caught a youth of about nineteen and, in answer to shouts, some of the group came out of the trees and joined him. The Maquis were brutal and ruthless. They punched him until the youngster at last confessed. He was a Frenchman, but had joined the Waffen SS, the German organisation for young men, and agreed to spy for them. So he joined the Maquis group, was given the name Cobra—which gives one an idea of what his comrades thought of him as a person—and waited his opportunity—when he knew three of the main commanders were present—to give away our position, using flares provided by the Germans. He was brought before Montréal, while Romans and myself were present. He was in a very bad way—I had never seen a man's head so swollen before.

He told his story again, and then went on to denounce several leading members of the Maquis in the area, all of which was false. Montréal gave his decision: it was his man and his camp.

'Kill him,' he said simply.

The battered youth was tied, sitting down, to an ordinary kitchen chair, and his back turned to the firing squad, picked from his own camp. Traitors were always shot in the back. An order was given, a volley was fired and it was over. Brutal and savage perhaps, but this was a war fought in desolate and lonely forests and mountains where a man's existence depended on the trust and loyalty of his comrades.

At the time when I joined Romans in the Ain, he had been

facing difficulties with the dependants of the men hidden in the Maquis, for they had no money, or at any rate, very little, and some of their wives faced hardship. Many of them, of course, were looked after by other villagers, and some of the richer people in an area would help too. Now Romans had been in touch with the FFI in Lyons, but the leader was arrested and Romans failed to make further contact with them, either to get money for the dependants, or arms for his men. Later we fixed family allowances for the wives and mothers left behind at home, which was always paid by the FFI. Only on one occasion was I asked by Romans, and by Belleroche, of the FFI in Lyons, if I could help to provide money for relatives, as cash they expected from London had not arrived and it was near pay day. London trusted me to ask for what money I needed, so it was a simple matter to get Paul, my radio operator, to ask for several million francs. He received a reply saying that an aircraft would make a special flight to France to parachute drop just the one packet, holding the wad of money. But a day before the flight was due, Romans told me the FFI's money had arrived and that SOE's money would not be needed. It was, of course, a splendid example of the French desire to be independent of British help—except they forgot that the FFI money and SOE's came out of the same coffer.

The families of Resistance fighters suffered greatly at the hands of the German and French police, as they were repeatedly interrogated about the whereabouts of their men. All a young wife would say was: 'I do not know where he is. He left here three weeks ago and I haven't heard anything from him since.' In many cases this was true, as the men realised that to give their addresses away would be a breach of security. The Germans and the police, of course, would not always accept this answer, and there were many instances of violence and brutality against relatives. The Mayor of Montgriffon, Marius Chavan, had a son who disappeared into the Maquis and he was repeatedly questioned, and beaten up with rifle butts. But he refused to tell the

Germans where his son was, and when they used the same treatment on his daughter, she, too, remained silent.

A farmer was dragged into his kitchen, put on the kitchen table and beaten so hard that the table broke. He stayed silent. His daughter was dragged in by her hair, thrown over a wooden chair, and beaten on the bottom so hard that eight or nine months—months, mind you—later, she was still suffering from the beating.

At La Cluse, right in the middle of our Maquis area in the Ain, one gang of drunken German soldiers went into a house to try to find out about a man, and raped all three daughters of the family. A great many of these atrocities were committed against Jews, or farmers known to have helped Jews, and the necessity of questioning them over a missing son or brother was a good enough excuse for the thugs to beat and rape. I have always admired the steadfast way in which the families kept quiet, even under severe pain, and I cannot remember one instance of a dependant breaking and telling the Germans the site of a Maquis camp. They were all very brave.

But I knew little about the organisation of the Maquis and its problems, as Romans and I talked that first day in Poncin with the family Leopold. I felt 'out on a limb', for I did not know the Ain, the Savoie, the Haute-Savoie, the Jura or the Isère, apart from one pre-war ski-ing trip to Pontresina, and the rapid rush-round of the previous fortnight. I had no friends or contacts and, until I made my own, I would be completely reliant on Romans and his groups. I trusted Romans, of course, but I was not really happy until I had vetted people myself. My SOE training and insistence on caution always made me reluctant to accept other agents' appraisals.

After Romans and I had our talk, I decided that I should take Paul, my radio operator, and Elizabeth, my courier, into the Haute-Savoie and set them up at a farm where Paul would be well protected and Elizabeth at hand to bring any messages received from London back to me. We set out in a car provided by one of the local Resistance group to drive over the Rhône at

The Miguet family – Jean, Xavier's transport officer, on left

(left to right) Maxime (Le Grand Jules), Paul (radio operator) Romans, Chabot

A maquis group at Corlier in the Ain

Henri Leopold

Leopold house at Poncin where Xavier often sheltered from Germans

Mme Leopold

Janine, their daughter

Seyssel, where there was no checkpoint that day, and on to Annecy. It was a delightful ride in beautiful September weather, and I felt that operations in the Haute-Savoie would at least be blessed by a little beauty. We finally reached Annecy, after a drive of about 100 kilometres, and went to a restaurant run by Jean Saulnier, leader of the local Resistance, and a stalwart man in every way. Then we drove farther down the Lake of Annecy to the village of Albigny, where he owned a small café, which was run by his sister, Emma, and his sister-in-law. We were made welcome and shown the two rooms at the back of the café which were to become my headquarters for many operations in the future. There was one large, empty room at the back, which I used as a 'classroom' or briefing room, and a small bedroom which was reserved for the couriers. Upstairs there was a big bedroom which I used myself and sometimes shared with other leaders. Whenever I went into the Haute-Savoie from the Ain my first stop would always be at Emma's café, as it was used as a postbox by contacts and Paul. Opposite the café, which was about two hundred yards from the lake, lived old Grandmother Saulnier, who was half-blind, but a keen Resistance helper, and I knew I could always take shelter with her if it was necessary.

The next task was to get Paul into hiding and, through Jean Saulnier's contacts and with help from Cantinier, who knew the area and the people well, we found a farm for him to live in at the top of the lake, in a rather gloomy, wooded area. I heard he had settled in with the farmer quite happily—Paul was a very easy-going person, liked by everyone, and he played a great part in our successes over the months to come. He was always calm and cool although his job was highly dangerous. Every time he went on the air he knew that his transmissions were being picked up by German listening devices. Normally he would hide his radio set—which was the size of a large suitcase and very heavy—in an outhouse or some other cache, then take it to his room or a barn when he had to keep a transmission time scheduled by London before he left for France. 'Skeds', as they were called, might be set for once a day or three times a day, depending on how much traffic was about, but he would not transmit if he had nothing to pass on, to cut down the risk of detection. Two of his sets had been brought in by the Hudson and taken to Annecy by members of the Resistance, and they proved very reliable. They could either be run off the main electricity supply or, in open country, off batteries charged from a mobile plant.

A few weeks after Paul moved in I went up to visit him, to see that he was well looked after, and I found him uneasy about staying on the farm. I knew the sort of feeling; you cannot pinpoint reasons, but I knew that Paul had a highly developed 'pifomètre', or nose, for danger, so I moved him right away. We had a fine understanding and, in the future, if I got a message by courier from Paul saying that he wanted to move, I did not hesitate but got him out, and into another house or farm.

At the end of those first few days in the Haute-Savoie, I felt that the organisation was beginning to take shape and that, because I had my own radio operator and an 'open line' to London, I was far better off than I had been after weeks of work in the Angers area.

At last I was in business in a big way, though there was much to be done before I could start planning offensive operations against the enemy.

10

I set out to meet new contacts in the Haute-Savoie and the Ain, to form new groups of Maquis in the hills and mountains, and choose dropping zones for the dozens of stores missions I would need if my new army was to be properly equipped and armed. Important, too, was the training of couriers to establish a network of communications, linking my 'radio station' with myself.

In the Haute-Savoie I met Tom Morel, who led one group, and his faithful companion, known as Pierrot. Morel, who was to become second-in-command in the Haute-Savoie, and Pierrot were always reckless, and on one occasion decided to ram a car with two German officers in it. Pierrot killed his man, and then saw Morel fighting on the ground in the best cowboy and Indian style, with the other one. Pierrot took out his revolver, leaned on the bonnet of the car, waited until the German's head was clear of his friend, and shot him. Morel was very angry: 'You might have shot *me*, you damned fool,' he shouted.

They were to lead the glory fight at the Glières later on in a mad, heroic stand against German infantry and crack paratroopers. Their group was well hidden and organised, and all they needed was arms and a target. I went with Jean Saulnier from Annecy to other small groups, and set up extra Maquis, scattered in the mountains and hills of the area. I did not tell anyone, even Romans, of the existence of these groups, because I felt that if we were overwhelmed in the Ain, I should have another organisation to fall back on—and the fewer people who knew of their existence the better for security.

Henri Leopold in Poncin, if Saulnier did not drive me, also

ferried me around the area on many trips at the beginning of my time in the Ain and Haute-Savoie.

I had one small adventure during my first weeks in the Haute-Savoie, which could well have led to my capture. A journalist in the Resistance gave me a lift in his small car from Annecy to Ain. As we drove through the village of Frangy, a little boy ran out of a house straight into the car, which was travelling at about 30–40 m.p.h. We hit him with the left wing of the vehicle and the little car shuddered with the impact. But we dared not stop because of all the formalities we faced. Farther down the road, gendarmes stopped us and asked if we had just driven through Frangy, as they had received news of an accident there.

'We have details of the car,' one man said, as two others walked slowly round the vehicle looking at its colours and inspecting the wings for dents or blood. The three of them had a small conference and the senior one told us: 'It wasn't you, the colour of the car is not right. *Au revoir*,' and he waved us off.

I was thankful to be moving again, but I decided that it would be unwise to stay with my friend, so when we reached the fields below Chaumonte, I left him and climbed up to see Jean Blanc, the Alpine guide, who helped me to get back to the Ain.

The journalist agreed to cover for me, if he was stopped again, by saying that I was a hitch-hiker he had picked up at a hotel in Annecy. But he heard nothing more, except that the small boy had only been slightly hurt. He also arranged for compensation to be sent secretly to the boy's parents.

I always enjoyed being driven through the Haute-Savoie because of the beauty of the area, and in particular I liked it when Romans drove me in a little Simca he used as a 'PTT inspector'. He and I would sing arias from all the operas we had ever heard, but we both noticed that we always stopped singing just before we reached a checkpoint.

I found several places for stores operation drops and had Paul radio back to London their positions for the RAF's approval and selection. All this reconnaissance took time, and I could not devote myself purely to the Haute-Savoie. The Ain needed me as well, and I was constantly travelling by road from one Department to the other, going through the normal checkpoints in my neat, grey suit—as became a traveller in diamonds for one of the best firms in France—and tucking my trousers into my socks to protect the turn-ups when we went into the rugged, muddy country areas which hid the *maquisards*. I worked closely with Romans in the Ain, and he and I chose various dropping zones, one of the best being at Izernore, where later we staged daylight drops, from dozens of aircraft at a time, and Dakota landings.

Couriers, too, were chosen. Some youngsters had been used in the past in the Ain, but I felt this was dangerous as they were always likely to be stopped by Germans in case they were avoiding service in the forced-labour battalions. Girls were better; they could mingle anywhere, and it is wonderful what a flashing eye or a cheeky smile can do to evade a search or a dangerous moment. Apart from Elizabeth, the most famous female courier was Michette, Cantinier's cousin. She was a strong, fine girl, an expert skier and horsewoman, who had lived in the area all her life and had many contacts in both the Haute-Savoie and Ain. I impressed on her and the other couriers that they must always have a reason for making a journey. With Michette it was easy; all she had to say was that she was going, for instance, to Nantua to see a cousin or a friend and that was that. The messages these girls carried, some in code, some in plain language, would have sent them to a firing squad if they were discovered, but not one of them was to lose her life. The messages were written either by myself, Romans, or Paul, usually on half a page of ruled paper from a school exercise book, and the girls hid them in various places. A few hiding-places I suggested were, under the soles of stockings, in a powder compact or, if the girl had long hair, in her hair. Some chose their own hiding-places, and I did not inquire too deeply into them. Of course, none of them were secure from a proper search, but their hideaways were good enough to escape the perfunctory examination of a handbag or bicycle carrier.

There were two or three occasions when couriers had to eat their messages, and Michette was one of those involved. She was returning by bicycle from the Haute-Savoie to the Ain when she came across a line of traffic and saw that everyone was being questioned and some were being sent to a near-by building to be searched. She kept her head and resisted the temptation to turn round and pedal away, as that would have drawn attention to herself. When her turn came she presented her papers. They were examined and found to be in order but, despite this, she was sent to a room in the building for a search. She sat in this room with two or three other people and decided that the only thing to do was to eat her message. Now this sounds very easy, but she had to smuggle the message out of its hiding-place, put it in her mouth, and chew away at it without letting anyone know that she was chewing paper. Having started to chew, she found that paper is not a very easy thing to eat, and it seemed a very long time before she managed to shred it with her teeth and swallow it. All the time she was chewing she was fearful that the door would open and a German would order her in for searching. When she told the story later she was laughing, happy that she had cheated the Germans, but she stopped laughing when I told her that she would have to go back and ask for the message again. She went, nevertheless, still game, still brave.

Another girl, Jane, was a courier in Oyonnax for a Maquis group of Communists under the command of my commandant of the northern sector of the Ain, Montréal. On one occasion thousands of German troops were brought into Oyonnax, and orders went out that no one must leave the town. But Jane got out and later told me that it was 'easy', as she knew the town better than 'any thousand Germans put together'. She always carried the traditional metal milk-can with her when she went on a journey, and concealed her message underneath the milk. Consequently, she always had an excuse for wandering into the town from the mountains, saying that she had been to fetch some milk. She was never caught, although several times she was severely questioned.

Elizabeth, my own courier, rarely carried written messages. She had a very good memory and was able to recite a message verbatim, which saved her a lot of trouble during the searches she went through. I was very fond of Elizabeth, for she seemed so English and appeared my only link with home at that time.

Before I met Romans, he had appointed Montréal and Chabot to take charge of the northern and southern sectors of the Ain, under his over-all command, as the area was far too large, and the groups too scattered, for it to be easily led by one man. These two kept control of the whole of the Ain, with permission to carry out small attacks without reference to either Romans or me, until 1944, when we decided to set up a western sector. This was necessary, as the number of groups had increased and there was more fighting. The sector was put under the command of Captain Ravignan, a man in his early forties who had been a soldier, but was a school-teacher when war started. He had few groups to control, but he did a valuable job. His command was small, as the Armée Secrète was strong in the towns of the western part of the Ain, in places such as Bourg. Romans and I came to trust completely these AS groups, as they were always willing to help us if we called on them, and when the Germans started to pull out in 1944 they fought some very bloody battles.

I let it appear that Romans was in charge and allowed him to choose the necessary leaders for the groups, although he would always ask my advice and we would discuss the capabilities of the prospective commanders between us. I did this to save any bitterness, for even though the Maquis were armed and trained, in many instances, by the British, there were many men who regarded the British as a bunch of traitors who had turned their back on France at Dunkirk. If Romans did the choosing it saved petty squabbles. I had a growing army, communications, couriers, and targets on which Romans and I decided the priority. The only things we lacked were arms, explosives, clothing, and ammunition. The time had come to ask SOE and the RAF to give us the weapons.

I sent a courier to Paul with a message asking for a series of drops to be carried out in the Ain, the first of which would be at Chougeat. Within a day or two I heard that SOE had authorised only a few of the drops I wanted. Someone in London was either bloody-minded, or the pressure on the RAF by other groups in France had caused a shortage of aircraft. Nevertheless, even a small number of drops would boost morale, for the news, despite the strict security, soon got round the groups. I supervised the first drop, and many others afterwards, until some of the Maquis leaders like Chabot, Montréal, and Verduras had been trained sufficiently well to handle the flare-paths and signalling arrangements. As usual the RAF was on time at Chougeat, and dropped their stores within the small target area.

I greatly admired the RAF; they always turned up when they said they would, and flew through dreadful conditions of weather and enemy defences to bring us our necessities. I learned later that the RAF became quite attached to us as well. If they heard they would have to fly in bad weather the crews would groan until they heard the drop was for 'Marksman', the code name that had been given my organisation. I contacted the aircraft on the 'S-phone', the radio telephone set, and heard them well, but they could not hear me, and although I heard and saw the aircraft circling for some time, they eventually flew home with their load intact. That one lost us our 100 per cent record.

Although I was dissatisfied with the numbers of drops made, the Maquis were delighted at receiving arms, and I found heated arguments going on in the groups as *maquisards* squabbled over the worth of the French FM and its equivalent, the bren-gun—both accurate automatic weapons with a high rate of fire. The time between drops was not wasted, as I was able to train the leaders to handle a stores operation and give lessons on the use of explosives for sabotage. We also formed a cadet group, where outstanding members of the Maquis could be trained as officers. Many of the recruits, of course, had never fired a gun, so they had to be taught to shoot and to care for their new weapons, Shooting ranges were set up and it was nothing rare to hear the distant stutter of an automatic weapon coming from the mountains towards the end of 1943. If I was a German I should have felt uneasy.

It sounds a very happy picture—arms being dropped, the radio chattering away, girl couriers dashing around on bicycles, men practising their shooting in the autumn sunshine, and even an odd party or two to celebrate a birthday or a saint's day in one of the Maquis camps. But the enemy was never far away, and there were sporadic attacks on Maquis camps from the time of my second arrival in France.

We had three main enemies. The German troops, of course, were the most feared, for at that time south-east France was not garrisoned by second line troops, but crack units, armoured divisions, and the like, all being held in reserve by von Rundstedt and Rommel to defend whatever part of France the Allies might choose to hit in the spring. Invasion, that autumn of 1943, was very much in the air, and both Germans and French realised that it must come within a few months. So we knew that we faced trained men, led by efficient officers, and that their attacks would be pushed home.

Our second enemy was the GMR, Groupes Mobiles de Réserve, a new Vichy organisation, hostile towards the Maquis, which was well-armed with light weapons, but whose men, in the main, had insufficient training as soldiers and too little heart to fight fiercely—although this depended on the officers in charge. Romans struck up a very good relationship with Commandant Vallin of the GMR at Nantua, who, in many instances, would contact us and say that he was going to attack a particular camp say, next Tuesday. 'We'll fire a few shots before we get too close, so please pull out,' he would say. He also promised not to burn down camps, and kept to his promise, but the *maquisards* were often furious, on their return from one of these dummy attacks, to find that all their pin-up pictures had been torn down and replaced by Vichy propaganda material. Vallin always put in a report to his seniors which seemed to satisfy them, but not all the GMR were like that, and there were some fierce fights with them over the months. Sometimes they were badly hit by the Maquis, and I remember receiving the report of a group who slaughtered dozens of GMR attacking a camp in the Ain. In their black uniforms, the GMR got out of coaches a few hundred yards away from the camp and made their approach on foot. They were badly led, bunched at the wrong times, and when the Maquis opened fire they fled, screaming with terror, climbed back into their coaches, and shouted for the drivers to take them away. All this time they were subjected to a steady and disciplined fire with automatic weapons until, finally, the Maquis commander ordered a cease-fire. The bloodied column went on their way, leaving many dead behind, and when I asked the commander, Lieutenant Roland, why he had called a halt to the massacre, he said, quietly.

'I have no heart to kill Frenchmen.'

The third enemy was the Milice, who delighted in snap checks and catching *maquisards*, couriers, or agents. They had as little mercy as the Gestapo, and the Maquis were happy to kill them whenever possible. The Milice did not mount frontal attacks on camps as the Germans and GMR did, but they were just as dangerous.

The first attack I faced was after I had been in France for a few weeks. Romans and I went with a handful of men to a village called Brénod, in the Ain, to set up a local headquarters where we could meet leaders, discuss future tactics, and receive messages from Paul or the local commanders. We were directed by the local group to a derelict farmhouse, which had a lean-to barn against it, a few miles from the village. There we made ourselves as comfortable as possible, making beds out of pine branches, and living on food and wine brought to us by the local Maquis. It was a pleasing situation, still autumn, still quite warm, and the farmhouse was perched nearly at the top of a hill, looking towards a pine wood, to the left down the hill, across open grassland and a small track with more trees in the background. It was secluded and easy to guard because of the open country in front of us.

Our first warning of danger came from one of the twenty men we had with us, acting as a lookout a short distance from the farm. He came running up the hill, crying: 'The GMR, the GMR.' When he could speak without gasping for breath, he told us that he had seen about 200–300 of the black-uniformed men getting out of coaches a mile or so away from us, the farthest they could go by bus up the track, which led from the main road.

Romans and I ordered the men to get out of the farmhouse and spread out, using what little cover there was for protection. I ran up the hill a few yards and snuggled into the grass, holding the sten-gun that had been handed me. Romans ran across the hill and got down about 100 yards away from me. As soon as we settled in, the GMR, advancing in a bunched group, opened fire then spread out in a long line across our front. We fired a few bursts at them, mainly to make them keep their heads down and to let them know that they had a fight on their hands, and, after two or three minutes, their officer-in-command knelt and shouted: 'I don't want bloodshed. Come out and we'll treat you as prisoners. Give yourselves up.' It would have been an easy matter to have shot him, but it was best to hear what he had to say in case he was 'good' GMR. There was no question of us giving ourselves up and, anyway, it was unwise to surrender as the chances were that the Maquis would be shot down. So we heard him out, then one of the men fired a burst over his head and he scrambled into cover. The fight started again, but it was a very inconclusive business. The GMRs had no heart for it and their attack lacked fury. Even their aim was wild, and during the hour they shot at us not one of us was hit. We managed to advance a little, and I believe we hit several of them. Eventually they backed away, scurried out of range, got back into their buses, and went off home.

We came out of hiding and went back to the farmhouse to collect our belongings and move off, in case the GMR or the Germans returned. As we walked through the woods, I realised that this was the first time I had been under fire, and I was surprised that my fear had not been greater. I was frightened when I saw the men, fifteen times our own strength, stretched out and firing at us, but the fear was more of the overwhelming strength of the unit than of the bullets. Mind you, I was not too keen on the bullets either—any man who says he does not mind being shot at is a bloody liar. My one real anxiety as we fought was how our men, many of them only boys, would behave when they had to carry out a rearguard action. Romans I had confidence in, and one or two others in the group, older men, would have been able to fight properly. But the rest were untested, and the soldier in me prayed that my lack of confidence would be misplaced. Fortunately I did not have to find out then, and I never again fought with this particular group.

By early November we had received more supplies, plastic explosives, weapons, and clothing, and I decided to harass the Germans. Both Romans and I had worked very hard, travelling like gipsies from one camp to another in the Ain, and I also went to the Haute-Savoie, showing the leaders how to use plastic explosives. I gave orders that 'targets of opportunity' should be blown, but only those that were undefended, as I did not want my untrained Maquis to become involved in stand-up fights over bridges, viaducts, and so on, at that time. This meant, in effect, that railway lines were the only easy targets to hit. Although the lines were patrolled during the night by groups of Germans, this was only near major junctions like Ambérieu in the Ain. On the more distant sections, it was rare to meet a patrol. So the bangs began all over the Ain and in the Haute-Savoie. Some were planned to derail particular trains known to pass at set times, others simply to blow the lines and so hold up rail communications. The best method was to place two charges, about eighteen inches apart, on one line. When the charges went off, they severed the steel and an 18-in. long piece of metal was chopped out of the line. If there was an up and down line, then the other line would be cut in a similar way about 200–300 yards away, thus preventing one exploding charge displacing the other.

London had impressed on Paul and myself that we must not take part in sabotage activities. 'Leave that to the troops, you are too valuable to risk over a piece of damned railway track', and that order was a sore point with the pair of us. On two or three occasions I am afraid I conveniently forgot these instructions and went off on sabotage trips. To ease my conscience, I told myself that I must keep my hand in, and that the Maquis would have more faith in me if they knew that I stuck my neck out a few times rather than staying in the safety of headquarters. The first one was really very easy. I was with one group near Neyrolles in the Ain, when someone suggested we blew a railway line. I agreed, and about a dozen of us moved off in the dark towards a railway cutting on the line that linked Nantua with Bellegarde.

I prepared two charges before we moved off, taping primers to the plastic sticks and putting them in my trouser pockets to keep them malleable, as I had been taught. I put the fulminate of mercury detonators in my beret, just in case I tripped and fell. When we reached the line, which had an up and a down track, we posted guards each side of the firing point and the others took up positions at the top of the cutting. It did not take me long to place the charges, squeezing them into the 'T' of the rails, push in the detonators, and move off. Twenty minutes later there was a very satisfactory bang which put both lines out of action for many hours. These attacks, of which there were probably hundreds during my time in the Ain and Haute-Savoie, did a lot of good. They always boosted the morale, an important matter in the Maquis, and they infuriated the Germans. Better still, they held up important trains carrying troops or supplies. Later on I received orders to keep, say, the Culoz–Bellegarde line blown for a week, to delay reinforcements heading for the north and the invasion beaches. In the main, they were very simple raids to carry out, and I do not remember one occasion where a line-blowing expedition was surprised by a patrol and shot at.

In the northern sector, Capitaine Montréal drew up a plan to blow a train carrying people being deported into Germany. His idea was to place a charge on the line which would not explode until the tender was overhead. He pointed out that it was hard to shift a railway engine, easier to blast a tender. Seconds after the tender was derailed a tunnel, a short distance from the stationary train, would be blown up to prevent troops arriving by rail, and also to block the main line. It was hoped that the deportees, all French men and families, would escape while the guards on the train were engaged by a Maquis group. The charges were laid, the men briefed, but someone (not anti-Resistance) heard of the plan and pleaded with Montréal not to blow up the train. 'The deportees will be mown down by the Germans; they cannot jump out of the train, it's all locked,' he said. Reluctantly, Montréal agreed to call the attack off and the charges were removed. As the weeks passed our sabotage of the railways increased, and later tunnels, turntables, workshops, depots, engine sheds, engines, signal boxes, and bridges were destroyed throughout the Ain.

On 9 November 1943 I told Romans I must take another journey into the Haute-Savoie as there was a particular job I had to arrange with Jean Saulnier at Annecy. Normally, he would have asked me about the job and tried to dissuade me from going. He felt that the Ain was the main area and that any time I spent away from it was wasted. This time he simply agreed, and I left. Late on the evening of 11 November, I discovered why Romans had raised no objections. He had carried out a mad, morale-boosting parade, with 200 *maquisards*, through one of the main towns of the Ain, laid wreaths at the cenotaph, made a speech, and already—only hours after the parade—the world was exclaiming over the heroic Maquis.

I learned the details. Romans had been perturbed by the German and Vichy propaganda, which denounced the Maquis and its leaders as terrorists, thieves, and rapists. France knew of the Maquis, but only by repute, and those Frenchmen who saw any of them in the early months had only seen poorly dressed young men, unshaven, haggard, vagabonds in appearance. Romans decided to put on a show to let France and the world know what the Maquis were really like. Unknown to me, he put out a rumour that the Maquis would parade on 11 November at Nantua, some fifteen kilometres from Oyonnax, a rumour sufficiently strong for the police and GMR to bring reinforcements into Nantua to deal with the Maquis when they arrived. But this was a smokescreen, and early on the morning of 11 November several groups of Maquis moved into Oyonnax. They moved quickly into the telegraph office, the police station, the two barracks holding the gendarmerie, and the town hall. The surprise was complete; no shots were fired and the town was in Romans' hands. He was helped by the commissioner of police, a member of the Resistance, who assisted the leader of the assault troops, Lieutenant Brun, to calm the police and persuade them not to fight. Romans then led his proud *maquisards* through the town. They marched in step, dressed in new clothes he had stolen in a raid on a Pétain youth organisation, freshly shaven, and with their new rifles, sten, and bren-guns glinting coldly in the November chill.

Romans wore the full uniform of a captain in the French Air Force, a commission he held at the outbreak of war, with polished boots, creased trousers, and spotless white gloves. With him was Belleroche, the FFI leader from Lyons, in full uniform, and three other members of the FFI, also in uniform. They were preceded by a standard bearer, carrying the tricolour, and a band of bugles and drums. Oyonnax went mad. Men and women wept as the well-disciplined men marched through the town centre. The *maquisards* were kissed and hugged; cigarettes, sweets and money were pressed into their hands; the crowds cheered and cried and waved. The parade halted in front of the cenotaph, where Romans took a wreath and laid it at the foot of the monument commemorating the dead of the 1914–18 war. It bore an inscription: 'From the Victors of tomorrow to those of 1914–18.' There were more tears, then the procession moved into each parish in a town of 14,000 people, and laid a wreath at each church before marching back to the town centre. There Romans told the crowd that these men, his *maquisards*, were no terrorists or thieves, but the men who would set France free. 'Look well, for you see in them the hope for tomorrow,' he told them.

He gave a few orders, the Maquis formed up again into military formations, and left the town. Lieutenant Brun, operating under Commandant Montréal, waited for them to disappear once again into the forests before calling off his groups and the men supplied by the Armée Secrète.

I returned to the Ain the following day, and Romans came up to me like a naughty schoolboy.

'*Vous avez entendu, Xavier?*' he asked quietly.

'Yes I have—and I'm bloody furious at your stupidity.'

I told him that there must have been collaborators and German plainclothes men in the crowd, and these people would now know the faces of the leaders of the Maquis in the Ain. In addition, the townspeople would be in danger, for the same spies would report the enthusiasm of townsfolk who gave money and cigarettes to the Maquis.

'You know as well as I do that security is all important in our task. Yet you chose to compromise every one of us by your recklessness. Why the hell didn't you ask me about this before you went ahead?'

Romans shrugged. I grinned. Even if he had talked with me and I had said a very firm '*no*'—as I would have done—he would still have gone ahead, and he knew that I knew this. It was his country, his France, and I had to accept it. As it happened, there were no obvious reprisals on the townspeople, but there was an enormous wave of excitement throughout the world when the news broke. Newspapers in Britain, America, and neutral countries all carried stories of the brave parade at Oyonnax. The spirit of France still lived, they said. It surely did.

I must write here of Lieutenant Brun—Bourret was his real name—the man who was in charge of the Maquis groups who protected Romans at Oyonnax and who took control of the telephone exchange and post office. He must be remembered, for his life was so typical of the gay, fighting Frenchman of the time, and the manner of his death such that will always make the people of the Ain hate and mistrust the Germans.

He was a bubbling, lively character, who gave up his business and left his wife and two young children behind so that he could fight for France. I met this small, dark man—then aged thirty—at the Camp de Granges in the Ain, in October, just before the Oyonnax parade. He had with him Polo—his real name was Sixdenier—a nineteen-year-old, big in frame with a low-pitched, but telling voice. These two were inseparable.

Their camp had been built on the side of a cliff which was covered by scrub. They and their *maquisards* somehow had managed to climb the cliff with enough materials to build a *barraquement* and why none of them ever fell off the narrow ledges when they were loaded, I never could understand. When I saw their camp for the first time they had, fortunately, transformed their mountain-goat path by building a flight of well concealed steps. There were 213 of them—I counted.

After the parade at Oyonnax I had a mild adventure with Brun and Polo when we got into a car full of sten-guns which we were taking from the Ain into the Haute-Savoie. We were all fully armed, but as it was so cold we wrapped ourselves and our arms under blankets.

We were checked through the bridge at Seyssel, as was normal, in a routine manner, went into Annecy, and had to return the next day with the car still filled with guns and grenades. We were stopped again on the bridge, our papers were examined very closely, and then the guards took me out of the car and insisted on cross-examining me. They asked me question after question, all based on my false papers, and the only one they nearly caught me on was 'what was your mother's maiden name?' I blessed my decision to run through my cover story at least once a week, and was able to remember the correct name in time. At last the guards were satisfied and they waved us on. Little did they know how near death they were, for Brun and Polo had both taken pins out of grenades ready to throw and had sten-guns cocked for firing to get me—and the arms—clear and back to the Ain.

A month before this, I had received a cable asking if I was willing to sabotage a major power station at Le Creusot, and Romans and I agreed we could do the job. But almost immediately we got another message from London saying that the attack was being made by the FFL. We agreed to give every help, and two of the three groups to be used in the attack were Maquis of the Ain. One was commanded by Brun and the other by La Brosse—a man who was to make his name later on. The other group was under a man named Mantin, who had over-all command of the attack.

Brun, accompanied, of course, by Polo and three other men—Dédé, Felix, and Lesombre—got into the power station, laid their charges, and escaped. They headed homeward by car, well content. But within a short time of the charges being placed, all had been discovered—one can only presume that there had been a traitor in the groups—and a general alert was put out by the Germans and special road blocks set up. Lieutenant Brun and his party ran into two of them but managed to talk themselves through, using their false papers. The group then lost their way and, suddenly coming over the top of a hill, ran into a third block. The first warning they had of this was headlights of several cars being switched on and illuminating them. They also saw, in the shadows, a group of German soldiers closing on them.

'When I stop the car,' Brun shouted to his friends, 'jump out and run like hell into the dark—it's our only chance.'

He stopped the car, but instead of making for the darkness, Brun ran towards the officer he saw in charge of the German group. This made the Germans switch all their attention to him and distracted them just enough to allow his friends to make a bolt for it without being shot down immediately. But the delay was only slight. The Germans opened fire. Brun was shot in the stomach, Felix and Polo were caught, but Dédé and Lesombre escaped. We never knew what happened to Felix and Polo, except that we heard two months later that they had been executed.

But we do know about Brun. He was tortured, slowly and systematically by the Germans, until he died. Then his naked body was flung on to the steps of the town hall at Le Creusot and the Germans ordered that no one must touch him or take him away for burial. The Germans said that he was a half-caste, because of his dark skin and sallow complexion, but we all knew that he had been the son of a Frenchman who had also died in the earlier war on the battlefield.

We found out from records after the war that neither he, Felix, nor the inseparable friend, Polo, gave anything away.

Romans and I were told of Brun's death and of the dumping of his body. We decided to go together to see his wife to break the news to her. We arrived to find that she had arranged a small Christmas party for her husband that night, as he had been given permission to visit her for the first time for weeks. I do not have to say any more.

Brun's death saddened us all. Death in battle was expected, but the method of his dying, like others to follow, will never be forgiven in the Ain.

At this time recruits were flooding into the Maquis, and I estimated that by mid-November we had close on 3,000 men hidden away in the Ain and Haute-Savoie. Nearly all of them were armed and had enough ammunition and clothing. Food was still something of a problem, but their main anxieties over the care of their families had been relieved by our system of dependants' allowances.

However there were two administrative problems that worried me as the numbers increased: medical treatment and transport. I had planned to blow up German food trains and to make large-scale raids on German army stores for food and clothing, but without a good distributive organisation this wasn't worth doing. It would be impossible to share hundreds of tons of food around the camps without lorries and vans.

Happily we picked on Jean Miguet to be our transport officer. He was a great driver and took me many hundreds of miles around the areas at high speed without causing me any anxiety. He was calm and slow of movement, good attributes in a man who had to plan the detailed movements of dozens of vans and lorries. In fact, in 1944 he had a transport section of more than 200 lorries and vans, for which he provided drivers and maintenance. And not once did he fail to produce the right number of vehicles to clear a wrecked food train or unload a laden Dakota of heavy equipment.

I always thought he was slow in reaction until one day when he was driving Romans, Montréal, and myself to Oyonnax. We had just left a Maquis camp and I was wearing my grey canadienne and rough clothes—not the sort of clothing one expects a diamond dealer to be dressed in—whilst the others looked just as tough. When we turned into the main road on the outskirts of the town, we saw, three hundred yards ahead (only a few seconds away at the speed we were travelling), a checkpoint manned by a handful of German soldiers carrying automatic weapons. Our guns were hidden under a blanket on the floor of the car, but the chances of shooting our way through seemed slim, as I knew that at this type of checkpoint the Germans always mounted at least two heavy machine-guns, hidden in a near-by building. They would open fire immediately if anyone tried to turn away from the check or fight it out. I heard Romans say quietly:

'*Merde.*' I looked at Jean Miguet, whose expression had not changed, and I thought all was lost. He had the look of a man who did not realise what was going on. But then the car lurched at high speed to the left and down a tiny lane, roughly surfaced, only fifty yards from the checkpoint. In my mind I apologised to Miguet. Using his knowledge of the area, he had worked out very quickly indeed how he was to avoid capture. He took us down to a farm where the car was hidden in case any German car decided to investigate our sudden change of direction, but nothing happened, and we were able to continue our journey a little later, using secondary roads.

This was the man we chose to run our transport which in early November consisted of only three or four camions, borrowed from local Resistance men when we needed to shift stores dropped by the RAF.

The medical problem was not so easy to solve. There were several dedicated doctors in both the Ain and Haute-Savoiè who would drop everything to go to the aid of a man in the Maquis. In particular there were Dr Rossand in Poncin, a friend of the Leopold family; Dr Touillon, a leading surgeon in charge of the hospital at Nantua; Dr Mercier, who was at the same hospital; his wife, who was a pharmacist; and Dr Le Tessier, who lived south of the Ambérieu–Bellegarde railway line, and treated me in the Maquis. These brave people, however, had their own jobs to do, and I decided that we must have our own doctor and our own hospital, for I visualised heavy casualties in the months to come, too heavy for a flying visit by one doctor to cope with. So I requested that a doctor be sent to join us, and waited a hell of a long time for London to react. It was not until July 1944 that a doctor was flown in to us, and until then we relied on our local doctors, who did a magnificent job. They were never short of drugs, for I radioed SOE to drop me whatever the surgeons needed, and we always had morphine, and later penicillin in large quantities, together with bandages, splints, and surgical instruments. The Maquis, in fact, were better off for drugs than the

German soldiers; but the Germans had their own doctors with them always, whilst we sometimes had to wait hours for a doctor to arrive.

Our first major chance to show London our full worth came in a message from SOE asking whether I was able to undertake the job of blowing up the main ball-bearing factory at Annecy, the largest of its kind in southern France.

I radioed back: 'Yes.'

I moved, therefore, out of the Ain and took up residence at Albigny, with Emma Saulnier, where I could be on the spot for planning and training of the operation. My first move was to talk with the local Resistance leaders in the hope of getting plans of the factory, so that we could work out the most damaging part to blow, and plot our way in and out the easiest way. I was lucky to be given a complete set of plans of the factory, which covered several acres of land on the south of Annecy, away from the lake, and near the railway station. Some of the experts in the factory would stop operating for some time, as the transformers were of a type difficult to obtain. This was a very important target, for the whole production was devoted to making ball-bearings for aircraft engines, and to destroy it would reduce the number of fighter aircraft that could be put in the air against our invading forces.

I took the plans back to Albigny and set them up in the large downstairs room of Emma Saulnier's café. I called together a small local group, and told them their target. We discussed the amount of plastic needed and decided that one large charge on each of the transformers would be sufficient. The raid was set for a Saturday night, 23 November 1943, when the factory would be deserted and the guards were most likely to be relaxed. Nothing ever happens on Saturday in the cold of an Annecy winter. The team of about twenty men were briefed, each one of them in Emma's café, on the charges, the way in, and the way out. Each charge, I said, would be given a twenty-minute delay by the usual time pencil. This would give the raiders time to get clear, but not enough time for searchers to find the explosives if the raid was detected. A man was detailed to each transformer, and the remainder ordered to fight off any opposition.

The raid was made easier because we found some sympathetic guards at the factory who obligingly looked the other way as our saboteurs went in. I waited nervously at Albigny until I heard repeated bangs boom across the lake. Then the report came in: 'Everything OK.' So I slept easily.

The next morning the telephone rang and Jean Saulnier asked me, guardedly, whether I would like to come and have lunch with him at his restaurant in Annecy. 'The restaurant is shut on Sunday, so you'll have to put up with a family lunch,' he told me. I hesitated. I was not very fond of going to his house, as the restaurant and bar were always filled with Resistance men who had no idea of security, and openly chatted about explosives, arms drops, and the like. But as it was Sunday I decided to go. I cycled down later in the morning and knocked on the side door of the shuttered house. It was opened by Jean, who was beaming all over his face as he ushered me into the main room in the house, with its bar and restaurant. He took me by the arm and led me towards his private dining-room saying: 'Come along in here, it's quieter.' I went in—and found every member of the sabotage team, standing with glasses in their hands and grinning like naughty monkeys.

I raved at them, said that they were a bunch of bloody idiots, and told Saulnier that by asking the gang there he may have compromised the whole operation and myself as well. Their faces fell, and the whole team seemed ready to burst into tears. I turned to Saulnier again and asked him: 'Where's my champagne—I want to toast a victory.' I just had to accept a *fait accompli*, and at least I knew they would never be so stupid again. So we had a party, and while we drank, Pan Pan, one of the team, took me aside. He did not look very happy, so I asked him what was wrong. 'I am afraid I failed to set off my charge. I forgot how to operate the time-pencil, I banged it, shook it, but in the end I had to pull out without setting it off. I know that one transformer was not wrecked.'

'You are a clot, Pan Pan. You know it's the easiest thing in the world to do—all you do is squeeze the end,' I told him.

'Ah, I remember now,' he said. He had been to my classes, but I suppose that under the pressure of the raid he muddled it.

'Forget it,' I told him. 'You and the rest have done a very good job, and the plant can't operate on one transformer.'

Pan Pan was silent for a moment or two, then he put his glass down, pulled himself up, and said. 'Xavier, I'm going to do it now.'

I told him this was absolute nonsense and brought Saulnier over and asked him to stop Pan Pan's madness—they were old friends. But Pan Pan would not listen. 'No, I failed. I shall now complete my job.' He left the restaurant, got on his bicycle, and made for the ball-bearing plant, about ten minutes ride away. We reckoned we would hear a bang in about forty minutes if he managed to get away with it, and if he was not back within an hour then he would have been caught. It was a very subdued party who sweated through the forty minutes. Then the windows shook, and ten minutes later a jubilant Pan Pan came in, grinning, and told me: 'I did it. It is no longer a failure. More champagne, Jean.' He then told us his story.

'You know my cover is that I'm an inspector of police. So I drove up to the guards, showed my identity card, and said that I wanted to see what had happened. "No," they said, "the Gestapo has telephoned from Lyons saying that they are sending investigators and that no one is to go near the wreck until they get here."

'But I persuaded them that I had to make certain things were safe, and walked through the guards into the transformer section of the factory. I took a time-pencil out, squeezed it when no one was watching and stuck it into my charge which was still, very conveniently, lying where I placed it the night before. I walked up to the guards and told them there was nothing I could do. They saluted me and I got on my bicycle and came away.'

It was a complete success. The factory was out of action for ten weeks and after that was only able to operate at ten per cent capacity. One interesting point here about the replacement of transformers, which just shows the stupidity of war. The only transformers that the Germans could find to replace those we had blown were in Switzerland, and an order for them was duly placed. When they arrived in Annecy, I got word to say they were being fitted and an astonished Frenchman said: 'Xavier, do you know that the damned things were made in America?'

Throughout late November and December the number of sabotage raids on the railways increased, and hardly a week passed without some section of the lines in the Ain being cut. I also ordered, as the men became more proficient, that attempts should be made to derail trains. This went very smoothly, and the Germans were eventually forced to use a pilot engine, heavily armoured and equipped with a device to strip charges from the rails, before any scheduled train passed over the main lines. Just to make life a little more difficult, we would wreck the pilots too. It caused more delay, and strained the rail recovery services to the full. You cannot pick up a 50-ton railway engine without special lifting equipment, which has to be transported to the wrecked engine.

My second escapade in rail sabotage took place when we decided to blow a food train scheduled to run from Ambérieu to Bellegarde. This was an ambitious project as more than 100 men were needed for the operation, some to unload the train after it was wrecked, some to fight the guards, and some to transport the merchandise from the scene, using Lieutenant Miguet's distribution service.

I led the group down to the rails late at night. It was cold, and although the snows had not yet reached this lower part of the Ain there was a sparkle of ice on the rails and the grass crackled as we walked through it. My task, as before, was to place the charges, and I set one which was timed to go off underneath the tender of the train. While I worked, some of the Maquis took up positions to deal with the German guards, and mingled with a section of the Armée Secrète who had been recruited—very willingly—to help with the attack and unloading.

I lay in the grass, fifty yards back from the railway track, after fixing my charges, and waited, sten-gun in hand, with the rest of the men. There was absolute silence—a tribute to the discipline of these partly-trained young men—and then I heard the distant hoot of a train. The earth beneath me started to tremble—the old story of the Red Indian putting his ear to the ground to detect the US cavalry was true after all—and then came the chuffing of the engine of a heavily-laden goods train. It rattled nearer and nearer; I saw the glow from the firebox of the engine, spotted one of the drivers as it drew abreast of our position, and then—*bang*. I saw the tender lurch, twist, and the engine topple. The goods vans tried to climb each other's back: there were screams, and, above all, the noise of metal violently twisting and snapping. Then only the hiss of steam and the moans of men could be heard. We saw German soldiers clambering out of the rear of the train in the darkness, and we opened fire. Some of them, bravely but uselessly, took cover behind the broken vans and fired back. They lived only seconds longer as the Maquis and the Armée Secrète poured fire into them. Some soldiers ran, screaming, throwing their guns away, and we let them go. Within a couple of minutes the train was ours. Miguet brought his vans and lorries as close as he could to the line as the trucks were broken open, and patrols set off in both directions down the line to see our work was not interfered with. The men worked quickly, stacking flour and sugar, tins of meat, clothing, butter, and vegetables into the transport. I chuckled as I saw this vast amount of food being ripped from the train. The Germans would be very unhappy. My main purpose for taking part in the raid—apart from the hell of it—was to see how the Maquis handled the situation, and I was delighted to see the discipline they exercised;

the speed and efficiency with which they got rid of the goods. London was right, it was stupidity for me to risk death or capture unnecessarily, so that was the last time I went 'just for the hell of it'.

Romans, Chabot, and Montréal, the main commanders, and I, agreed that the time was ripe for German patrols to be ambushed, so orders went out to selected groups in the Ain for attacks to be made on German parties who ventured into Maquis country in search of camps. They were not to engage heavy concentrations, only groups of, say, platoon strength. Several groups of Germans were caught in this way in later months, and in each case there were no survivors. The objective was not just to kill Germans but to affect morale in the German forces. After a month of these attacks, they became very jumpy and we played on their nerves by spreading the word that there was an armed man behind every tree, waiting for the strolling soldier or small patrol to wander into the woods of the Ain. By the end of the year it was very rare for a German patrol to go into Maquis country; they kept to the roads where they thought it was safer. In fact, in 1944 the only time Germans went into the Maquis country was if they were in overwhelming strength of 700 men or more. So the ambushes had the desired result, and we knew that no small group of troops would ever surprise a Maquis camp again.

Our own morale was of great importance. Romans and I realised that hidden men, living in dreadful conditions, with little comfort, monotonous diet, and no relaxation, were likely to become discontented. So together we visited as many camps as possible, partly to brief commanders, partly to cheer the men up. It was virtually their only 'entertainment', for they were not allowed into the towns, they never saw a girl or went to a dance or a cinema. Apart from a game of cards or a sing-song, our visits became highlights. I had not realised how important they were until Christmas loomed, and Romans and I were inundated with requests and invitations to visit the dozens of camps in the Ain. Obviously, we could not go to all of them, but we did manage to go to four, in a rumbustious twenty-four hours which left me full of food, wine, and confusion. The French celebrate at midnight on Christmas Eve, so an hour or two before then Romans and I, with Miguet, our transport officer, and Montréal, the area commander, went up to the Grand Michel's camp outside Brénod. He had his headquarters in a dilapidated farmhouse, with a kitchen set up on what remained of the ground floor, and was living in the first floor, two rooms in the shape of an 'L'. There we found about sixty men talking and laughing by a long, deal table laden with cutlery, plates, and wine glasses. They provided benches for 'the officers' and there were seats of all kinds, boxes, tree stumps and the like, for the rest. The Maquis had decorated the room with pine and spruce, and over all was the rich smell of cooking, and the emotional, family Christmas feeling. I cannot remember the menu, but it was special, with splendid sauces, the finest wines, coffee, liqueurs, and cigars—all stolen from the Germans. We were all full, flushed, and happy at the end of the meal, when Romans burst into some very rude songs in which we all joined. Eventually I was asked to do my party piece, which was known the length of the Ain and the Haute-Savoie. 'It's a long way to Tipperary . . .' I sang it with great enthusiasm whenever I went to a camp on a social visit. I always had to sing 'Tipperary' and I was always given bacon and eggs to eat. No one believed that the English could survive without eating this dish at least twice a day.

We went to our beds of pine branches at about 3 a.m., filled with the pleasures of a damned good party. Not all the Maquis of course, were able to get sozzled. Grand Michel had his patrols out as well as his normal guards, just in case the Germans tried to sneak troops in.

On Christmas Day Romans and I went on a dazed visit to three more camps, and at each camp they waited dinner for us. We could not eat, but sat and drank with them as they enjoyed their Christmas fare. The last camp of the day, which we reached at about 4 p.m., was at Les Plans and was run by Lieutenant

Minet, and here we found two Italian soldiers who had deserted to join the Maquis. One, a captain, was an Italian ski champion, and before it got dark he gave us a demonstration of his skill on skis by slaloming his way down the mountain in deep snow. I envied him, for I loved ski-ing, but my wretched ankles were so weak that it was dangerous for me ever to put on skis. Once or twice I would have been saved a lot of worry if I had been able to get away from German attacks on skis rather than by wading waist deep in snow.

After Christmas I reported on our organisation to London and said I had about 3,500 men under arms—an increase of 2,500 in less than three months. I demanded more stores, more guns, explosives, drugs, and clothing. Strangely, I got approval for every operation I demanded and, though delighted, I could not understand why, for I had been trying for weeks to have the number of drops increased. Then I remembered the VIP captain who had passed through the Ain a little earlier. This man was on his way to Switzerland to carry out a mission there, and London warned me that he would be parachuted into our landing ground at Izernore, where there had been an airfield, and asked for arrangements to be made to get him into Switzerland. He arrived late at night by parachute, and landed on the field only a few feet from where I stood, revolver in hand. He had a gun in his hand, too, but we quickly exchanged passwords, and he was helped off with his parachute whilst his various small packages were picked up by the Maquis. A great groan went round the area later, I heard, for I had arranged for hundreds of men to protect the airfield that night, and several camps were specially brought in to provide defence in depth in case there was an attempt to hit the landing zone. All the men said was: '*Merde*, all this trouble for one British officer and a few packets. We thought de Gaulle was coming in.'

There hadn't been sufficient time to arrange for the captain to cross into Switzerland—normally done by arranging for one of the Swiss customs officers to look the other way as one of our contacts crawled under the wire—so Romans suggested that he might like to spend two days looking at some of the Maquis camps. The captain was delighted, so we gave him a guided tour. He was highly impressed at the discipline, training, and arming of the men, and asked me what else was needed. I told him that London was being bloody-minded about sending me extra weapons and clothing: either that, or there were not enough aircraft to go round. He told me he would contact London the instant he reached Geneva, and add his insistence to my request. Now I believe he kept his word.

11

Romans and I were in the Haute-Savoie in late January, at the end of another quick tour to visit various camps and to see how Cantinier was getting on in his area. As I was expecting more drops in the Ain, the result of my plea, and because Chabot had been left in control of the whole of the Ain in our absence, I decided that I must get back to the main centre of operations. I left by road with Jo, one of our girl couriers, to find that there was such a tight check on the bridge at Seyssel over the Rhône, that it would be stupid to risk a major interrogation. We went over by boat and our veterinary friend drove us on to within a few miles of Chabot's command post. Jo and I then walked through the deep snow until we found the headquarters, Chabot, Paul, and other Maquis group leaders. Chabot decided to shift camp a short time after we arrived, as he had been there a few days and it was unwise to stay in one place for too long. So we all trudged off through the snow towards Brénod, where we found yet another dilapidated farmhouse and outbuildings at Le Molard, about three to four miles to the south of the village.

We settled in and I had long talks with some of my friends and leaders. There was Maxime, the adjutant, who, with the Roche twins, coped with the vast amount of administration for the area, keeping pay-lists, dependants' lists, food requirements, and so on, as well as details about ammunition and availability of weapons.

There was also Tin-Tin, whose real name was Georges Perrin, our chief cook and a doughty fighter. He was one of the first three men to join when Romans started the Maquis de L'Ain at

Montgriffon, as the Germans wanted to deport him to a labour camp in Germany. He was middle-aged, always grumbling, but a fine friend. There was one incident that Tin-Tin was involved in which always brought a grin to any *maquisard* if it was mentioned. A little earlier in the campaign he had been cooking in the ground floor of a broken-down farm and was bent over a large iron cauldron, making soup, whilst the rest of the group were settling in above him on the first floor of the house. One youngster, known as Bidule, 'The menace', was playing around with his revolver when it went off. There was silence for a second, then a great roar of anger came down from below. The group rushed down and saw Tin-Tin, white with rage and waving his soup ladle at them. 'I'm shot, I'm shot,' he bellowed.

'Where? Where?' they asked. Tin-Tin turned round and jabbed his finger on his backside. 'In my arse, you bloody young fools,' he screamed. The group rocked with laughter as Tin-Tin raged at them. Tin-Tin's backside was part of the tradition of the Ain. He was killed in a major attack three weeks after I met him that day in Le Molard.

At first light next morning, Chabot and I were shaken awake by Mimile Carrier, son of the local baker at Brénod, and a well-known skier, who shouted. 'Get out of bed, you sluggards. Don't you know the Germans have arrived at Brénod. Get out, get out.'

Carrier, who later worked closely with Jean Miguet on the transport side of the Maquis, told me that they had marched in during the night and were preparing to move out into the Maquis when he left the village to give us warning. The first thing I did was to send a courier over to the Camp Michel, which was to our right a few miles away, to warn Michel that there were Germans about and to prepare for a fight. I sent a small patrol out to see if they could get any news, and they reported back that the Germans had left the village and were climbing up the hills in the deep snow, heading for Belleface on our left, and towards the Camp Michel, at Ferme Du Fort on the right. There

Colonel Romans

General Koenig decorates Verduras, a major Maquis leader

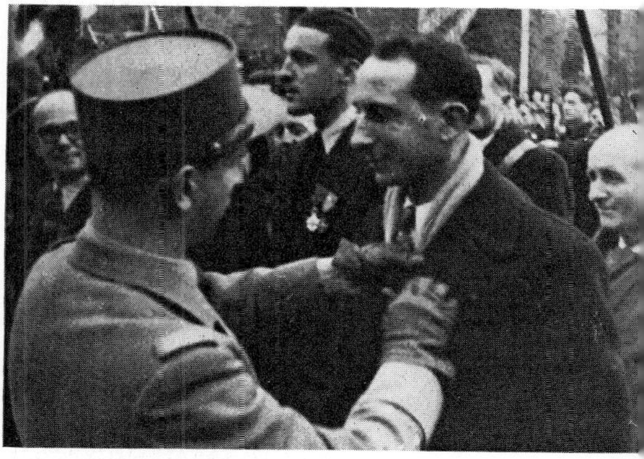

Above, Prosper and his wife, who lost an eye after a beating by the Milice

Right, Verduras in light-hearted mood

Crew of the first Dakota to land in occupied France. Xavier was flown in this aircraft to and from France

A parade of the Armée Secrète under Plutarque (front right)

was no point in our small group attacking the Germans, and I decided that the best thing for us to do was to sit tight and try to evade involvement if we could. If the Germans did stumble across our post, then we would clear out as quickly as possible. I was concerned, however, as the deep snow, which came up to our knees, was difficult to wade through and left perfect trails for the soldiers to follow.

After a while we heard heavy firing from our left and guessed that Michel had been attacked. A runner came through to confirm this, and he said that the Germans, having fought their way uphill for some three or four miles, were not now pressing hard, and Michel was quite able to hold them off for the time being.

Chabot, Maxime, and myself decided that we must make our own recce of the area, just in case the Germans were preparing an attack on the command post. We were sliding through the snow, gliding from tree to tree when we suddenly saw German troops not a hundred yards away from us. We froze as these men, in green field uniform and with arms at the ready, stumbled uphill on a course that was taking them away from us. They were close enough for us to hear their conversation and see their breath steaming in the cold January air.

We had to get away, as only one of us had a sten-gun and all I had was a revolver. So we fell back, quietly, and to our amazement we were not spotted. I was surprised to see that the Germans were in green; if they had worn the proper snow equipment of white smocks and trousers, as they did on the Russian front, we would have walked right into them.

We regained the command post and spent the rest of the day listening to the battle going on at Camp Michel, and receiving reports from that camp. We were not unduly worried at the noise of fighting, as this meant that the Germans had not pressed home their attack. If the firing became more distant, then we would know that Michel was being forced to retreat. One of the runners was Ludovic, one of Michel's officers, who dashed into the command post, grinning all over his face, and waving the epaulettes of a German major he had killed two or three hundred yards away from us. 'I have killed three of the Boche,' he explained, as he handed round the epaulettes for inspection, 'this one, and his driver and a soldier.' This was the first blood drawn in close fighting by the Michel group, and Ludovic was enormously proud to be the first man to kill a German officer.

As night came on the firing died away and we assumed that the Germans were retreating back to the village. Even skilled German officers disliked keeping their men, however numerous, in Maquis country at night. At 7 p.m. Paul told me he had just heard from London that my stores operation was on for that night and that arms would be dropped at the Verduras' camp, called Le Terment. This meant that I had to travel some ten to twelve miles, at least, to take charge of the drop, a damned hard walk in the deep snow at night. There was also the chance of running into German patrols, so I was pleased when Chabot suggested that I take as escort two of his men, one being Carrier, who could not return to Brénod as he would be unable to explain his absence during the day to the Germans, and the other Paulo, a relative of Jean Miguet. Carrier's bakery was burnt to the ground, and his wife as well as Mimile's wife and two children were literally thrown out into the snow when the Germans found Mimile was missing from home.

I did not like leaving the post, as I felt that attacks would be resumed in the morning, but I was the only person available to run the stores operation. We left at 7.30 p.m. to walk through the forests in the high hills, to Jean Monnier's farm at Aranc, which was about ten miles away. He was the only person in the area who knew where Verduras' camp was, and I cursed security on that trek, and wished that Verduras—an excellent commander who gained a fine fighting reputation in later months—had been a little more forthcoming in passing on his position. We reached Monnier's farm at about 10.30 p.m., to be greeted with hot soup and a glass of brandy to warm us.

'Jean, I have to get to Camp Verduras tonight and I want you to take me,' I told Monnier, after the three of us had rested for ten minutes.

'Of course, Xavier. I'll get ready now.'

But Jean's elderly mother, frightened no doubt by the heavy firing she had heard during the day and the news that the Germans were in the area, did not agree.

'No, Jean. You are not to go. You stay here. If this mad Englishman wants to go and risk his neck, that's his business. Let him go alone.'

Mother and son had a great set-to, and it seemed to me that Jean was about to submit to his mother's demands, so I intervened. I was a little harsh, I am afraid, but I told her: 'You call yourself a French patriot, and yet you won't let your son out of the house at night in çase he should face danger. What sort of a Frenchwoman are you?'

Jean's father came to our support and the old lady, told to stop grousing, subsided. At last we got on our way, and after another ninety minutes in the snow, we reached the camp to find that Verduras had heard the BBC message, and prepared bonfires on the field where the drop was to take place. Some of his group of sixty *maquisards* were at hand for the drop and, to be on the safe side, I took my torches with me, as I never trusted bonfires. They frequently refuse to light when you want them to. I took up position in the middle of the field at a quarter past midnight, snuggled down in a hollow to try to get out of the cold, and waited for the RAF. I was using two new pieces of equipment that night: S-phones, which enabled me to talk to the pilots of the aircraft direct, and a Eureka, a portable set which sent out a beacon on which the pilots could 'home' when they were within some ten miles of the field. At the end of an hour and a half a blizzard started, and the icy wind blew the snow into drifts. I was bitterly cold, despite my canadienne, and wished I had remembered to bring some brandy with me. But I hung on because I had enormous trust in the RAF boys, and sure enough, at about 2.15, I heard aircraft engines. I lit the bonfires, set up torches, and thought that the field looked like peacetime Piccadilly Circus. I spoke to the pilot of one of the three planes sent to carry out this big drop, and I could hear him calling me. Once I saw the shadow of a plane, low over the field, as the snow swirled thinly above me, and there was a light, flashing the correct signal. But he did not see my reply, nor spot the bonfires, and after a while the three flew off. I was bitterly disappointed, for the plane crews had made exhausting flights in dreadful conditions, and their navigation had been absolutely spot on. I waited another hour, just in case they returned, but nothing happened. So I went back to the camp with Verduras and Jean Monnier, had a good warm-up and a brandy, and then Jean and I walked the four miles back to his farm through the blizzard. I was very grateful to get to my bed that night.

I heard the next morning, by courier, that the Germans had launched a major push against the Maquis and that several camps were under attack. But Chabot, who got the message to me, said that the attacks were not being pushed home and that everything was under control, so I decided to remain with Jean Monnier at Aranc. I knew that the BBC would put out the same message in two or three days, and I hoped that I would have more success with the stores operation then. Staying there at the time were two ladies, who had come for a 'rest' in the farm and to sample the good food which was served even in wartime —for a price— at the small restaurant. We were joined, too, by Jean Chavan, son of the Mayor of Montgriffon, whose sister, Dedt, was engaged to Jean Monnier. The bad weather continued and for two or three days the farm and village was virtually snowbound, so I was able to have a rest.

The German attacks continued but they were still not being pushed home, although several hundred trained troops were being used. Having to fight uphill in deep snow, which reached a man's waist in many places, affected even the German soldiers' efficiency.

On my fourth morning at the farm I woke early, as usual, and looked out over the flat valley in which Aranc lies, across the open fields to the trees some 1,000 yards away. The snow had stopped and, as I admired the beauty of the view, I saw men moving out of the trees, dozens of them, walking slowly within five yards of each other and spread in a wide front, heading towards the village. I shook Monnier and Jean Chavan. 'Quickly, get dressed. The Germans are heading this way.' As they dressed, Madame Monnier, who was a patriot despite her concern for her son, hastily cut some bread and cheese for us, which I stuffed into my canadienne. Within five minutes of my seeing the soldiers, the three of us slipped out of the back door and started on our way—and I blessed my habit of waking early. Once clear of the protection of the tiny hamlet, we were in open ground and we broke into a weaving run, heading for the woods. We were spotted immediately, and the Germans opened fire. However we were at extreme range for light weapons, and reached the shelter of the trees without any of us being hit. We pressed uphill into the mountains, heading for Montgriffon and the ravines and caves in the area, where we knew we could hide out until the Germans had gone through. On the way we climbed up, out of the shelter of the trees, to the edge of a ravine, which was about 100 feet deep. As we reached it, we saw twenty to thirty German soldiers lining the opposite side directly across from us. We were only saved because they were all looking down when we burst into sight. We dropped, crawled back to the trees a few yards away, and hid until the group went away.

We reached the caves and grottos around Montgriffon before it got dark, had some of the bread and cheese and wine that Jean Monnier had brought, and then crept up towards Montgriffon to see if the Germans were in the town. They were, so we went back, found a cave known as the Bear's cave where the entrance was well protected by boxwood, and stayed there the night and until late the following afternoon.

We then visited a farm at near-by La Breuvière, owned by

Fernand l'Herbe—one of the local Resistance men—in an effort to find out more information about the Montgriffon area and the German attacks. Much later on we discovered that l'Herbe's son was a member of the SOL—Service Ordre Légionnaire—the Milice. The son, happily, was not about and, of course, Fernand did not talk of our visit. He, however, was as badly informed as we were.

Jean Chavan then decided that he would go into Montgriffon to try to find out what was going on and also to get some more food for us. He came back an hour later, with tears running down his face and sobbing like a small child. We comforted him as best we could, until he was able to talk. He said he saw no Germans in the village so he went to his home where he found his sister, Dedt, weeping and almost hysterical. He asked her where his father was and without speaking she pointed through the window. He ran out on to the small square and opposite the Mairie lay his father, dead, crumpled, his blood running down the cobbles. Jean went back to his sister and she told him, between sobs, what had happened. The Germans had come into the house and demanded to know where he, Jean, was hiding. They had asked this question off and on for nearly two years and, as usual, her sister and the Mayor both denied that they knew where he was. His sister was not beaten, although guns were pushed into her stomach. But when the Mayor refused to talk about his son, he was systematically beaten, as his daughter was held back. Angrily an officer shouted an order and his father, elderly, dazed, only semi-conscious from his beating, was pushed into the square. There he was shot down.

I kept Jean Chavan in the grotto for half an hour to give him time to get over his immediate grief, and then took him and Monnier into Montgriffon. I saw Jean's sister and comforted her as best I could. I told her what I believed—that sacrifices by people like her father were making certain that France would again be free. '*Mort pour la Patrie*,' I told her, 'is the finest epitaph any Frenchman can wish for.' I did my best. But daughters love their fathers, and my stumbling sympathy did not do much good.

I went round the village to try to find out what was happening from local Resistance people, and found that the southern Maquis area of the Ain was being put to the torch. As the Germans swept through the area there were stories of atrocities, burning villages, and fleeing Resistance men coming in every hour. All Monnier, Jean, and I could do was to take to the mountains and try to evade the Germans, who were darting from village to village, with no apparent system, flushing out Resistance men and shooting villagers when they felt like it.

So we were on the run. We headed for Nivollet, up in the mountains, and received further news there that the southern section of the Ain was still under attack. That night Monnier, Jean Chavan, and myself stayed in an empty barn with a handful of other Resistance people who, like ourselves, were on the run. The following day the three of us went into Corlier, and it was a most distressing sight. Most of the houses had been burnt down, some were still smouldering, and many of the villagers were numb with grief over the German atrocities. They had taken nine villagers, picked at random, and shot them down in the village street. If you go through the village today, there are plaques under the trees showing the names of the murdered hostages and the places where they fell. They had also taken two fifteen-year-old boys, friends since they were babies, and given them a stick each. The boys were ordered to beat each other, and, urged on by threats and the menace of submachine-guns stuck in their ribs, they did so. The weaker finally collapsed, knocked unconscious by his friend. A German then shot both of them—and all because Corlier had a reputation for producing Resistance fighters.

The two Jeans, myself, and some half-dozen other men on the run, grouped here and moved off into higher slopes to a little village called Saint Jérôme, which was quite close to Boyeux There we met Père Ravier, an elderly man who had a small mill called Le Mollard in the village, and he agreed to help by giving us shelter and food and promising me to get as much information as possible. Two days later I was told astonishing news which made me think London and SOE had gone stark, staring mad.

'Xavier,' said Père Ravier,' the RAF is dropping arms all over the Ain. Guns and ammunition and clothing is being dropped indiscriminately. It is stupidity. Most of it is being picked up by the Germans.'

I agreed with Ravier. Whoever thought that we needed this sort of support must be a typical Whitehall warrior with a cavalry mind, believing that guerrilla fighters stayed tight in their own little forts when under attack. I hoped Paul had got a message back to London, telling them what had happened, but it was not until later I found that Paul, too, had been on the run.

On the third day I was told that one of these indiscriminate drops had taken place the night before, a few miles from the mill, so I decided to see if we could beat the Germans to it and salvage some of the stores. As soon as it was dark, I set off with a guide to wade through the snow to the dropping zone—a zone, incidentally, that had been used for organized drops earlier. We scouted around, found some containers, and loaded ourselves with as many arms as we could manage for the trek back through drifts to the mill. I had a bren-gun over one shoulder, a ·303 rifle over the other, and five bandoliers of ammunition wrapped round my body. In that area the hills are very steep and each small farm, with its own small vineyard, cuts the hills into terraces, and small walls at the end of each terrace stop the good earth from eroding. But it was impossible to see these, as the snow had drifted around all the walls and on other parts of the hills. Which was why I stepped into a drift and—because of the weight of arms I was carrying—was thrown forward and cracked my shin against one of the damned walls. It did not hurt much at the time, partly because my legs were nearly frozen from constantly falling into drifts, and we finally reached the mill, quite exhausted. I lurked in the mill for two more days, sleeping on the one mattress with three or four other Resistance men, while others slept on the bare boards. On the third day my leg, which had been badly gashed in the fall, became infected, swollen, and began to hurt very much. I had little sleep because of it, so Père Ravier decided to move me to a small farm near his mill, run by an elderly farmer, Marius Genin, who liked his wine, and his sister-in-law, Ottulie Ladoucie. The leg got no better, despite being bathed often by the housekeeper, but I was cheered to hear that Chabot, our southern area commander, knew I was alive in Saint Jérôme and that someone was coming to see me. The man turned out to be Dr Le Tessier from Jujurieux, a very frightened man who risked his life walking five miles through burnt-down villages to find his way to me after a runner from Chabot asked him for help. I thought he was the more courageous for conquering his fear. He wasted little time with me, lanced my leg, shoved a bowl underneath it, and said: 'Let it bleed.' As he left, Chabot and others from his headquarters walked in the door and sat one on each side at the end of my bed. They were describing the battle at the command post and talking of Paul, of Maxime, the adjutant, and of Ludovic, the officer with Michel, when suddenly their faces became blurred, misty, distant—and I passed out. Stupidly, I had not asked Dr Le Tessier for how long I should let my leg bleed, and all the time I had been listening and talking, my blood dripped into the bowl. I was on my way to bleeding to death. However, Chabot took charge, bound my leg, and in a few minutes I regained consciousness.

Chabot told me that before light, on the day following my departure to conduct the stores operation at Verduras' camp, firing broke out again at Camp Michel and, a little later, the Germans found his command post and started a fight which lasted for the rest of the day. Michel was so heavily committed that he was unable to spare any of his sixty men to join the command post force of about twenty men, and the two little groups fought isolated battles throughout the day, facing some 700 highly trained German troops. The Germans forced home their final attack and Michel, and later Chabot, were driven out of their posts into the mountains, taking different directions so as to split the German pursuit force. Chabot, with Maxime, Paul my radio operator, Tin-Tin, and the rest of his command post—the girl, Jo, fortunately, had been sent away earlier on a courier mission—headed for another derelict farm some miles away, called La Ferme de la Montagne. As its name suggests, it was perched high on a hill, and it was surrounded by a clearing before the open fields ran into a pine forest. When they reached the farm the following day, the whole group, worn out with fighting and marching through heavy snow with their arms, collapsed inside the shelter of the old buildings to rest. Chabot let them lie while he made a reconnaissance of the area and, as he walked through the trees, he was surprised to see a large party of Germans between him and the farm. Immediately the Germans attacked, and there was nothing Chabot could do except hide, and pray that his command-post staff would get through.

I heard from Paul and Maxime what happened in the farm. Surprised, caught—some literally—with their trousers down, half the group were catching a quick nap when the first bursts of machine-gun fire crackled through the old buildings.

'If they had walked in quietly without firing, the chances were they would have got the lot of us without a shot being fired,' Paul said. Maxime and Paul took charge. Paul, although a W/T operator, was a damned fine soldier, and was the only one in our Maquis groups at the time with an American carbine, which was a very efficient and accurate weapon. During the hours of the battle, he would squirm from cover to cover, wait for a German to show himself, shoot him, and then crawl back. All the time he and Maxime encouraged the rest of the group, many of whom were no more than boys. They fought some two or three hundred Germans who were very wary and did not rush them. In the farm were the twin brothers, Julien and Marius Roche, who were inseparable. Julien died, and it was many weeks before his twin got over the death.

The group held on, completely surrounded, facing heavy machine-guns, automatic weapons, and rifles for hour after hour. Then they heard a swish, and a mortar bomb burst close to the main building. More bombs followed until the field round the farmhouse was pockmarked with craters and the air was filled with flying, whining splinters. Paul told the group they would have to make a break for it or be blown to pieces. Maxime agreed, and Paul chose an escape route which would take the ten remaining men through the sector with the least attackers, across an open field and into the woods.

'Follow me, at the run, in single file—for God's sake don't bunch up,' Paul shouted. He ducked out of the farm and ran, jinking from side to side, across the open field as the Germans concentrated their fire. He reached the woods; so did Maxime, but half the rest were caught in the heavy fire and brought down. Romans and I, a few days after this, went to the farm and found our good, grumbling friend and cook, Tin-Tin, dead in the snow, lying on his back with his hands and arms held to his face trying to stop the blows from rifle butts.

Paul, Maxime, and the rest of the little group kept going, but there was no pursuit. The only person they met was Ludovic, Michel's second-in-command, who was lying in the snow with a bullet wound in his thigh. Ludovic and Paul were great friends, so Paul insisted on dragging him to the outskirts of the small village of Boyeux, which had been partially burnt down, while he and Maxime went to see if they could get help. This was a dangerous thing to do, as the villagers, following the roasting they had had from the Germans, were unlikely to be very helpful. But they were lucky. One of the village firemen immediately found bandages, food, and wine for the group and hid Paul, Maxime, and the wounded Ludovic in the huge, communal bread oven.

Chabot was told where Paul and his group were hiding and made his way to the village.

Within two or three days, the Germans pulled out of the Maquis areas and returned to their bases, leaving behind dozens of dead villagers, hamlets and villages destroyed or badly burnt, and it was estimated, at least 200 of their own dead, killed by the *maquisards*. There were also dozens of Germans seriously wounded, and through our intelligence system in the main towns we were able to get a complete breakdown of the injured from the records kept in local hospitals. Our own casualties were slight, perhaps forty dead and a handful of wounded. The Germans always suffered at our hands, for we were fighting on ground we knew, from good cover, and nearly always the Germans had to attack uphill, which takes the steam out of soldiers.

Romans joined Chabot and myself, so at last we were able to take stock of our situation and make plans for the future of the southern Ain. Romans, incidentally, had heard firing while he was in the Haute-Savoie some fifty or more miles away, and decided to come straightaway to the Ain with Elizabeth, my courier, to see what was happening. There were Germans and checkpoints all through the area, and they had a hard time reaching us, travelling part of the way by rail and part on skis, as both were expert skiers.

We changed command posts several times in the next few days while we assessed reports of casualties and damage, and worked out our needs for re-arming and resupplying. One morning Maxime and I were standing outside one of the derelict farms, dressed in Maquis clothing. I had two guns at my hips and Maxime a sten-gun in his arms, when Maxime said: 'Xavier—look, bloody Germans.' And there were two German soldiers in uniform, but without weapons, wandering not ten yards from us. They were rather elderly gentlemen and we presumed they were on wood collecting fatigue. We did not shoot, as that would have brought others to our camp. They saw us, but took no notice, so we had a quick look round the farm and found a contingent of soldiers a couple of hundred yards away. We decided it was best to move.

I found, when the last reports reached us, that the damage to our groups had not been all that great, although some of the *barraquements*, Maquis camps, had been burnt down and some arms lost—mainly due to the foolish London decision to drop arms indiscriminately into the fighting area. I agreed with Romans that we should move out of the sector that had borne the brunt of the German attack (the first major attack ever launched on the Maquis) into the Dombes for regrouping.

I was very impressed by Montréal's action in the northern sector. He had used his head, and instead of rushing down to help us, decided that the number of Germans operating in the south must have weakened the forces in his area. So the Maquis in the north made repeated sabotage attacks on German rail, road, and telephone communications, which puzzled the Germans considerably, for they believed the main section of Maquis was in the south of the Ain. I praised Montréal later for his initiative.

We found, from reports we received through the Armée Secrète, that the Germans had used two full divisions in their sweep through our southern sector, with armoured companies in tanks patrolling some of the main roads.

The German tactics had been to set up road blocks to restrict circulation of our forces—which was a stupid plan as they were not used by the Maquis groups, only by people like Romans and myself to move from area to area. We always had warning of road blocks and it was not very often that we ran into one we did not know about.

The Germans split their attacking parties into groups of about 300 and designated to each one specific targets, like a camp or a village. Reconnaissance was carried out by ski patrols dressed in white camouflage smocks, and from the air.

All these groups were armed with heavy machine-guns, automatic light weapons, and 77 mm. guns firing, of course, explosive shells. They also used mortars and machine-guns fitted to sleds and pulled into action by their troops.

We lost only thirty-six men killed in the Maquis in this sweep through the south, despite the overwhelming number of German troops attacking us. The Armée Secrète also had casualties, far more than the Maquis.

It is always hard to assess the enemy's losses, but we knew they must have lost several hundred killed and many hundreds of others wounded.

In the Dombes we started to reorganise, and I managed to get in about six major parachute stores operations, with as many as nine aircraft a time dropping weapons, ammunition, plastic explosive, and so on. The Dombes was a fine area for drops as it was clear of the mountains of the Ain, and was fairly flat and open.

The RAF had improved their techniques by this time, and were able to send six or nine aircraft at a time and during all stages of the moon—they no longer needed a moon to guide them as we used the homing device, Eureka, and S-phones to direct them to their targets.

I used the S-phone successfully for the first time in one of the six aircraft-drops on the Dombes. I called up the leader of the flight as I heard aircraft approaching. I nearly dropped the equipment when I heard an English voice reply: 'Hello, hello, hello, Raymond—how are you?' Raymond, of course, being my cover name in Britain. It was Jerry Morel, the man who had escaped from hospital with stitches in his stomach and whom I had last seen when he brought me back to London the previous September. He and I had a great chat, for his was the first English voice I had heard for six months. I was very sorry to hear him say: 'Goodbye, see you later.'

I was impressed by the readiness with which London responded to my request for more and more arms, and I suppose we must have had something like forty plane-loads of goods dropped to us in about a fortnight. This enabled us to re-arm the groups, who were nearly out of ammunition after the German attacks, and also to arm the flood of recruits which came into the Ain demanding to fight with the Maquis. Our command grew in size and by the end of March, or the beginning of April, there were something like 5,000 fully armed men, many with battle experience, ready for action in the Ain. A formidable bunch.

The day before Romans and I were due to leave the Dombes and move back into the southern sector, Belleroche, the head of the FFI in Lyons, came to confer with us about the Armée Secrète. The administrative section of the command post had already left and all that was left was a group of about twenty fighting men who made up the rest of the post. One of our guards ran in and shouted: 'The GMR, the GMR,' and, sure enough, there were two or three hundred of the black-uniformed Frenchmen settling into cover. I grabbed a sten-gun and Belleroche was given a ·303 rifle. We spread out close by the post, and Belleroche and I, together in a small wood, watched one group of the GMR disembarking from their buses at the end of a track, about half a mile from us.

One of my fondest memories of the Maquis is of the sight of Belleroche standing in a wood, wearing his businessman's coat and hat, with an umbrella over one arm and a rifle over the other. Anyway, the GMR made their attack and we fought a rearguard action, slipping away in ones and twos to fall back on the place to which we had already sent our administrative staff. The attack was not pressed home, but Romans and I were very nearly hit as we crouched in a hollow, hidden by bushes, listening to the GMR coming towards us. There was a burst of firing, the bushes around us crackled, twigs flew, and we fell flat on to our faces. He looked at me and raised one eyebrow as though to say '*Merde*, that was too close.' It was not the last time that Romans and I were nearly caught by random shooting.

It was at this time that Romans found that there was not enough money available to pay the full allotment of 1,800 francs a week to the wife of each *maquisard* and 500 francs for each child, as the FFI in Lyons, under Belleroche, had run into trouble with the supply of cash. We discussed this, for it was very important to keep the morale high in the Maquis and if men knew that their families were going hungry, they would have been anxious and not fought so well. I told Romans I could get him the money if he wanted, but he decided that the French should handle their own affairs.

'I think we'll rob a bank,' Romans told me. 'They'll have some money.'

He and Belleroche got together and discussed the bank raid, and decided they must find a manager who was pro-Resistance. The Sous-Préfet at Saint Claude in the Haut-Jura, who was brought into the discussions, said that the bank manager at the Banque de France in his village would probably be just the person to help. So approaches were made to him and he agreed to assist the Maquis by leaving his keys on his desk and not giving the alarm signal when the Maquis broke in.

On the day chosen, Romans led a group into the village, posted guards to keep anyone from interfering with them, blew down the main door of the bank, and held all the tellers up at gun-point. The manager was tied to his desk—but not too tightly—and with his keys, the Maquis opened the safes and strong-boxes.

They cleared one hundred million francs—about £500,000 sterling—which was more than enough to pay the dependants.

No one was caught after the raid and the bank manager was never suspected of being involved. The German and French police put it down to the 'Terrorists'.

We were by now back in the Ain, in a new HQ, with a new cook called Marc, the son of a baker, to replace our friend Tin-Tin.

We were ready again, with our men fully armed, and with weapons much better than the faithful sten, such as tommy-guns—one of which I appropriated for myself—bazookas, brens and grenades. We were ready, but the next attack was to fall on the Haute-Savoie.

12

I had been unable to devote as much time as I wished to the Haute-Savoie, where I wanted to weld the groups more firmly together. As it was, there were Communist, Armée Secrète and Maquis groups, all squabbling politically among themselves and not liaising as well as they should have done. Every camp I visited asked me about my political views and which party I supported for the rebuilding of France. I told them I had no political affiliation to any party, that I was a soldier, not a politician, and I asked them to forget their politics. Cantinier and Romans' deputy in the area, Captain Lachenal, did what they could, but they had a very difficult task.

In this disrupted area I attempted to set up a system of 'personal' groups, and I managed to recruit a handful of them under my direct control, quite separate from Cantinier and Romans, who knew nothing about them. They were small groups of ten to fifteen each, centred around Chaumonte and Jean Blanc, the small farmer and mountain guide I met on my reconnaissance visit to the area in September. I also arranged arms drops to him and to some of the other groups, but I found that, compared with the Ain, it was much more difficult to bind the groups together, for they were all very suspicious of the British. 'Perfide Albion' was always in their minds. Romans was in charge of the area and, with his great energy and drive, he did make an impression. If he had been able to remain in control of the Haute-Savoie, perhaps we would have produced the same cohesion as there was in the Ain. But, quite rightly, he left the Haute-Savoie, as the Ain was obviously the main centre of the Maquis and Resistance in the area. At the beginning of 1944, I too was forced to leave the Haute-Savoie mainly to its own devices, but still controlled their operations from the Ain.

Some of the parachute drops in the Haute-Savoie had been on the Plateau des Glières, a high mountain plateau ideal for operations but a death trap for guerrilla warfare as there were normally only one or two exits and, because of the snow, footprints showed up easily from the air. It was to this area in January that Tom Morel, my good friend, Pierrot, and Lashenal, Romans' deputy, decided to gather together all the groups, set up a concentration of forces, and use the plateau as a base to attack the Germans and carry out sabotage. The inevitable happened, for the groups ceased to be guerrilla fighters and became a static force. Firstly, the GMRs attacked them, fighting on foot through the high mountains and deep snow as no transport could reach the area, except mules. The Maquis and Armée Secrète groups beat them off, and word seeped out of France to Britain and America that a great and glorious uprising had taken place in south-east France which was destined to control the area. The news, which rapidly spread round France, brought more groups to the plateau to join in the uprising, including some of those run by Jean Blanc.

Hundreds of Maquis and Resistance fighters made their camps on the plateau, defence in depth was arranged, ammunition and weapons hauled up, with food, clothing, and medical supplies, and the force settled in ready for a siege. The Germans, not liking the world publicity this stand was receiving in case it gave encouragement to other occupied countries, then stepped in. They bombed the area, and their fighters strafed the camps with cannon fire and machine-guns. They made frontal attacks up the two main exits to the plateau, causing casualties, but losing many men themselves. It was glorious, bloody, but not guerrilla warfare. Slowly we were losing well-trained Resistance fighters, plus their arms, and wasting ammunition by the hundredweight.

Cantinier had been against the idea from the start and sent a courier to me in the Ain telling me of Morel's decision to fight. I told him to do all in his power to stop the operation, foreseeing nothing but disaster for our men, but Cantinier could not stop it. As the fight progressed, I got courier after courier from the Glières, asking me for support, and time and time again I sent the same message back—'sorry'. If I sent arms and ammunition, it would only delay the inevitable. Finally, I relented, stupidly, perhaps, but I could not harden my heart enough. I arranged two or three heavy drops by RAF aircraft, which brought arms and food to the beleaguered groups. My only hope was that the weapons might give the men a chance of breaking out of the ring of Germans encircling them.

The arms were used in the last desperate fight against airborne troops, the toughest fighting men in the German war-machine, who were parachuted in to mop up the area. Many Frenchmen, including Morel and Pierrot, died in hand-to-hand fighting and in the fire fight which developed on the rugged, snow-covered mountain top.

Looking back at this action, I am forced to take the same view I took at the time, that it was nonsensical. The groups would have done far better to have continued their normal activities, although those who praised the operation pointed out that the fight mauled two German divisions who were sent to clear up the Glières and, at least, prevented them from being used anywhere else for a period of three or four weeks. Nevertheless it was madness, a glorious stupidity which is still spoken of in France with awe and pride.

Earlier, in the Haute-Savoie, I met Andrés, a Spaniard, who had formed his own small group of fellow countrymen, and very good they were. He and I became great friends, and he was so reliable that I asked him to rent me a villa on the lake shore at Annecy, which he did. No one, apart from Andrés, knew of this hideaway, not even Romans. I used to go there for a day or two if I was awaiting a stores operation, as it gave me a break from the hurly-burly of Maquis life, the fighting, and the enormous drag on the human body of working without sleep for days on end. I used to keep in touch through Andrés, who received messages from Paul, Romans, and the Ain, and left them for me in a dead letter box I selected in the yard of a garage which had a selection of used cars for sale. My hiding-place was the toolbox on the running board of an old car with a 'For sale' notice on it, but which the garage owner never encouraged anyone to buy.

I went there one day and the owner, a good Resistance man, came up to me and said that Andrés had been shot, but he did not know if he was dead. I thanked him, and went to Albigny, to the restaurant run by Jean Saulnier's sister, Emma, and moved in. Later I went to Annecy and saw Saulnier, who told me that Andrés was dead. Apparently he had decided, rashly, to take a radio set by road to an operator who was waiting for it, and had, of all things, chosen a main road. Rounding a bend, he saw a German checkpoint ahead, hesitated, slowed down, and then tried to turn round to run away. But the two machine-guns that the Germans always mounted before a checkpoint opened fire, and Andrés died. When they searched his body, they found a piece of paper on which he had written the address of my villa on the lakeside. When I heard this I thanked God I had stuck to the rule book and not gone back to the villa to pick up my revolver and one or two other small items. For the rule was—if anyone is shot or captured, pull out immediately.

Andrés and Morel were great characters, fine fighters. They are still remembered. As is Simon, the son of a general, who had one ambition—to kill Germans. He had a small group of about fifteen men who lived close by Annecy, and he always went about with two or three of his men, who were fully armed, even in the villages. Simon, for instance, was never without his sub-machine-gun, and he was likely to shoot down any isolated German officer or man he saw. He was an individualist and refused to link his group with any organisation, but he did sometimes listen to myself and Romans when we criticised his rashness. But our lectures made no difference.

One episode which rang round the Haute-Savoie concerned the small village of Thorens, where Simon had gone with one of his gang to have a coffee and a meal. He sat with his back to a wall, facing the door, with his submachine-gun on the seat beside him, when a German officer, an NCO and a soldier walked into the café and demanded identity papers. Simon had papers of a sort, but it was obvious to him that his gun would soon be seen. So he shot the three down, much to the terror of the restaurateur and his patrons. The two ran out of the café and found a German staff car outside with yet another officer sitting in the back. They shot him, took the car, headed towards the mountains and, at a quiet place, ran it over the edge of a ravine with the German dead inside.

Simon was well known to the Garde Mobile, the gendarmes, who were fine people, and to the GMR. Strangely enough, both groups allowed him to pass at will through checkpoints, after making a vague inspection of his obviously false papers. One day he came to a checkpoint run by the GMR, and the officer in charge, as Simon's car stopped, called cheerily: 'Ah, *c'est Simon*—come and show me your papers.' Simon smiled, got out of the car, and was shot down by the GMR officer. He was taken to hospital at Annecy, where he lay desperately ill for several days with a member of the Milice at his bedside. One night he disappeared, and Romans and I believed he was taken out by the Germans and shot. His body was never found.

I was at Frangy in late January when I was asked by London if I was able to put on another sabotage raid at the ball-bearing factory, now running again. I told them that we could, and got together the gang that had blown it the first time. Pan Pan chuckled when I told him and the rest of the group our objective, and said he now knew how to set off a time-pencil. We were within a few days of setting our date for attack when I got a message from SOE which said: 'Sorry, Xavier, factory raid is off. It will be bombed.' The head of Bomber Command, 'Bomber' Harris, quite understandably, believed that his aircraft could do a job as well as a sabotage group and avoid the risk of hostages being taken and shot, which was fairly normal after sabotage by the Resistance.

I passed the news on to the group that the raid was off, but not, of course, that an air raid would be made, just in case someone opened their mouth too wide. Secretly, I was rather pleased that the group were not going to make the raid, as security precautions had been tightened. There were many more guards about, and none that we could trust to look the other way. I felt we might have heavy casualties, and it is hard for a commander to commit his friends on a venture which might kill many of them, though of course I would have sent them in if the job had to be done.

By chance I was at Albigny when the raid took place early one morning. I heard aircraft and went out on the balcony and looked towards the town to see what I could of the bombing, so I could pass on details to London later. The aircraft were from the United States daylight force and their approach seemed rather casual and haphazard, but there were certainly a lot of bombs dropped. During the raid, Janine, aged about thirteen, one of the Saulnier family, came running up the outside stairs to my balcony, obviously rather frightened, as this was the first raid in the area. She took my hand and said: 'I know I shall be all right with you, Monsieur Xavier, for the bombers must know you are here and they wouldn't do anything to hurt you.' I agreed with her to give her confidence, but breathed a quiet prayer that the pair of us would not be hit by a stray bomb.

I went into Annecy after the raid, saw various contacts from the factory, and found that the USAF had not scored one hit, or even a near miss. I sent a message through to Paul telling him this, and a week or two later, the RAF raided the factory again. This time ball-bearing production was brought to a standstill.

But, as I explained, I had to leave the Haute-Savoie and concentrate on the Ain, where it was obvious I was most needed and where it was also obvious that more attacks would be made during the weeks ahead. The Germans could not risk letting thousands of trained, armed men rampage around in their rear if France was to be invaded.

We had to wait, in fact, until the beginning of April for the next major attack. There were several small actions against the GMR meanwhile, but nothing to cause any real trouble. Romans and I were in one of the mountainous command posts in the north of the Ain with Montréal, our area commander, when news came through that thousands of German troops were moving into the sector. We heard that they had gone into Nantua, Oyonnax, and Bellegarde, and were pouring through the Jura, down the Col-de-la-Faucille, wreaking havoc in the villages, and venturing into the Maquis country on the hunt for *maquisard* camps. Reports talked of 'several thousand' motorised troops, and we knew that we were in for a dose similar to that received in the southern part of the area. Montreal sent couriers to some of the main camps passing on the information, and the whole area was warned to stand by. I also sent news to Chabot's headquarters in the south so that he could carry out diversionary raids on railway lines and trains to harry the Germans and, perhaps, make them reduce the strength of their attacks in the north. Chabot did exceptionally well. The Germans were so pressed in his area that they were forced to send an armoured train ahead of any other train. But that did not stop Chabot. He cut the lines in front of the armoured train, then cut the lines behind it, so that it became isolated and of no further use until the tracks had been repaired. That took up more German time.

The Armée Secrète in the Belley area came to aid us when we called on them. Under their chief, Plutarque, they sabotaged the railways, and on one day, 8 April 1944, they derailed two trains laden with German troops, and another troop-train filled with Milice, in the area to the east of Ambérieu, causing many casualties and blocking the line for a considerable time. All in all, the liaison between the Armée Secrète and the co-operation between our northern and southern sectors was excellent, and showed Romans and myself that all our journeyings and talks over the past months had been well worth while. We had a force which was well-balanced, well trained, and fighting for the same end. I felt very proud.

Fortunately for the Maquis, the Germans concentrated their attention on the towns and villages. They fired some villages, took hostages, shot Resistance men known to have been involved with either the Maquis or Armée Secrète, and tortured others in attempts to learn more about the Maquis. They terrorised the population, and there was nothing we could do, for our weapons were too light to take on Germans armed with mortars, artillery and tanks. But when they came into Maquis country they paid heavily for their bestiality; the Maquis showed no quarter and fought savagely to revenge the townsfolk. The Germans took hostages and warned the countryside that they would be shot if there was any resistance. We ordered a proclamation to be drawn up in German and French which was posted on all the notice boards in the towns and villages. It told the Germans that we had soldiers as prisoners in the Maquis—they knew this, of course, as word was sent to them by comrades of these men—and that for every hostage shot, two German soldiers would die. We also offered to exchange prisoners and hostages, but this offer was not taken up.

One group of Germans in Nantua went to the hospital where Dr Touillon had under his care nine wounded *maquisards*, as well as some German soldiers, also wounded. The German officer bitterly reviled the doctor for looking after 'French terrorists' and demanded that he throw them out of the hospital. Touillon, a very brave man, stood on the steps of the hospital, refused to let the Germans in, and told them that his task as a doctor was to heal people irrespective of race or creed. 'I shall continue to nurse and doctor both French and Germans here,' he said emphatically. And he did, for a time. But another German group came during the fourteen days of terrorism sparked by their major attack and took away the nine injured Frenchmen.

They were put in a tip-up lorry, driven to a lay-by outside the town, tipped out, and massacred by machine-guns.

The Germans also took our friend Dr Mercier, who had given us such great help in the mountains, and shot him outside Nantua, after a traitor denounced him. His wife, the pharmacist who did so much work for us, later came into the Maquis to work at our hospital.

The northern sector attacks lasted longer than the attacks on Chabot's sector earlier, but although the Germans had overwhelming superiority and used four or five hundred men to attack a camp sixty strong, their successes were fewer. This was partly because the ground they fought over was much more mountainous than in the south, but mainly because the Germans had become chary and, perhaps, frightened at the losses they incurred. Not once did they overrun a camp, although several had to be abandoned under pressure of attacks, and the camp *barraquements* were duly burnt. I was with Romans at the command post with Montréal during this period and was delighted to see that the sector held together. There were no stories of lost *maquisards* wandering the country, no disruption of communications between the commanders and headquarters. It was a very disciplined force, hitting hard and often, in true guerrilla fashion, and then disappearing into the trees. I found Montréal had everything so much under control that there was little for me to do; so I decided to go into the Saône-et-Loire area, which was north west of the Ain and the Department next to the Haut-Jura, where groups I had been unable to visit were clamouring for arms. I spent three to four days touring the area and selected two dropping zones between the two rivers. They were ideal, flat and level, and well away from towns. On the whole, I found the groups well disciplined and had no hesitation in recommending to London that arms and supplies be dropped. I supervised several drops myself.

My guide was a young milkman in his early twenties, who took me about on the back of his motorcycle, which was very frightening. One morning I had to go into Mâcon. He drove me on to a long, wide bridge over the river Saône and half-way across we saw that there was a big collection of police at a checkpoint on the other side, and with them, a group of plainclothes men—which meant either Gestapo or Miliciens. My milkman slowed down, and muttered '*Merde—les policiers*.' I liked to avoid all checkpoints if it was possible, and I suppose here, because it was quite a busy bridge with heavy traffic we might have turned round and got away with it. But my milkman said: 'Let's go and get it over with.' The police checked our papers, asked him where he was going, to which he replied 'my early morning milk round', and we were through. It sounds easy, but I felt the usual tightening in the stomach and, as usual, found my guts had tightened after we passed through.

I returned to the command post in the northern Ain without any real difficulty, and found that fierce fighting was still going on. Montréal was still very calm and still had the situation firmly in his grasp. He told me, without a flicker of a smile: 'Xavier, I have just learned that we are under attack by two divisions amounting to some 20,000 men. They must think we are important.'

I knew there must have been several thousand Germans involved because they had gone into so many towns and villages. But 20,000 trained infantry was quite a number to set against the 1,500 men we had in the northern sector. I was very pleased we had provoked such a German effort and even more pleased that my *maquisards* held firm and fought so well.

The Germans pulled out at the end of a fortnight as though they had been given orders to create hell for fourteen days, and then quit. After they pulled out, we set to work to find out exact figures of troops involved, German casualties, and the numbers of Resistance men and hostages who had been shot. The figure 20,000 was correct and this force had killed seventy civilians in the towns and villages, and eighty-five *maquisards*, whilst we had killed 1,000 Germans, including several officers. We were unable to get an accurate figure for their wounded, but a conservative estimate was one injured for every one killed. In other words, we had achieved a minimum of ten per cent casualties on two divisions. A very creditable effort, I thought. In addition, of course, were dozens of Germans and Miliciens who had been killed by Chabot on 8 April when he derailed the three trains. I know, from what I learned later, that the German command was appalled at their losses and decided that the Maquis de l'Ain must be exterminated. This they tried to do at a later date, using three divisions.

I arranged more arms drops for the sector to replace the ammunition expended in the fourteen-day fight and we found some more camps to replace those burnt down by the Germans. Within a week we were fully prepared again to take on whatever might come next.

We were ready, and our successes brought a flood of recruits to the Maquis, not all of whom could be trusted. There were many Frenchmen, unfortunately, whose loyalty was in doubt, either because they believed in a German victory or because they had been frightened into betraying their fellow countrymen by threats of torture against them or their families. These traitors, for they were all traitors even if they were working under duress, and the too inquisitive German, caused me much heart searching during my stay in France.

One of the first cases which Romans and I had to judge concerned a gendarme at Pon d'Ain near the village where the family Leopold lived. The police, of course, had to try to discover the whereabouts of young men, liable for forced labour, who disappeared before they were due for call up. The large majority of gendarmes made cursory inquiries and simply reported the boys were untraceable. But not the one at Pon d'Ain. He had tracked down two or three lads who were sent to German labour camps. After the last capture, the local group sent him at least six warnings in writing, telling him to stop his activities, but reports kept coming in telling of continued zeal in his search for lads. I decided we would send him one final warning telling him he would be shot if he went on. He would not stop, and we said he must be killed.

A boy aged eighteen volunteered for the job, and I saw him with Romans in our command post in the Ain. He was a member of the Maquis whose brother had been caught by the policeman and sent to Germany. The boy's father suffered many interrogations and threats by the gendarme, who was trying to find out where both his sons were. I asked the boy how he would carry out the killing. 'It is easy. I have seen him morning after morning leave his home on his bicycle at 7.30 a.m. to ride to the gendarmerie. I shall ride up to him on my bike, taunt him about catching my brother, and then shoot him with a ·45 revolver which will be hidden in my pocket.' I told him to go ahead, and it went as easily as he predicted. I wondered over the years whether becoming a gunman had affected the lad, but I was pleased, when in France a year or two ago, to find him working contentedly on his farm. I asked him if the shooting had changed him. He shrugged and said quietly: 'The war was the war.'

On another occasion, a Maquis patrol sent out from our command post in the southern part of the Ain, came across a young French girl aged nineteen to twenty walking with a man in plainclothes aged about thirty-six. The two were surrounded and brought back to the post, as we did not like people wandering in the woods near our headquarters. I questioned the man, who eventually said he was a captain in the German Army on a day's leave, which he had decided to spend in the woods with his little friend. I did not believe him, as we had received more than one report in the past week of a couple wandering around various parts of Maquis country. He finally confessed that he had been sent to spy out our camps.

The girl, we found out later, was well known in the area for her affection for various German officers. But we faced a problem: we could not let the girl go as she would certainly pass information to the Germans, and we obviously could not let her live in the women-starved Maquis. The German was a problem as it was impossible to keep him a prisoner in the headquarters. Romans and I talked it out, and in the end I said: 'They'll have to be shot. There's no other course.' Romans agreed.

We told Romans' bodyguard, a young killer by the name of Dédé de La Butte of our decision, and late at night he took them, one at a time, into the woods, shot them in the back of the head and dug a grave.

These were very difficult decisions to have to make. It was against our principles to shoot people—it was one of the very reasons that we were fighting the Germans—but we were under pressure, and if the lives of our own patriots were jeopardised it was necessary to kill. It was not a matter of revenge, but survival.

There were other times when I had agreed with the order to kill—once at a small hamlet where the local gendarme was too inquisitively anti-Resistance and had been warned many times. I was given the details of his activities, checked them with other Resistance people in the area, and we finally ordered him to be shot. Every day the gendarme went to the hamlet's only café, which stood beside a mill stream. One day the executioner walked into the café, shot the gendarme through the heart, and walked away.

Towards the end of May, with the invasion date approaching, I was increasingly aware of the need for security and I talked with all the commanders and many of the camp commanders about the need to keep as silent as possible on our future plans. I also emphasised, as did Romans, the problems caused by the increasing number of very pretty girl couriers we were using in the Ain and Haute-Savoie and of the importance of there being no involvement with them by the men. Love and sex could play no part in guerrilla life, for a man in love might take undue risks to go to visit a girl friend in a town or village and lead traitors, Gestapo or Milice to the site of a Maquis camp.

La Brosse, one of our top saboteurs, became very fond of Jo, the courier who went with me to the command post near Brénod just before the major attack, but he had sufficient sense not to prejudice our security by rushing off to visit her whenever she was in our area.

I received a personal message at this time to say that my wife had given birth to our first child, a daughter, and I was, of course, delighted, so planned that the next BBC message announcing an arms drop would be: 'I see everywhere green eyes—*Je vois partout des yeux verts*.' This was in honour of my wife, Vi, who had green eyes.

I told one or two people about this message and Romans said: 'Ah, La Brosse is going around saying that he sees nothing but Jo. She has green eyes. We'll have them both in the command post and when the message comes through we can have a laugh at the pair of them.'

When the radio message came through we told La Brosse that it had been aimed at him. He took it well, but poor Jo did not know where to look.

I sent several messages through the BBC which had sentimental value to us in the Maquis. One was in honour of Miguet and *le garage*. They were magnificent throughout my whole time there and never failed to get through with stores and arms after drops or in clearing an enemy train after it had been wrecked. This message read: 'The garage hands are full of guts—*Le Garage est gonflé à bloc*.' It went down very well.

Another one concerned Michette, Cantinier's cousin, who at the beginning of my second visit to France, helped me to find a safe place to hide if ever I was forced to leave the Saulniers. She walked with me through snow up to our knees, for miles above Lake Annecy, until we came to a small shepherd's hut which had one plank to take a palliasse, a stove, and a cupboard. It was the ideal place for a man to hide out, as it was never occupied, like many other small huts in the area used either by shepherds or climbers. We set out back to Annecy and in the darkness at about eight o'clock, we approached a small alpine hamlet.

Michette asked if we might stay in the small hotel there, a place with two or three bedrooms and a large kitchen where the guests ate with the owners. As we were both exhausted from the heavy work of walking through the snow, I agreed and asked the owner for two rooms.

'I have one room with a double bed, that's all,' he said.

We looked at one another and shrugged.

'We'll take it,' I said.

Michette and I had an enormous meal, a bottle of wine, and were nearly asleep over our food. We finally went up to bed. I did not know whether to get into it first or let Michette, but we eventually slept in the vast bed in the small hotel called the Soleil d'Or. We were very good and treated each other as soldiers, true comrades, and completely sexless.

Later, when another drop came along and Michette was at the headquarters, I asked for the BBC to send the the message: 'I'll see you again at the Soleil d'Or.' She grinned as she heard it, but it was not until long after the war, when she, Jo, and about a dozen other ex-Maquis types were gathered in Paul Johnson's, my radio operator's, lounge in Paris that that story was repeated. Michette told it and then turned to me and said: 'Just to think, you and I went to bed and didn't do anything.' This was the nearest I got to breaching my own security rules.

These seem trifling incidents now, but in wartime Maquis life there were few amusing events and these trifles did bring some light relief.

I faced another problem just before D-day and this concerned my own courier, Elizabeth Devereaux-Rochester, the American girl who looked so like an Englishwoman, who wore a tweed suit, carried a knapsack on her shoulders, and strode through the countryside. She had worked very gallantly for me and was always on the search for work. She never liked to sit about and if she had to stay in the command post for any length of time she would pester me to give her a task to get her moving again.

But as the weeks went by I had more and more discreet and diffident inquiries about her. A person would say: 'Ah, Elizabeth, what a wonderful girl she is and how well she's liked. But doesn't she look English.'

Romans, too, made one or two remarks about her Englishness, until I felt that it would be wise to have her sent back to London, partly for her own sake and partly to relieve the minds of those she worked with, who were anxious lest their activities be compromised if the girl was captured.

I did not want to sack her because of the great assistance she was to me, and anyway I did not have the heart to. I took the coward's way out and asked London to recall her, having explained in my cable the growing concern about her Englishness.

When the cable arrived ordering her to return to SOE, Elizabeth asked me why she had been recalled, but I was evasive and embarrassed and made some poor excuse. She then pleaded to stay, but I told her it would be folly as her mother was under constant surveillance by the Gestapo and French police as she was known to be a foreigner. Reluctantly Elizabeth agreed to stay away and finally she left me.

A few days later I heard that she had been arrested and taken to Fresnes Prison. I guessed that she had disobeyed my instructions and had been caught while visiting her mother, and I found later that this was correct. She had a good cover story, a simple one, which was that she had taken a false identity and had lived in the Haute-Savoie for months. She was not badly treated, because the Germans did not consider that she had been involved in the Resistance, and later she was freed when the troops liberated Paris.

Some months later I was in Baker Street in Buckmaster's office, when one of the staff told me that a girl wanted to see me in the next room. I went in, and before I had shut the door, Elizabeth had stood up and said: 'Xavier—you were right, I should never have gone near Mother, it was folly.'

I have always been very fond of Elizabeth, I have to this day a great respect for her work and for the guts she showed in France. If only she had not looked so English . . .

If any blame is to be attached for this incident, it must lie with London in recruiting a girl who looked so un-French. But it was wartime, and Elizabeth did have the qualifications for the job.

13

The climax was fast approaching. After four years of occupation, terrorism, brutality, and clandestine warfare, the French were preparing to come into the open to fight for their country. In April and May even the doubters of a French victory began leaving their boltholes, declaring they had always known the Germans would be thrown out of the country, and expressing belated willingness to fight. The first signs of this change of heart showed in the GMRs—the Pétain-supporting reserves. Up to April we had come across only one or two of their commanders who were pro-Maquis, and willing to help France by looking the other way, or warning us before attacks came in. But in the spring of 1944, group after group of GMRs made only feint attacks on Maquis camps and, in many instances, a commander would say: 'Leave a couple of guns for us to capture, go away for a couple of hours, and we won't even burn your camp down.' In the main they kept their word, and only occasionally were the Maquis double-crossed by a commander who pressed home a fierce attack. When that happened the GMRs always suffered badly, for the Maquis did not take kindly to treachery, and in one fight they killed 300 or more GMRs in a cold-blooded counter attack. This, too, helped to make the GMRs less aggressive.

Some weeks before the Allies landed, Romans and I began the talks which produced our master plan: Le Plan Vert. In the 10,000 miles square of the Ain, we would kill all the Germans in the area, and put an end to all rail transport through the Department. It was an ambitious programme to launch, and Romans and I spent many hours talking with commanders, civilians and members of the Armée Secrète, before every detail had been worked out and every person briefed. Put simply, we intended to eliminate all the Germans who manned outposts—like the one at the crossroads at La Cluse—take over the towns of Hauteville, Bellegarde, Nantua and Oyonnax, and run them on a proper basis, maintaining the normal services like electricity, and producing more food and clothing which would be shared out by ration cards and clothing coupons we would print ourselves. We also arranged to set up a military tribunal to try offenders against our laws (which were based on the laws of France) and to bring in the gendarmerie to police the towns. We talked with civilians in these towns whom we knew were pro-Maquis and pro-France, and appointed them to head the various civil government departments, like electricity, water and so on. Chiefs and deputies at the main headquarters of the gendarmeries were approached to gain their support, or get their word that there would be no attempt to dispute our control.

The aims of our talks with the Armée Secrète were twofold: to ask them to garrison the towns, and to carry out attacks against the Germans in towns like Bourg and Ambérieu, where there were main garrisons too big for us to take over. The Armée Secrète were eager and agreed with every request that Romans, who was their commander, put to them. They promised to put up road blocks on the main roads out of the towns, to try to prevent German troops recapturing our area. They were to fight hard at these blocks, and the Germans were astounded to find Resistance men actually battling in the streets, for they believed all the fighters were in the mountains with the Maquis. The Armée Secrète were briefed also to attack certain railway lines and so sever rail communications in areas outside the Maquis control.

The main task of the Maquis was to blow up every railway line running through the Ain and to keep them cut, if necessary, for weeks at a time. This was done, and when London requested a particular line to be put out of commission for a week, then it *was* unusable for a week. In addition, the Maquis were to man road blocks on every road into the Ain to prevent the Germans entering the liberated area. Chabot and Montréal, our commanders, were briefed on the outposts held by the Germans, and instructed to draw up plans to wipe out every man. This delighted them and they were overwhelmed with volunteers for the task.

The successful feeding of the townspeople—there were about 15,000 in all taking in some of the larger villages—depended on two things: intelligence reports on German food trains which we planned to derail, and the preparedness of Jean Miguet and his transport section. We had talks with our friends the Cheminots about future train movements and, as always, they were only too willing to do anything which could embarrass the Germans. As for Miguet, this quiet, capable man, he declared himself ready to handle any transport problem we might run into. He told us, proudly, that he could provide 200 or more lorries and vans with drivers and mates, and, providing we had the men available to act as loaders, he would always have sufficient vehicles to clear a wrecked train, and handle parachute drops at the same time.

At this time Romans and I were pestered by former French officers who, realising that the invasion was upon us and that France stood to win, came out of their homes dressed in their best army uniforms and demanding entry into the Maquis. Many of them came to us and said: 'Right, I am a colonel as you can see—give me troops to command to fight these damn Germans. What men and equipment can you let me have?'

Romans and I were amazed at their effrontery and we knew that even if they were fine soldiers, none of the Maquis, some of whom had been living a life of hardship and hard fighting for a couple of years or so, would accept them.

'Give *you* command! You, who have sulked in your homes throughout the whole of these times—nonsense,' Romans would explode. 'My men don't want you, and I'm not even going to suggest to them that you lead them. They would think I was mad.'

We christened these former officers the 'Mothball Brigade'—'*Les Naphthalinés*'—as all their uniforms had been carefully pressed and stored in mothballs for years. You could smell them.

I thought, however, and Romans agreed, that they should be given the opportunity to make up for their timidity, and it was suggested to them that they made up their own groups. They readily agreed, and I was able to arrange for stores operations to be given to them so, when the Plan Vert was put into operation, there were several hundred other men under arms. Some of them fought well, but their losses were high as they had not learned the proper guerrilla tactics. They insisted on the stand-up-and-fight method.

One incident, I think, shows the attitude of the Frenchman in the Ain at that time. On 19 May, a farmer called Prosper—his real name was Claudius Charvet of Saint Julien-Sur-Veyle-Vonnas—ran a small AS group, but lived and ran his farm with his wife at the same time. Prosper was known as '*Un point, c'est tout*'. He got the nickname at an arms drop I conducted some time earlier in which the SAP men—part of the FFI supply force—wanted to claim some of the stores and arms sent down. Prosper told them: '*Non. Les Colonels Xavier et Romans ont dit . . . Un point, c'est tout.*'

Anyway, Prosper was at home late one evening with his wife when a machine-gun opened up outside and grenades crashed through some of the downstairs windows. Prosper had been given away to the Milice by a collaborator, and they had launched their attack to capture him and force him to give information. Prosper put all the lights out and slipped away from his home through the farm buildings, leaving his wife behind. He feared she might be killed, but he knew he could not deal with the Milice on his own and decided to try to find some of his men. The Milice broke into his farm and started to ransack his house for papers, which they believed gave details of the Armée Secrète and his own group.

They beat Prosper's wife so badly that she lost an eye, but she told them nothing. Eventually they gave up their search and emptied the larder of its good wine and fresh meat—both most difficult to come by in those days. They sat at the great wooden table—thinly lined with linoleum in the French custom—and started to eat and drink, ignoring the injured woman.

Prosper, in the meantime, rounded up twenty of his men, all armed with guns and grenades, and the group made their way back to the farmhouse. On their way across the fields they met a farmgirl who told Prosper that his wounded wife had slipped away. Only the Milice remained in his house.

'Come,' Prosper told his men, 'we're going to attack my farm.' The Resistance men hurled grenades and poured fire through the windows, killing seven of the Milice, who then withdrew. The following day they returned and burnt down the farm—but Prosper had left and taken to the Maquis.

He always laughed at the raiders. 'There was the Milice eating at my table, drinking my wine, and damned good wine too, much too good for them; and all the time my papers were under their soup plates.' For he had spread out his papers beneath the linoleum.

During the last part of April and through most of May, sporadic attacks were made on individual Maquis camps by 400–500 Germans. But our men in both the north and south of the Ain were now experts in this sort of warfare, and although they lost a few men and had their camps burned, they inflicted heavy casualties in those early spring days, when the nights were warm and the trees green once more.

At the end of May, I was at one command post in the northern Ain when a courier came in. 'Xavier, the Germans are pulling out of La Cluse,' he said. This was odd. Then, over the following few days, we got reports of the Germans pulling out of the whole Maquis area of the Ain. One of the commanders suggested that someone had informed on us, but then I pointed out that the Germans would reinforce their posts if they believed they were in danger, not pull out. I thought that the German commander of the Ain was being very sensible, for he too must have realised D-day was not far ahead and that the Ain, geographically, was asking to be taken over by the French. He knew how strong we were from the losses they had suffered since February, and continued to suffer during the April and May attacks. But all of us, particularly Montréal, were angry that several hundred Germans would escape death at the hands of the Maquis. As it was, there were only two or three very small pockets of Germans left on D-day and Montréal had no trouble in annihilating them.

June the fifth dawned clear, and brought the SOE message that we had so long awaited: Stand by for D-day. I alerted Romans, Chabot and Montréal, as soon as Paul, very excited, brought me the signal. Romans passed the word to his commanders in the Armée Secrète and, for security's sake, these men were told to say nothing but be ready for action at any moment. I felt very emotional, for the endless journeyings through the sectors had made me very tired. Every trip had become a major expedition, every checkpoint a major anxiety, and the national habit of the French—to be late for every appointment—made me more and more frustrated. I knew it was impossible for me to be relieved, as no one would have a hope in hell of taking over from me at that time, and I realised I must go on until I was either captured again or the Germans were thrown out of France. So the message brought me succour. It would not be long now, I thought, before I would be with my own countrymen again, freed of the burden of living a secret life. To be an 'agent' sounds romantic, but it was a very wearying task which had been getting me down up to the time that signal came through. Now I had a new vigour, and I prayed that the worst was over.

I was astonished to receive an SOE message early the next morning that the Allies had landed in Normandy. I expected we would have had to wait at least two or three days after the stand-by. What excitement; I have never seen such excitement as there was in that derelict farmhouse HQ in the early hours of 6 June. Romans and I laughed together, long and loud, so immense was our feeling of relief. There were toasts, shouts of '*Vive La France, Vive l'Anglais*', and my hand was shaken time and time again. Laughing men slapped each other's shoulders and kept repeating: 'They've arrived, they've arrived.' We drank champagne. But at the end of fifteen minutes or so, I restored order and sent our couriers out to our commanders to put into operation our own D-day, Le Plan Vert.

If the landings had been made a few minutes earlier, just before midnight on 5 June, I would have won a bet with twenty of my officers. As it was I had to buy them all dinner. Within an hour or so of the landings the area was isolated from the rest of France. Every road into the Department was blocked, and no one could use one without a *laissez-passer* issued by our headquarters. All trains came to a halt, and the two main lines to the north, through Bourg and Bellegarde—the only rail exits—were immobilised. For more than four weeks not one ton of supplies, or one platoon of soldiers, managed to reach the north—and the invasion sector—from our area of south-east France.

The first major disruption to German communications came that same night of D-day, 6 June, less than twenty-four hours after we had celebrated the Allied landings.

Some weeks before, while drawing up Le Plan Vert, Romans and I had decided that the railway junction at Ambérieu, heavily guarded and with reinforcements readily available from the German garrison there, could form one of our main targets to disrupt communications. We called in our friends the Cheminots, the railway workers who were some of the most patriotic men I ever met in France. They were all anti-German and went out of their way to help the Maquis, the Armée Secrète, and escaping prisoners alike. We asked them for details of the railway works in the town and they supplied us with detailed drawings of the machine shops, engine sheds, marshalling yards, signal boxes, a turntable, and, better still, told us that normally there were fifty to sixty railway engines most nights. These locomotives, they explained, were usually grouped together in sidings waiting to be hitched to trains the following morning.

This would obviously be a prime target for us, and if we could blow up fifty engines as well, our first strike against Germany on D-day would be a severe one.

We called in Chabot, in whose area Ambérieu was, and told him the Cheminots' news. He, as usual, was enthusiastic when we told him that his first task would be the attack on the junction. He brought in La Brosse, an explosives expert, and we discussed plans with him. La Brosse then raised his own team and trained them to blow up particular objectives at Ambérieu with plastic. Railway engines, for instance, required one small charge on one of the cylinders to immobilise them, and it took special parts and hours of work to get them going again. I worked with La Brosse in training the team and showed them the correct methods of fixing their charges and putting in fuses.

The Cheminots told us that there would be fifty-two engines on the sidings on the night of D-day, so the day we had chosen fitted in very well with the Germans' transport arrangements.

Chabot brought in Verduras and his men to his command post, which he had set up at a farm at Balvay, which overlooks the depot, as well as Mazaud, the man in charge of Les Enfants d'Autun, the camp used for training the Maquis. Verduras and Mazaud and their men, some 150 in all, were the fighting force to be used to fight off the German guards and the reinforcements that were bound to be brought in from the barracks, which were only a short distance from the junction, the instant the first guns started firing.

Romans and I watched the two groups, the saboteurs and the fighters, go off from the command post late at night and we had nothing more to do except wait—always a difficult task for me. Later we heard heavy fighting, explosions, and saw flashes of tracer round the railway depot and red glows as fires started.

We had no news until the next morning, 7 June, when a runner said that the attack was a success, but that he had no details.

Later in the morning, Romans and I were sitting at a table talking in a tent when Chabot came in. He drew himself to attention in front of us, saluted and said: '*Mission accomplie.* But I regret to say that we only destroyed fifty-one locomotives out of the fifty-two there. I am very sorry.' This report was given in such a solemn, sad way, that I looked at Romans and we both laughed. '*Mon vieux*—it is magnificent. Well done,' we both said. At which Chabot's serious face creased into a smile and we drank to his success in wine.

Chabot then gave us the details. The explosives group slipped into the depot after the fighting force dealt with the German guards, some of whom were shot. The noise of the shooting brought dozens of Germans to the depot and a running fight developed as the Maquis fought to protect the saboteurs. Chabot, first into the depot, shot down a German NCO and later in the fight, jumped a German officer and killed him too after a hand-to-hand struggle on the ballast of the tracks. The Germans fought at a disadvantage, as they did not know the size of force they were against, and most of the Maquis had good cover behind heavy machinery or a railway engine, whereas the Germans had to advance over open ground in the sidings, or try to enter the machine shops through the doors. They were shot down as they were silhouetted against the night sky. All the charges were placed and Chabot instructed the sabotage team to get out as he led the rest of the men in a rearguard fight. Finally they disengaged, leaving a handful of dead Maquis in the depot, and cleared the town without further trouble, dispersing to their mountain camps. Chabot stayed behind to get accurate reports, and the Cheminots told him that the turntable, workshops, and fifty-one engines had been destroyed. The charge on the fifty-second failed to explode, and he and I thought that in the darkness, and under heavy fire, the saboteur had failed to set off the time-pencil.

It had been a great raid and, as a bonus, Chabot and his teams killed dozens of Germans.

A little later Montréal did a similar job in his sector with the aid of a group of Armée Secrète, hitting the sidings and marshalling yards at Bourg, which is in the north-west of the Ain, and on the western fringe of Montréal's area. He mounted the same type of operation as Chabot, went in with the first wave of Maquis, and gave covering fire to his sabotage team. Again it was a success and he destroyed fifteen engines and a turntable. The target was smaller than at Ambérieu, with no machine shops, but, again, the raid hit rail communications very heavily.

These actions were typical of the loyal, brave, and efficient groups, and the commanders who ran the Ain. They stirred up no trouble in the political field, and gave Romans and myself little cause for anxiety over security. I wish all the men I met had been as co-operative. Our operations against communications were highly successful. German rail traffic had to be diverted farther to the west, where other groups—of which I knew nothing—did their part to hamper communications.

The line through Bellegarde—a town close to the Swiss border and on the edge of the Pays de Gex—was blocked by sending in two railway engines at high speed, one from each end of the long Bellegarde tunnel. When they met in the middle, with a very satisfying bang, nothing could get by. It took the Germans a long time to clear that tunnel when they finally fought their way back into the town. And we did not restrict our line-cutting to the Ain. Groups of the Armée Secrète and the Maquis ranged out of the liberated area to attack trains and tracks all around the edges of our 'box'. We fought almost nightly battles with guarded food-trains, shooting soldiers and cleaning every ton of supplies from the trucks. We kept this up for four weeks, and Miguet and his transport team, as efficient as the Royal Army Service Corps, distributed thousands of tons of food to the towns, villages and Maquis camps in the area. More important, we kept other railway lines, linking east and west, cut for weeks; nothing moved except our own transport.

In the towns, local government was smoothly taken over. Many of the police worked with us, and those that did not were content to stay in their own barracks without interfering.

We also set up a military tribunal in Nantua to try both civil and military who offended against the laws. The law was based on the laws of France before 1940 and under this, of course, traitors could be, and were, sentenced to death.

The tribunal was established by the Procureu de la République, a man called Davenas, and he arranged for it to be run by members of the Maquis, with a Maquis officer as president, four NCOs and some soldiers forming the rest of the court. The Commissaire de Gouvernement from Belfort, Monsieur Netter, was brought down from Belfort, and he sat as the equivalent of the Judge Advocate. All the people who faced charges were given the opportunity of choosing a defence lawyer from advocates in Nantua.

I spent one day at the tribunal, just to see how it was operating, and watched the usual string of small cases—breaking curfew, theft, and the like—dealt with swiftly and correctly by the court. One other man was tried for embezzlement, and during the trial it was also discovered he was one of the Milice, the French 'Gestapo', and we found out that he had been guilty of denouncing French people to the Germans—which was part of his job. He was found guilty of embezzlement and treason, was sentenced to death, and later executed. Other Miliciens were tried during the five weeks that the tribunal sat and they too were executed.

When the Germans took control of the town later, they carried out reprisals on some of the civilians, but none of the officers of the court were accused. It was enough for them to say that they had been forced to carry out the work—which was not true—for the Germans to leave them alone.

Printing presses produced our new ration cards, stamped with the mark 'FFI', and the population was very happy as they received more food during our liberation than they had done in the previous four years of occupation. We were able to increase their rations because we raided the dumps at the Germans' quartermaster stores and added this food to the tons of flour, rice, and tinned stuff from derailed trains. It was, of course, late spring, and we were able to distribute fresh vegetables from the country areas.

A by-product of our train wrecking was the discovery, in nearly every one, of large piles of mail written by German soldiers to their families back in Germany. Much of this was examined and we gleaned some secrets from it, as the security of the German soldier was not very good, and the censorship was poor. Many of the soldiers wrote about 'Maquis atrocities', which was part of the propaganda line fed to them in their barracks. There were no atrocities committed against the Germans in our area that I ever discovered—even though every German was hated by the Maquis. Certainly no soldier was ever beaten or tortued in the way *maquisards* were treated.

We always burned all the mail after we had examined it. This must have had some small effect on morale in the Fatherland because little Fritz had not written his usual Sunday letter.

Romans was appointed Le Préfet de l'Ain, and he and I worked closely together, running both the military and civil affairs from our various command posts. We did not move into the towns, as much as the luxury of a bed, with sheets, and restaurant meals appealed to us. We stayed in the Maquis with our commanders, where Paul could communicate with us and where the couriers knew where to find us. We knew the Germans must react at some time and we couldn't risk being caught in a major attack on a town, which might separate us from Chabot, Montréal, and Ravignan, the commander in the west.

Romans and I were lucky to have survived the first day of the Plan Vert, for we were nearly killed by mortar bombs. He and I had gone on a reconnaissance in the southern sector at the Col-de-la-Lèbe area, which is north of Virieu-le-Grand on the 3,000-feet high road. We were with Chabot, Jean Miguet and Dédé de La Butte, lying in a hollow watching a German probing attack. Suddenly there were two major explosions a few feet from us, which blew Romans and me several feet. Mortar bombs. We heard fragments whine over us and around us. We had been seen and had to withdraw. If we had been hit, the whole control of the area would have passed into our commanders' hands—and they did not know the whole picture, the contacts, the radio methods and so on. We were lucky to have escaped—the Maquis of the Ain was even more lucky to have missed chaos.

The next day we were with Verduras in the south and had climbed some 3,000 feet up the Col-de-la-Lèbe again and were inspecting a Maquis road block which had been set up on the road leading from Artemare, when Verduras crawled towards us and grinned like a schoolboy.

'Ha, Xavier,' he laughed, 'have you ever heard anything like this. Three of my Jugoslavs (he had a small number of them in his Maquis) smelled a plastic today for the first time and liked its perfume of pear drops. So they ate some. I've had to send one off to the doctor and the other two have a splendid guts-ache. They won't do that again.'

The Germans were very active around the Col and Verduras fought them for three days, losing two killed and three wounded. His Maquis, including a boy of twelve, fought so well that the German group of about 500 men finally withdrew without pushing through the road block and forcing their way into the Ain.

Chabot was also with us that day at the road block where trees had been cut down to hold up any vehicle short of a tank. It had been planned to give the Maquis the advantage of height, and when I arrived the *maquisards* were in good cover in the trees, looking down the road to where the Germans had spread out and were firing with machine-guns and automatic weapons, trying to discover the strength of the Maquis. Later in the day they brought up an artillery piece, mounted on wheels, rather like the old French seventy-five or the British twenty-five pounder, and it became a damned nuisance. La Brosse, the man who led the saboteurs against the fifty-two railway engines at Ambérieu, was called in by Chabot. 'Get that bloody gun,' he told La Brosse. The big man took a bazooka, and crawled through the trees until he could see the gun firing in an open field. He destroyed it with his first shot.

The Germans eventually pulled out, leaving some dead, as they did on all these small, reconnaissance-type attacks.

For three weeks we had our way. The Maquis and the Armée Secrète fought a great guerrilla action which considerably helped the Allies by reducing the number of troops available to Rommel in his defence of the Atlantic Wall. Then reports came in from our intelligence workers outside the Ain: 'German troops are massing. They must be planning to attack you.'

The obvious was to take place. The Germans were about to react. The first probes were made in the south, and all were beaten off by Chabot's men. The next attacks came from the west, striking out of Bourg, a town which always had a big German garrison, now strengthened to deal with the Maquis takeover of the Ain. They were faced with Ravignan and his groups, and some of the 'mothball' groups. Again they were held, sustained losses, and retired. The 'mothballers' fought well, but they suffered more than the *maquisards*, who were better trained and more used to guerrilla tactics.

Meanwhile the Armée Secrète in the towns played a valuable part in harassing the Germans. They sent out patrols to attack tired German troops—who had been marching and fighting the Maquis all day—as they went back to their barracks. The Germans became more and more puzzled by these attacks as they thought all the Maquis were in the hills and mountains and would not dare to operate within a mile or so of German headquarters.

The attacks spread to the north, and Montréal faced more probes which came down the main roads. Again, one or two companies of German troops would make feint attacks to test the strength and disposition of the Maquis, and then pull out. Romans and I studied all the action reports from the Maquis commanders and, in our view, the main attack would be made in the north sector. The Germans needed the railways; they were not concerned with the towns and the population. Bellegarde, Nantua and Oyonnax, in German hands again, would free one of the main routes to the north, and they would once again be able to move troops and supplies. We warned Montréal, and asked for information from our friends in the Armée Secrète on troop concentrations and movements.

We finally got word that the Germans were massing to the north-east of the Ain and that it seemed probable they would try to make a drive down the Col-de-la-Faucille, towards Bellegarde. Romans and I were in the west sector with Ravignan, so we decided to leave for our command post in the centre of the Ain, where we would be more easily available to the northern sector if the threat developed. When we reached our post, couriers from Montréal reported that the Germans were launching a major attack with a large force, so we drove through the night to the Col, arriving at dawn. The Col, one of the best-known features of the region, sweeps down from the mountains in a steep, zigzag road, like the lacing of a shoe. We saw Montréal at the foot of the Col, where he had his command post, and he was unhappy about the pressure on his groups defending the higher regions. He led the way up to the 'front', to the local command post within sight of the Germans, and there we found Michel, *Le Grand Michel* as he became known, partly because he was big of heart. He was one of the more able commanders, and I approved of Montréal's generalship in putting his group at the spearhead of the defence.

'We badly need more bren-gun ammunition,' Michel told me. I explained that I had already asked for more parachute drops, as so much ammunition had been used up beating off the reconnaissance attacks. He took us to the front group, well hidden on the mountainside, and with a wide field of fire against the attacking Germans. I saw hundreds of German troops cautiously climbing along the 'laces', stumbling on the rocks, to join up with the troops already in the firing line. These troops, professionals (vastly superior to the ragbags that German regiments became later in the war), were not at home in their exposed positions against guerrilla fighters tucked into niches in the mountains. They showed their nervousness by firing long bursts from machine-guns and automatic weapons, in contrast to the *maquisards*, who replied with single shots, showing they were unworried and using their heads. I turned to Michel: 'There's no need to tell your men to conserve ammunition; they couldn't be more sparing than they are. Well done, your men are excellently trained.'

Some of the group noticed that regular 'convoys' were driving down the road to the Germans, consisting of four or five lorries with stores and guards, and a staff car, with two or three officers, sandwiched for protection between the lorries. Half a dozen *maquisards* went off to attack one of these convoys. They hid themselves at the top of a cutting, as steep as a cliff, by the roadside, and waited. When a convoy came through they dropped a 'gammon'—a large piece of plastic timed to explode within a couple of seconds—and it landed squarely on the staff car, killing the officers and the driver. But the *maquisards* barely got away. One told me: 'Those Germans were so fast. They came straight up the side of that cliff as though they were walking down the Unter den Linden. We had to get away quickly.' This alone showed the quality of the attackers, for rabble would have needed orders from an officer to set them moving.

After several hours Romans and I went back to Bellegarde and, sitting in the car with Miguet and Romans' bodyguard, Dédé de la Butte, we discussed the situation. It was obvious that the Germans were going to force us to give up the Col; there were far too many of them to hold. So we agreed to fight a rear-guard action for as long as possible.

Once the Germans got clear of the Col there was nothing to stop them moving into Bellegarde. But there was no point in using guerrilla fighters for a house-to-house battle with troops expertly trained in this sort of warfare, so all we could do was to use delaying tactics. Montréal agreed. 'But, *mes Colonels*,' he said, with his Errol Flynn-like gestures, 'we will give them a very sore head before we let them in.' He was right. With the groups of Michel, and Maxime, the former adjutant, he fought thousands of crack German troops for five days and nights, giving ground foot by foot, crevice by crevice, in one of the finest organised rearguard actions ever fought by the Maquis. Company after company of German troops were sent in waves to try to break through the slim line of Maquis, never more than 150 strong. The *maquisards* held firm, firing single shots and making every bullet count and bombing the Germans with grenades when they got too close. Finally, Montréal gave the order to pull out, and the Germans once again took over Bellegarde.

For a month the men of the northern sector had controlled the town, and it was a month worth the sacrifice of the handful of *maquisards* who died in the fight for the Col. The Maquis action had gained priceless time for the invading Allies and saved them from suffering far greater casualties.

The Germans immediately started to clear the Bellegarde tunnel of the two wrecked locomotives, to re-open a south–north line through the Ain which could be used to reinforce their armies in the north. It took them some time to shift the tons of twisted steel, and, as soon as the tunnel was clear, the Maquis hit back, blowing up the track with plastic, day after day. Only a small force of Germans occupied Bellegarde; the rest, still many thousands strong, switched their attack south-west, towards Nantua. The Maquis went into action again, tired after a week's solid fighting, but encouraged by their successful rearguard of the Col. Montréal and I gave the orders to attack, and the groups were led by Michel and Maxime.

The first objective of the Germans was Trebillet on the way to

Nantua, where another tunnel had been blocked. They came on with great determination, and it seemed as if they must win control of the village within hours when Romans and I, still being driven by Miguet, arrived at the front.

We met Maxime walking down the road towards us, grinning. 'We've held them,' he said. Again the same 150 men had proved a match for several regiments of German troops. I watched the *maquisards*, and was again impressed by their disciplined fighting. I told the two group commanders: 'You must pull out if it looks as though they may overrun you.' They agreed. But those magnificent men held Trebillet for five days, broke the spirit of the troops opposing them, killed many dozens, and only withdrew when a major frontal attack, made by hundreds of troops, was launched. They might even have held that, but the Germans, desperate now to break through, made a secondary attack on the flank with a force brought down from Saint Claude to the north of the Maquis defences. These men joined up with units from the German garrison in the west at Bourg, after marching through the villages at Dortan and Thoirette.

Typically, the Germans showed their fury and frustration by attacking civilians. They burned, pillaged, raped, and tortured in the way that had become expected of them. They set fire to Dortan and Thoirette, and, at Sièges, a tiny hamlet en route from Saint Claude to Bourg, they captured three members of the Maquis who had somehow become detached from their group.

Two of the *maquisards* were shot down straight away, but the 'treatment' was reserved for Lieutenant Naucourt. We found his body after the Germans left. He was naked, his eyes had been gouged out, his arms broken, and a fire had been lit under his testicles. Such bestial treatment only stiffened the hatred and resolve of the Maquis and the Armée Secrète. If high morale meant hatred, then morale was very high.

For all the German might, we still held most of our liberated area. We had lost Bellegarde and control of the strategic road which runs from Nantua to Bellegarde. But the rest of our section, apart from an indentation on the eastern fringe, was still clear of the enemy. We intended to hold on to it if we could, but we badly needed more supplies. I had arranged some drops in June and had, for instance, been able to give Michel the bren ammunition he needed. The drops had all gone well, but the supplies only allowed us to keep abreast of expenditure in ammunition and weapons. I wanted a really big drop so that we would have 'something in the bank' with which to meet the major push the Germans must surely be planning. I told Paul to impress on London that this was an absolute necessity. He smiled, said 'Sure thing,' and wandered off in his ragged clothes. He was still giving away his good clothes to those he considered more deserving than himself, and he was also being 'mother' to the crew of an American Liberator which force-landed in the area. 'I'll take care of them in case they get into trouble,' he told me when the bunch of tired, surprised Yanks were brought into the camp.

I received an almost immediate, and very surprising reply to my demands. 'Can arrange to send you thirty-six aircraft. Can you deal with them in daylight?' the SOE asked. This was magnificent; it would bring close to 400 tons of supplies in one go. Certainly it would be a major operation, in sight of the Germans, but Romans and I agreed that—providing we had defence in depth and transport available—we could handle a daylight drop. I signalled back, naming two dropping zones, one at Izernore and the other at Port, and SOE agreed to both zones. We would only know which one they would use on the morning of the drop.

I worked out that something like 700 men would be needed—representing a dozen Maquis camps—to protect both zones against any German attack. I also decided that the supplies would be divided on the spot and sent in lorries and vans to the various groups. Miguet borrowed extra lorries from friends in Oyonnax for the occasion, and as it was essential that our transport should not be held up by crowded streets, everyone in Nantua was ordered to stay indoors on the morning of the drop. Nantua was only eight miles away from the level ground at Izernore, a smooth plateau some 3,000 feet high, and the thunder of thirty-six low-flying aircraft would quickly awake the highly excitable citizens of the Ain.

The Port ground was left to the Maquis to handle, and the 'mothballers' brigade—who were to receive a large proportion of the cargo—were responsible for defending the ground at Izernore. I saw the commander of this brigade early on the morning of the chosen day and told him, truthfully, that I did not know which ground would be used. I do not think he believed me. Anyway Romans and I, using our well-developed *pifomètres*, felt certain that Izernore would be chosen, so I left the chief 'mothballer' and went there. It was a sunny day, with wisps of white cloud, and the whole of the plateau was green and beautiful, and filled with excited members of the Maquis.

It was almost 10 a.m. when we heard the hum of approaching aircraft from the north. Then we saw them, a fleet of American Liberators protected by dozens of wheeling, diving fighters. They flew, line abreast, in three squadrons, and as they roared over Nantua, the townsfolk crowded on to rooftops and balconies, waving, cheering, crying with emotion and excitement.

The planes flew towards us at a height of about 500–600 feet, and it was a wonderful sight to see the glinting wings, in perfect alignment, and then the blossoming of the great, multi-coloured parachutes as containers tumbled from the bellies of the aircraft. It was all over in a couple of minutes, then the armada wheeled, and climbed towards home. The sight of them immensely improved the morale of the people of the Ain, for it showed that the Allies could operate over French territory just when they wanted to. Also the fact that the Maquis could call on such massive support, in daylight—without interference from the Germans—showed the strength of the Resistance and its value to the Allies.

The next six hours were spent sharing out the supplies and loading them into Miguet's transport fleet. By four o'clock every gun, round of ammunition and pair of boots had been cleared. Only once was I interrupted, and that was by the furious commander of the 'mothballers', who claimed I deliberately misled him and that his men had wasted a day sitting at Port. He could not be persuaded otherwise, and I had to tell him, very firmly, not to be such a bloody fool. Anyway, his group got a large share of the supplies, so he went away reasonably happy, nursing the remnants of hurt pride.

The drop made an enormous difference to our groups which—with the 'mothballers'—now numbered about 5,000 men, of which 3,500, I reckoned, were shock troops who had seen much action. From then on we were able to fight without the anxiety of running out of ammunition, for I still organised the normal night drops by six to nine aircraft, and further mass daylight drops in July kept us well stocked.

One thing only dissatisfied me; I had been clamouring for weeks for mortars, heavy machine-guns, weapons which would put our men on a par with the Germans in fire-power. Artillery could not be used easily in the mountains, and the Germans rarely tried to bring up mountain guns. London kept telling me that the weapons I needed were too heavy to be parachuted, and that we could only be supplied if a plane could land. 'So why don't you land a plane?' I asked them, and—perhaps encouraged by the Liberator drop, from which all the aircraft returned safely—they finally agreed to send in a twin-engined, slow-flying Dakota, if we could fix the landing ground.

Romans and I had taken over an empty château, the Château Wattern, at Izernore, when this message arrived. It lay on a steep hillside overlooking the landing zone and faced another château on the opposite side of the valley. It was the first comfortable headquarters we had during the whole of our months together and was partly furnished, with decent beds, and some good wines in the cellars. We moved in with Paul, the crew of the

Liberator he was 'mothering', and the remainder of our HQ staff.

Paul radioed SOE our selected field—Izernore—and this was immediately accepted. I ordered a Maquis group to clear a landing strip on the nearly level plateau, and they dug out boulders and stones and levelled hummocks and scrub. I also asked Montréal to arrange for the Dakota to be camouflaged for a day as such a slow aircraft could not land, be unloaded, and get back to England in one night. His plan was ingenious. He decided that the Dakota should be taxied to a small copse of pine trees close by the landing strip. *Maquisards* would then cut down many dozens of pines from another part of the area and 'plant' them around the plane.

I laid out a flare-path of torches and, exactly on time, I spotted the plane in the summer night, crossing over the mountains. I flashed my recognition signal, got the right reply, and saw the landing wheels come down. Then the powerful beams of the landing lights split the darkness and she came straight in, as though the pilot was touching-down on thousands of yards of concrete runway. It was a fine piece of flying. A man with a torch guided the plane until it was tucked into the copse. The pilot killed his engines, opened his window, and called down in a good American voice: 'Hi there!' He clambered down, introduced himself as Colonel Heflin of the USAF, and I shook hands with the rest of his crew, a major, a captain and one sergeant. The main door of the aircraft was opened, and there stood half a dozen men in plain clothes. 'Bloody politicians,' I muttered to Romans. I hated these political figures who turned up in increasing numbers as the war progressed. They added an extra element of risk to our security and, to my soldier's mind, it was better to finish the fighting before starting to squabble over the prizes.

There were three more men in the background, and these I welcomed. One was the surgeon I had been pleading for London to send me for months. Parsifal was his code name; otherwise Major Parker, who had a surgery in Harley Street. He organised our Maquis field hospital and, in the weeks of heavy fighting that lay ahead, he saved many lives with his skill. Not least, he boosted the morale of the *maquisards* who knew that from then on their wounds would be treated more quickly.

The second man was Bayard, or Captain George Nornable, aged twenty-nine and born in Sheffield, where he worked as a local government officer. He was the small arms and demolition expert and instructor I needed, for all the senior officers in the Maquis simply didn't have time to train the dozens of new recruits who kept coming in. He had been seconded from the London Scottish to SOE and was wearing glengarry and full uniform. Of medium height, with a broad forehead and curly hair, he set up at Saint Martin-du-Fresnes and, within hours, was caught up in the great German offensive, launched on Bastille Day, 14 July. He joined the men of his command post in a fight against a German patrol and was injured in the chin and hit in the arm by a mortar bomb splinter, which is still there. When things quietened down, he moved to Cinq Chalets, and later visited Parsifal, the surgeon, at the hospital. There he met a lovely girl, Yolande, and he told me: 'To me, Xavier, she is France, and I shall never forget her.' He returned to France in 1956 to try to find her, but he never did, for he knew only her Resistance name and could not find out where she lived.

Bayard did an extremely worth-while job conducting courses at a recruiting camp run by Captain Colin, and dealt with many unexploded plastic charges, wrongly assembled by recruits and liable to blow at the slightest touch. That is real courage, the cold-blooded sort.

The third man was Yvello-Veilleux, a French-Canadian radio operator, requested as an assistant to Paul who—with the heavy fighting and frequent requests for drops—was much overworked.

Our nine passengers were taken to the château whilst Romans and I stayed to see what presents London had sent us. We had a very full stocking. There were heavy machine-guns, mortars, boxes and boxes of mortar bombs, and hundreds of belts of machine-gun ammunition. But the prize present was a jeep, able to trundle over territory in the mountains which none of our ordinary Citroëns could negotiate. Romans and I annexed that.

We joined our visitors at the château, fed them, produced some of the absent owner's best wines, and made arrangements for the politicians and the others to move out the next morning. I saw the rest of his crew to a point above the château, looking down on the landing ground. I pointed to the landing ground and asked: 'Where's your aircraft, Colonel?' There was no sign of the Dakota, and he was immensely impressed when I explained how it was hidden in the false copse.

We took the four Americans on a tour of two or three near-by camps, where they were warmly welcomed—and surprised by the spirit, cleanliness, and discipline of the Maquis. The colonel should have flown back to England that night, but the weather deteriorated over northern France, and London told him to stay a further twenty-four hours.

Another packet aboard the Dakota held several up-to-date, British-produced films, and *The Blue Angel* with Marlene Dietrich. These were shown one night at a cinema in Oyonnax and Nantua, and the locals saw *Desert Victory*, *The Landings in Normandy*, and other films. Montgomery was loudly cheered, and when Paul, Romans, Bayard and Parsifal walked in half-way through, there was a loud cheering for minutes on end. The show ended with the National Anthem, which was greeted with more wild cheering and shouting, and some wag decided to play the German national anthem too. But by mischance the French anthem was replayed, and the place went mad. A little later Montréal, to whom I had given the films (as the main towns were in his area), came to me and said he had received a request from Switzerland to show them. Geneva, of course, was only some forty miles away, and I thought about this deeply as it could be tricky for a neutral country to show the latest British propaganda films. Eventually I told Montréal that he would have to make his own decision—and winked at him. Later we heard from contacts in Switzerland, and in cables from London, that our films were much appreciated.

In the fortnight following D-day, London asked me several times to return to England to give an on-the-spot report of our fighting and the liberation of the Ain. They argued that they could learn far more from a personal interview than they got from the brief messages I sent through Paul. But I kept putting them off as I felt that, though we had won a battle, the war was far from finished as far as the Maquis was concerned. Romans told me the decision must be mine, and now, with the Dakota about to leave, I considered the possibility of making a short trip to England. Colonel Heflin offered to take me, but I was worried about getting back to France. 'I promise I'll fly you back,' he said. 'It might be within forty-eight hours, certainly within a week. And I'll bring you right back here.'

I had a feeling I might be deserting my friends, and I told Romans I would leave it until the last moment to make up my mind.

'Xavier, no one will ever think that they have been deserted by you. If you feel you must go, go. If you are on the spot you will be able to tell London what we have done and plead with them to provide the extra arms we need,' Romans said.

Colonel Heflin was due to fly out the night after his arrival, but London signalled me that the weather over northern France and southern England was going to be bad and ordered him to stay another twenty-four hours. I had already arranged for Paul's 'orphans', the crew of the crashed Liberator, to be flown out, and the delay meant that I could send out one more passenger. This was Loulette Miguet, sister of our valiant transport officer, Jean Miguet. Earlier London had asked me to send a French girl to London who was intelligent, knew the Maquis and could describe its work, I presumed, at lectures. We had selected Loulette as all her family were in the Maquis or Resistance and she had worked as a courier in the Ain. She was reluctant to leave

France, but I persuaded her that she could be trained in Britain and might be able to parachute back in later in the war.

On the night of 10 July, Heflin's Dakota was de-treed, and the engines were run up. I laid a flare-path in a straight line down the bumpy runway for his take-off, saw the Liberator crew were on board and Loulette. I raised my hand to give Heflin the all-clear, but stopped it half-way. I turned to Romans.

'I've decided. I'm going, too.'

We shook hands, he wished me *bon voyage*, and I climbed aboard just as I was, in my dirty grey suit, battered tie, scuffed boots, and my grey canadienne. I hoped to be back within forty-eight hours.

14

Heflin gave us an uneventful flight back to Tangmere in Sussex, where I was met by bacon and eggs and a group of friends from SOE, as Paul had radioed ahead that I was coming. I was then taken to Baker Street to see Buckmaster, other officers, and Vera Atkins. Vera is a dear, serene person, who held the rank of GSO III and was one of the most respected officers in SOE and certainly held in high regard by Buck. She, because of her gentleness, was often used to interrogate agents on their return from France and she was used on this occasion, with the others, to find out what the Maquis of the Ain, Haute-Savoie, and Jura, had been doing under the tripartite arrangement.

I spent the next two or three days telling London of the work we had been involved in and trying to impress on them our needs for the future. I found that the brief cables I had sent over the months had not been enough for them to gauge the enormity of the task we had undertaken or of our successes. I found, by talking about the people and by bringing the fight down to the individuals, that they appreciated more and more our way of life and the hardships of Maquis existence. I told them a simple story of the brothers Juem who were present at one attack on Chabot's headquarters in the south of the Ain, with their little white fox-terrier-type dog. One brother was killed. So was the dog, a Maquis mascot. The simple tale moved them.

I spoke about the foreigners who had joined up with the Maquis, the Italian ski-ing champion who had given us a demonstration over Christmas, of Andrés, the Spaniard who had been my friend in the Haute-Savoie, until he was gunned down.

I talked of the Russian group, whom they had not heard about, as they played only a small, if colourful part, in our over-all command. Their leader was Nicolas, Lieutenant Retznikov, a twenty-five-year-old taken prisoner by the Germans and imprisoned in Lithuania, who had escaped and made his way through Luxembourg into France. He was taken into the Maquis and later put in charge of the twenty or so other Russians who all had similar stories of escape from the Germans. They were formed into a special ski group, as they were all brilliant skiers, and were used as a recce patrol under Montréal in the northern sector. I used the story of my first encounter with them, to illustrate the night conditions in the Ain and our methods. I was climbing with Jean Miguet and another of the 'garage' group, up towards the Prairie d'Eschallon to carry out a night parachute stores operation, when we heard chattering in the distance and footsteps on the small track through the woods. Miguet and I slid into bushes and crouched in the bright moonlight as the noises got louder and louder and the marching feet thumped into the hillside. The chattering grew louder, too, but neither Miguet nor I could make out the language—it was not French or German. We then saw men on the path, but just as we would have been able to recognise them, the moon went behind a cloud and it was dark. The group passed us and Miguet followed them at a distance, leaving me and my companion in the woods. Miguet was worried not so much at the strange men of the night, but that he had left a car down the bottom of the hill which might be stolen. After a while Miguet returned and said: 'Xavier, all is well—it's those bloody Russian skiers. I saw them when the moon came out again.'

That story showed London that it was not just French and British, but men of all nationalities who had suffered under the Nazis, who were anxious to fight to regain their freedom. Nicolas and his men were seen by me a little later on and I told them I had passed within a few feet of them that night and that if I had been a German patrol, they would all have been dead. I warned them to be quieter and to have a scout out ahead of a bunch so he could give warning of other forces.

I told London of George Millar, a British soldier who had escaped from a prisoner-of-war camp and made his way through into our area in the Haute-Savoie. I had heard that he was being hidden by Pépette at Frangy near Annecy, so I went to see him to check his story and to arrange details of his escape. There was no doubt that he was English and I told him that I could get him through to Spain on an escape route run by my friend the alpine guide at Chaumonte, Jean Blanc. Blanc eventually took him and a group of airmen through France, into the Pyrénées and to the border where they made their own way into Spain and an eventual return to England. Millar had wanted to join me, but as his French was not perfect, I told him that it was best for him to go and fight as a soldier. I saw him once more, on 20 September 1944, when I met him at Ambérieu and arranged his transport back to England for the second time. He had parachuted into the Maquis on the night of 1 June 1944, and had fought with them until, his job done, he was recalled.

This story, which was told partly for the records on Millar, I related to show how a British agent was dragged into every sort of activity in wartime France. Escaping prisoners were not my concern, but no agent would turn his back on a fellow countryman. The story also showed how Resistance-minded civilians, like Pépette and Jean Blanc, were risking their lives to help the British.

I told London about the increasing political pressures that were building up as the day of the final liberation of the country grew nearer. Romans was constantly being pressed by the Free French in France, to throw in his political hand with de Gaulle and was always being asked to attend political meetings in Lyons, the real hot-bed of intrigue at that time. Romans used to go occasionally but, although he was personally a Gaullist, he refused to take any political sides. Whatever favours were offered him in the way of future political power, he would ask whether the politician had two or three hundred pairs of boots to spare to shoe his Maquis. This always silenced the tempter who might mutter: 'Ah, I'll see what I can do in the near future.'

Romans' answer was always the same: 'I am fighting a war. I am allied to the British and will remain faithful to that alliance until such time as you politicians can provide me with mortars, machine guns, clothing, and money. When you can do that, then I *may* join your party.'

This answer was to gain for Romans the name and reputation of *L'Homme de Londres*—London's Man.

I warned Romans against going to these meetings as security in the city was poor and political meetings, supposed to be secret, had often been raided by Gestapo and Miliciens in the past. Happily, he only went to a few and was not involved in any raids.

The political pressure was so great on both Romans and me—for I, too, was asked to support de Gaulle's party—that in the end I told the Free French that if they did not stop their constant badgering, I would tell London not to supply them with any more arms or money. This eventually silenced them.

London had known, through my cables, a little about the pressures, but had not realised how forceful the FFL had become. I was told, however, to tread very warily as de Gaulle and SOE were starting to operate together under one command, and not separately as before. I told them that I would not discuss politics and that I still insisted that the Maquis were there to fight, not talk.

Later, on my return to France, Romans and I had little trouble in keeping our Maquis out of the towns, whereas the FTP, the Communist groups, and the FFI rushed into any town for the political value of the capture. This, I feel, was due to our insistence that the Maquis remained non-political.

I told all things to London, as well as giving them a full description of the various fights and acts of sabotage that our Maquis had carried out since I had flown into France in the

September, of the atrocities carried out by the Germans, of the morale on both sides and of our needs for the future in the way of heavier, and more, arms. Everyone was so pleased by the way we had disrupted the south-east of France at D-day onwards, that I was promised everything I asked for, even down to more daylight operations.

I also saw General Koenig, de Gaulle's deputy in London, on two or three occasions and told him and his officers the same story, but leaving out the political part. Koenig was also pleased and handed me the Croix de la Libération, the highest award possible, for me to take back to France and give to Romans. He also decorated me with my second Croix de Guerre with Palms, which made me very proud.

On 14 July, after I had been in London three days, a message came to SOE that the Ain was under heavy attack and I was called to Baker Street to stand by in case I could assist, verbally, by assessing signals sent from Romans and the other commanders. Later that day we received a message from Paul, my operator, saying that three to four German divisions supported by armoured units had massed.

This attack, which was to last seventeen days, was fiercely pressed home by the Germans, for their objective was to clear the area, not out of spite against the 'bloody terrorists in the Maquis', but to secure a retreat route for their units in the south of France who were beginning to pull out and head towards the line of the Rhine, through the Belfort Gap.

I was able to be of use during this time by organising major drops by air to places where I knew it would be easiest for our Maquis to protect the dropping zones and easiest for Miguet to transport the arms for distribution. I also persuaded London, at long last, to drop large pieces of equipment, like mortars, mortar shells, and heavy machine-guns, in these operations. God alone knows why it took London so many months to agree to my constant demand for heavy equipment to be dropped; they had the arms, suitable aircraft, and large enough parachutes. But *They* decided against it until Romans and Montréal, on whose area the main German attack developed, were really up against it. If we had had heavier equipment earlier, we would have been able to have inflicted much heavier losses on the Germans in the big attacks through the Ain.

I was also able to take part in discussions about another major daylight drop, and I recommended the Prairie d'Eschallons, an area some 3,000 feet high about five kilometres south-east of Oyonnax. This drop went through and lightened the anxiety about ammunition expenditure which had pestered Montréal during the early part of the big push.

I did hear of one extraordinary lapse in security by SOE headquarters during this period, when I discovered that one important message, announcing the time and place of a night parachute stores operation, had been sent out *en clair*. What possessed the staff officer in charge to allow this to go, I do not know, but fortunately the operation went through without the Germans ambushing the reception committee. I played hell when I heard about it and I am sure that no other message was ever sent in plain language again.

During the fight I had constant cables from Paul reporting the strength and direction of the German attacks, and he was also relaying to me messages sent by Yvello, the Canadian who had come out just before I left for England, who was with Chabot's headquarters in the south. I gathered from these cables that Romans had been surrounded, with Paul, and that the main battle was being run by Montréal. This news, of course, increased my wish to join my friends in the Ain, and I pestered Buckmaster to get me an aircraft to fly me out to take command again.

Eventually, about ten days or so after I had left France, Buck got my aircraft for me—the same Dakota piloted by my American friend, Colonel Heflin. We took off with one other passenger, a cameraman from Metro-Goldwyn-Mayer, who had been asked to take a full documentary of life in the Maquis, and headed for Izernore, where Paul had been told to prepare a committee to receive me. We flew without incident to the area, but there was not a light to be seen. We circled for about half an hour and, as our fuel was running short, headed towards Corsica, which had already been liberated. It was not possible to return to England as the Dakota was so slow it would not have got there in darkness.

We reported by radio, on landing, that I had failed to get in, and asked for another rendezvous to be made. While I waited, I enjoyed three magnificent days lolling on the beach and living in the holiday home of the Duke of Westminster. We were told that I was to go back again to Izernore, and three days after our first attempt, Heflin put his aircraft down on the bumpy, grass field. Romans was there to greet me, so were Paul and Jean Miguet, and they took me out to their command post at Girons, which was in our northern sector south-west of Oyannax and on the edge of the small town of Champs Fromier. I regret that the MGM cameraman did not come with us. He decided that a man can have enough of a good thing, and flew back to London with Heflin. This was a great pity as the opportunity was missed of taking some historic ciné film.

On the way to Girons, and when we finally settled down there, these friends, Romans, Paul, and Miguet, told me about their seventeen days of hell under attack.

Quite early on, Romans had decided to leave our comfortable château on one side of the valley which overlooked the Dakota landing ground, and head for Girons which, he believed, was a better place to command and also because German reconnaissance planes had been spotted over the château area. These planes eventually brought in aircraft which bombed the château on the opposite side of the valley from our headquarters. Such was the efficiency of the German air force at that time.

Romans found that the Germans had launched their attack, four divisions strong, had retaken Bellegarde—a town they had vacated after they had fought us for it after D-day—had pushed by rail through Nantua and Oyonnax, swept into 'our' villages of Brénod and Corlier with one swing of the attack, and launched another hook of the drive from Saint Claude in the Jura, down the Col-de-la-Faucille and, after driving down the main road towards Bouchoux, linked up with the first force.

These two prongs had been attacked savagely by Montréal and Le Grand Michel, who then commanded four major groups comprising about 600 men, inflicting heavy losses on the spearheads. But the numbers were overwhelming, as were the 88 mm. guns, mortars and tanks that the Germans used. The Maquis fought, retreated, fought and retreated through the whole area for seventeen days as the Germans took over village after village, and destroyed camp after camp. But despite the heavy pressure, the Maquis remained intact and were making raids on the Germans throughout the whole of the period.

Two immediate gains were obtained by the Germans, although they did not know it. Romans had gone with Paul and his headquarters group, into a forest called Crêt de Chalame, which is west of Oyonnax and on the edge of the river Valserine, to set up a temporary command post in good cover, to which his local commanders would send couriers to keep him in touch with the battle so he could plan future moves. But he had not been there more than an hour or two, when one of the outer *piquets* reported that a large body of German soldiers had bivouacked in the area. Romans was surrounded, his only link with the outside being Paul and his radio. He lived with the rest of the crew for a week on starvation rations and water which had to be obtained from a small stream by crawling through the undergrowth only a handful of yards from the Germans, who never found out that the Frenchmen were in the forest. Paul had managed to keep contact with London throughout the period and also to relay messages through to Yvello, who was with Chabot in the southern area.

The second gain by the Germans was the disruption of the medical services. Parsifal, Major Parker, who was our doctor from Harley Street, had been forced to evacuate all his wounded from our tented field-hospital and move them into a battered old farmhouse and buildings near the forest. He was caught with Romans in the forest and had to stay away from his charges until the Germans cleared the area.

When I had heard the main part of the story, which included the news that the Germans had pulled out and many of them were retreating eastwards towards the Belfort Gap, I handed Romans two things—his Croix de la Libération together with a signed order from General Koenig setting out his future mission in the Ain, on which I had already been briefed by SOE before flying out. The decoration moved Romans deeply, and he was not able to speak for a minute or two as he examined the handsome medal. But then we had a drink or so of wine, a brief celebration before moving to the important matter—the future.

We called a 'Grand Conference' of all our main commanders, including Chabot. He, of course, had done a very fine job during this major attack on the north, by attacking railways, trains, and German parties in the south, together with units of the Armée Secrète, to take some of the pressure from Montréal in the north.

We checked our needs in terms of weapons and ammunition, as well as medical supplies, and we made out a 'shopping list' which I had Paul send off to London. Immediate drops were agreed by SOE, including more heavy equipment, and within a few days the Maquis of the Ain, which had been so badly mauled, was ready yet again to take on its next task.

This was to harass and embarrass the Germans whenever and wherever possible, with priority to be given to disrupting road bridges and railways according to the orders set out by Koenig and SOE, and thus hindering the German retreat towards the Rhine through the Belfort Gap. This we did, and nightly raiding parties from the Armée Secrète, which was still under Romans' command, and the Maquis went out blowing railway tracks, wrecking trains, and shooting up any small group of enemy they discovered. The Germans, of course, were shattered by the constant attacks. They must have felt as baffled as a small child trying to pick up a ball of quicksilver.

Having made our new decisions and having seen the groups start their offensive actions again, Romans and I moved out of Girons and set up another headquarters at Champdor, five kilometres south of Brénod. It was the last command post Romans and I had.

He told me in some greater detail of some of the actions that had taken place during the big attack, including the story of Chevassus and his second-in-command, Daty. Chevassus had set up groups in the Haut-Jura consisting mainly of students, and when I came to France in the September I had seen him, approved of his plans and arranged for arms to be sent to him.

Chevassus, hearing the firing and receiving a message by courier that the Germans were attacking along the Saint Claude road, had drawn out two of his groups and joined up with two other groups of the FTP—Communist groups—under a man named Martin. Chevassus and Martin launched attacks against the moving German column, hitting them as they moved through road cuttings in the highlands. The Maquis were attacked from the air by fighter aircraft who bombed and strafed them with machine-guns, but there were very few casualties. The fighting went on throughout the day, until the Germans brought up an armoured car, and more troops in an attempt to pin the groups down. Bazookas were fired at the car, it was damaged, but the Germans kept firing until ten o'clock at night, when Chevassus ordered his men to cease fire to give the enemy the impression that the Maquis had gone away. The Germans relaxed as the fight ended and many trucks, troops and officers moved down to the village of Troillet, where the officers took over the only hotel, the Dupont.

The Maquis allowed everyone to settle. Their small recce section heard the German officers drinking and singing in the hotel, and reported back. Chevassus launched an attack in the early hours, fired bazookas through the windows of the hotel, threw in grenades, and drenched the rooms with small-arms fire. Every German in the hotel was killed. The Maquis then slid away without one man being hurt.

This fight showed the spirit and co-operation between the Maquis—who, in the main, were Gaullists—and the Communists. If they had concentrated more on the fighting and less on the squabbles over political power, then life in the areas outside the Ain would have been much simpler.

Romans and I, together with Paul, were in our command post Champdor, when, over the radio, we heard in a message from London, that the American Seventh Army, under General Patch, and the French had landed in southern France. This was Operation 'Dragoon'.

There was great jubilation in the command post. We drank another bottle of wine to celebrate the landings, and Romans and I, surprised as the others had been by the new move, stood apart to work out what we could do to help the Allied Forces. We consulted our maps, and decided that the Americans must make for the Belfort Gap and then head towards the Rhine in pursuit of the German forces, which were heading on the same route following the defeats they had suffered in northern France at the hands of the Normandy-landed armies of Britain and France.

Our plan was obvious. The spearhead of the invading force must be armoured and, therefore, had to have the use of the roads, for the country of the Ain was not suitable for tank warfare except in certain parts. The Maquis, we said, must protect the roads for the invaders and clear any road block or small collection of defending Germans to allow the Seventh Army a free run through. The orders, therefore, were sent to Chabot and Montréal to clear the roads—but to continue to cut the railways to prevent German reinforcements being brought southwards, through the Ain, to meet the invading forces.

I was driven down to the south to meet the American spearhead, and, just south of Grenoble, our car was pulled into the side of a road and we listened. We heard, not far off, the jangling of rolling tanks, with the distinctive noise of squealing metal and deep engine note. I got out of my car and walked down the road until I saw the leading tank, waving as I went. The first tank stopped, with its guns trained on me. The turret was opened, an American wearing the rounded—almost German-shaped steel helmet, stood up and shouted in French: 'Who are you—what do you want?'

I called back, in English: 'I'm a British officer—I must talk with you.'

The American climbed out, jumped down on to the road and waved some of his tanks up covering positions in case I was the head of an ambush.

This man turned out to be Colonel Johnson, the man at the head of the invading force who had orders to drive for the Belfort Gap. He and I had a long talk and I told him about the Maquis and the orders we had given them to make certain he had a clear run.

'We cannot take on major defences,' I told him, 'but any road block or small force which looks like interfering with you—those we can handle.'

'Great, great. Thanks, Colonel,' he said.

I told him how we could be contacted by courier, if necessary, but told him that he and his force would be shadowed all the way through our areas and if he really wanted immediate contact, then the odds were that he only had to shout: 'Anyone about from the Maquis?' and men would, almost literally, appear from behind every tree. We had a very fine relationship, and I and the Maquis had a great respect for the American armoured columns that we helped through the Ain.

There was one small incident at this time in Sandrans, where I was in a house owned by Madame Serveigne, a widow, whose son was the local wheelwright. The village was suddenly invaded by German troops and their commanding officer stopped right below the window where I was, and talked to Madame Serveigne. He was looking for rooms to put his men, but Madame talked him out of entering her house by saying there was no room to spare. I thanked her, after the Germans had left, and she said: 'I hear you have just been promoted, Xavier. How pleased your mother would be. Let me embrace you, for her,' and she did. I found this very touching.

The Americans, of course, did not have things all their way, and German resistance, particularly around the garrison town at Bourg, stiffened after the American spearhead had gone through. One Panzer division, trying to make its way eastwards in retreat, ran into an American tank squadron of two tanks and fifty men at Meximieux, near Ambérieu. The Panzers forced the American commander, Colonel Murray, to surrender, but not until he had knocked out five German tanks. At this stage the Maquis, who had stood at the edge of the tank battle, engaged the German Panzer division with bazooka and mortar fire and delayed them sufficiently for an American force to come up from the south and engage. The fight at Meximieux developed into a major tank battle and the Germans were severely mauled by the Americans.

One amusing incident, at this time, concerned the French First Division who had forced their way up into the Ain on the right flank of the American Seventh Army. They had landed at Marseilles and it was not until they reached Bellegarde, in the northern Ain, that they were fired on. And their attackers? The Armée Secrète, one of Romans' group. Fortunately only three Spahis were grazed but the divisional commander was not very amused at being fired on by Frenchmen.

At about this time, as more and more areas were liberated by the advancing American and French troops, some of the ill-feeling of years of occupation was got rid of on some of the known collaborators. The first of these occurred at the village of Matafelon and concerned a postman named Plachet. He was anti-Resistance, so, when seeing armed men among some ruined houses which were used to store food and one of the Maquis five-ton trucks, wrote a note to the police at Brénod informing them. But the police were pro-Maquis and told us of Plachet's treachery. The Maquis, under a man named Annibal, found him on his postman's round and ordered him to strip. They then tarred and feathered him, painted a swastika on his back and front, and clipped another swastika by shaving his head. He was then ordered to march to the post office, naked as he was. When he protested, he was told that if his message to the police had not been passed on by a friendly gendarme, then he would have been shot out of hand.

'March—think yourself lucky,' he was ordered.

The next day a postman made of straw was hanged from the belfry at the church tower at Brénod.

This sort of collaborator, black marketeers, prostitutes who had served the Germans—all of them—were known as the Matafelonages, because of the first offender so treated at Matafelon.

I was spending a large amount of my time rushing by car from one camp to another giving orders for them to attack certain targets and also passing on information about future parachute drops I had arranged through Paul. This gave me an opportunity to check on some of the atrocities the Germans had carried out, as was their wont, during their major push while I was absent. I managed to gain corroboration of stories of tortured prisoners from both the Maquis and the Armée Secrète, of homes of innocent villagers being burned, of looting and—perhaps the worst of all—the rape of a tiny, fourteen-year-old schoolgirl at Izernore by five German soldiers. The stories seemed without end, and I duly reported these to London when I returned with as much evidence as I had collected.

This was a hectic period for me, rushing from camp to camp, driving to link up with Colonel Johnson to persuade him to let us have some petrol for our lorries, obtaining information from our own intelligence groups about German positions and passing this on to the invading forces. As his task of training Maquis had disappeared overnight, Bayard, my demolition officer, came with me on petrol-scrounging expeditions to the Grenoble area, and was of great general help to me.

The last major fight I was involved in was outside Bourg, where the Germans fought hard to keep control of this garrison town and the railway. Romans and I moved to the outskirts of the town to a village called Jasseron, eight kilometres to the east, with a Maquis group whose orders were to be 'a bloody nuisance' to patrolling Germans. But, early in the morning, our position was discovered, we were surrounded, and we were immediately shelled by the very accurate 88 mm. guns. This went on until about four o'clock in the afternoon, with us unable to get away and the Germans causing us no casualties but a lot of fright. The shelling suddenly stopped, the soldiers pulled out, and Bourg was in Allied hands.

At the same time as this, Colonel Johnson got in touch with me and asked if I could supply 2,000 men from the Maquis to try to ferry him through the Belfort Gap as we had done through the Ain and Haut-Jura. I agreed immediately, sent for Montréal, and asked him if he would be willing to take on the job. He was, and within hours had 2,000 volunteers to go with him. But the request was cancelled—I presume the gallant colonel found his own way through. A few days later, however, I had another message asking me to send the force to the Italian front, south of the Swiss border. I agreed, and Montréal sped off with the groups and fought hard and well, as he had done for the past year in the Ain.

As this was happening, I got a message from General Koenig in London asking if I would take Lyons. I saw Romans and we both agreed that it would be madness to commit the Maquis to a house-to-house fight with trained soldiers. I told Koenig we were not prepared to do this. London cabled again, insisting that we take on the task. I again refused. I then learned that London wanted the Maquis, who were non-political but mainly Gaullist in outlook, to take the town to prevent the Communist

FTP's armed groups having it and so increasing their political bargaining power. I was grateful that I had insisted on the Maquis remaining non-political—I did not want my guerrilla fighters, at this late stage, to start fighting among themselves or with other groups for the spoils of being *préfet*, or *sous-prefet*, or mayor.

The FTP, however, decided they had a chance of occupying the towns and launched attacks on them, but they were beaten off with heavy casualties. It was left to the American forces to free both of them.

All these events had taken place during the space of a fortnight or so and had left me weary, slightly bitter because of the political wrangling, and anxious to get the job over. I knew it could only be a week or so before my task as SOE's chief in south-east France would come to an end as the Germans were driven or retreated, out of my sectors. Romans was in the same state and was delighted to get a message asking him to come to London to see Koenig. He left and took three of our leading *maquisards* with him, Verduras and La Brosse being two of them. Romans upset London and the security forces during his week in the capital. He was approached by the BBC who, God knows how, found out that he was in town and was a big noise in the Maquis. Romans agreed to give a live broadcast over the French network describing the work of the Maquis and some of his part in it, without consulting his superiors. There was uproar when it was known what he had done, but Romans just shrugged in his normal way and disregarded all the complaints. 'Nothing is secret now—the war in France is nearly over,' was his answer to his critics.

By the time Romans returned to the Ain and our main command post at Champdor, Ambérieu was in our hands, as well as the fighter airfield. I had started my own airline—'Xavier's Express'—and was happily running Dakotas and Hudsons in and out of the former German Air Force field. I handled supplies for the Americans and the Maquis. I brought in mail for the troops, I even handled some hush-hush flights direct from Switzerland. These loads all had manifests which did not ring true to me and I suspected that we were shipping out clockwork fuses for use in shells.

I also ferried out of Ambérieu and out of our old landing zone at Izernore, a host of VIPs, politicians returning to London for consultation with de Gaulle and Koenig, as well as some of our own people. I saw Colonel Cammaerts, another British SOE colonel who had run groups to the south of me, as he left to return to England, and finally saw off George Millar—Horned Pigeon Millar, whom I arranged to get into Spain earlier—and Bayard, my sabotage expert who helped me running the Xavier Express at both Ambérieu and Izernore.

Slowly the Ain was dying down, towns and villages were free, some villages were deserted and only here and there would one run into a pocket of German soldiers, left behind in the general German retreat. Some of these fought hard, to be annihilated by the Maquis. Others surrendered.

It was in this atmosphere of victory, of seeing our job coming to a successful close, that I talked with Romans in our command post at Champdor. It was morning as we discussed the action reports that had reached us of the night's activities, when three uniformed French officers from the Free French de l'Intérieur, were shown in to see us.

One introduced himself as Colonel Carré. One of the other two I did not have to be introduced to.

'Good God, Cantinier, what the hell are you doing here? You're supposed to be in the Haute-Savoie,' I said to the smartly dressed Parisian.

Colonel Carré interrupted, 'Colonel Romans,' he said, 'we have come to arrest you.'

There was an astounded pause. Then he turned to me.

'Colonel Xavier, you have thirty-six hours to leave France.'

Then all three started smiling and laughing at the preposterous statements Carré had made. We joined in, until Carré stopped smiling and said: 'I know it sounds ridiculous, but these are my orders. I do have to arrest you, Romans. I know you only have to raise a finger and the three of us will be thrown out of here very fast. But I advise you to come with me quietly and let things sort themselves out.'

Again Romans and I were speechless. Finally Romans roared: 'Arrest me in my own command post after all these months? Who the hell wants to arrest me and why?' he demanded in his most autocratic, French-colonel voice.

Carré explained that he did not know why he had to make the arrest, only that he had been ordered by the Free French de l'Intérieur in Lyons—the Gaullists.

Romans argued with him, trying to find a reason.

Suddenly he said: 'Xavier, I'll go quietly. I could do with a rest. Let someone else find out what it is to run the Maquis. All right, Colonel Carré, take me away.'

Carré told me again that I had to leave France, and I told him I would leave when I was good and ready to go—not before and certainly not on some flimsy demand from an unknown political group in Lyons.

Carré shrugged, and went away with Romans.

I asked Cantinier what he was doing with the group, but he merely shrugged too, and told me that he was insistent on working for a new France now that the Germans had been driven away. He, too, left after Carré with the third officer.

Paul, who had been listening with me, said: 'We could have arrested those three—why didn't we?'

But I wearily told him that the soldiers were about to be displaced by the politicians who, no doubt, would make just as big a hash of things as they had after the First World War.

'Send this off to London,' I told him and handed him a signal which told Buckmaster that I had been ordered to leave and that Romans was arrested and asking what instructions he had for me.

While I waited for a reply, I found Chabot, outraged, storming into the command post.

'Why have they arrested Le Patron?' he demanded, as though it was my fault. 'Say the word and I will free him.'

Over the next twelve hours something like 500 members of the Maquis of the Ain, leaders, group commanders, and ordinary *maquisards*, came singly and by groups to protest to me and offer their services to free Romans from Lyons Prison, where he had been taken.

'Xavier—you are his friend,' they would say. 'You cannot let France make this sort of mistake and imprison one of her finest heroes.'

Patiently I tried to explain that we could take no military action to free him—it would only make his position worse and lead to a bigger row than the one I saw ahead. All reluctantly agreed.

I went to Lyons with Jean Miguet to see if I could do anything to get Romans released, but I was told by the FFI that Romans was their business—'and please, Colonel Xavier, do not forget you have only a few hours left before you must leave France.'

I returned to Champdor to find a cable from SOE which said that 'it would be better if you came back to England'. It had taken many hours to receive this and I assumed that my cable had started a long conference involving the Free French and SOE leaders, before Buckmaster had made his decision.

I saw Chabot and formally placed him in charge of the Maquis of the Ain, to replace myself and Romans. Later Montréal came to me, shook me by the hands and said: 'Ah, Xavier, to think that France treats you so badly.' Chabot stayed in the army and is now a full colonel.

I decided to leave at once and arranged a car to take me to Paris. I shook hands with Chabot again, and with some of the command-post staff. I got into the car and was driven out of the Ain, away from the Maquis and away from my life as a British agent.

I was quiet on the drive to the capital, trying to work out why

Romans had been arrested, as I had not had time before to think of the reasons.

It was fairly plain, to my mind, in the end. Romans had become known as *L'Homme de Londres*. Any leading Frenchman who seemed to have too heavy an emotional link with England was automatically excluded by General de Gaulle as a possible future leader in the new France. And, on top of that, Romans had snubbed de Gaulle's representative in France. This was Yves Farge, a leading Communist, a Commissaire de la République, and a man de Gaulle was befriending in the political battle for power, to gain the support of the Communist section of France. Farge, under the code name of Grégoire, had visited the Ain and had seen Romans, who was an important and well-loved person in the area. The two did not get on.

Farge announced, in a stiff, autocratic manner as he met Romans for the first time: '*Moi, je représente le pouvoir publique.*'

Romans did not like overbearing people, and replied in terse, Maquis language: '*Et moi, je represente les gens qui se font casser la gueule*'—which roughly means, 'I represent the people who have done all the fighting and all the dirty work'.

Farge was angry at this reply, and I am sure carried back a very unfavourable report of Romans' attitude to de Gaulle, which, allied to his reputation of *L'Homme de Londres*, was sufficient to have him removed from his job.

As it happened, Romans had a splendid stay in jail. His warders allowed him to be visited by dozens of people every day, he had the best food and wine in the district brought to him, and if he wanted to go for a walk, then the gates of Lyons prison were opened for him. As he told me later: 'I had the best holiday of my life.' But I did not know that until very much later.

I arrived in Paris with quite a lot of money and wearing my canadienne, my battered grey suit, a frayed tie and crumpled shirt, and scuffed, black shoes. I resolved to have a good meal, a few drinks, and some good conversation to try to make me forget briefly my friend Romans back in his prison cell.

I had my meal and went to the Hotel Scribe. I was talking to two or three people at the bar, including the *Daily Mail*'s war correspondent Evelyn Irons, when Ike—General Eisenhower—walked in. He, of course, was wearing a well-pressed uniform, but after eyeing my dirty, shabby clothes, he walked over and chatted to some of the group. I prayed that he would not turn to me and ask me who I was and what I had been doing in the war. For, Supreme Allied Commander or not, I would have had to tell him a cover story and not the truth. As a spy, one can never relax.